50 Years of

EXILE

The Story of a Band in Transition

by
RANDY WESTBROOK

Acclaim Press
MORLEY, MISSOURI

Acclaim Press
— *Your Next Great Book* —
P.O. Box 238
Morley, MO 63767
(573) 472-9800
www.acclaimpress.com

Book & Cover Design: M. Frene Melton
Cover Background Photography: Tracy L. Melton

Library of Congress Cataloging-in-Publication Data

Westbrook, Randy.
  Fifty Years of Exile / composed by Randy Westbrook.
    pages cm
  ISBN 978-1-938905-22-3 (alk. paper) -- ISBN 1-938905-22-9 (alk. paper)
  1. Exile (Musical group) 2. Rock musicians--United States--Biography. 3. Country musicians--United States--Biography. I. Title.
  ML421.E95W46 2013
  782.42164092'2--dc23
  [B]
                                        2013005572

First Printing: 2013
Printed in the United States of America
10 9 8 7 6 5 4 3 2 1

This publication was produced using available information.
The publisher regrets it cannot assume responsibility for errors or omissions.

Contents

FOREWORD

*T*HERE ARE MANY BANDS that could tell a similar story: teenage boys form band, members come and go, band finally gets big break, has a hit record, differences divide members, group splits up, band fades into obscurity.

I believe Exile is the exception to the rule. They are not just a garage band that formed in Richmond, Kentucky in 1963 and went on to do some pretty big things, then faded into oblivion—no. They have always been and always will be thought of as "Central Kentucky's Own Exile." They represent an entire region of the Bluegrass State. This is where I grew up, and I remember very well the night they played on NBC's "Midnight Special." I had such a sense of pride knowing that guys who grew up in the same area as I was from had "made it." That gave me hope that maybe someday I could do the same thing in the music business. Almost 10 years to the day I saw that TV appearance, I would become a part of the band. (The "Midnight Special" aired August 25, 1978; I joined Exile on August 1, 1988). They told me I was the 21st member, and I ended up being one of the last to join before we decided to stop touring in early 1994.

This is a story of triumph, failures, personal heartaches, tragic losses, and even redemption. Most importantly, it is about several men who poured heart and soul (pun not intended) into a band over the past 50 years—a band that is still able to perform with the energy and musicianship it has always been known for.

With any band, there are all kinds of struggles. That can fuel many types of problems and distractions, which usually brings a decisive end to most groups. Exile has never been one of those groups. As you read this book, you will understand that issues existed here, too; but deep down, everybody that has been a part of this band through the years stands on the sidelines to this very day, cheering on J.P., Sonny, Steve, Les, and Marlon while they are still carrying the torch. I personally hope we can all somehow keep it going for many years to come. Can't imagine the world without Exile.

What Exile means to me is quite unique. Did it make me a multi-millionaire? No. Am I a household name? No. Usually people expect you to say that an experience like this brought you fame and fortune. But, what I gained was much more rewarding. It made a positive impact on my music career: I'm still able to make a living doing what I love to this very day because of the credibility of being a part of Exile. It forged unbreakable bonds for those of us who spent countless hours together on the bus; and we are still close friends, even if we don't get to see each other for long stretches of time. Our "brotherhood" grows more special to me each passing year. This experience also gave me something even more personal: because of Exile, I met my wonderful wife of 18 years, and have four healthy, beautiful children who love music as much as their ol' dad. (They love to look through the old pictures and tease me relentlessly about my wardrobe and hair, too!) For these reasons, I say to my Exile brethren: "I love all of you for allowing me to be a part of this story!"

I think I hear a voice in my head…maybe one of Kentucky's radio legends Ralph Hacker or Karl Shannon, saying:

"Ladies and Gentlemen: Central Kentucky's Own EXILE!"

Paul Martin
2013

FOREWORD

"*H*AS RANDY CALLED YOU?"
"No. Who is Randy?"
"Randy Westbrook. He's writing a book about the band."

This was the first time that I had heard of Randy Westbrook. As it turned out, I had seen him before but I did not know his name.

Mike Howard asked me that question several months ago as we were beginning to practice in the basement of a friend. As it turned out, Randy came to practice (he is an accomplished keyboard player), and eventually performed a gig with us.

At first I wondered why he would want to write about the band. Wouldn't it be better if some member or former member did the book? Upon further thought I realized that actually a better account and a non-biased view could be done by an "outsider."

Randy put in many hours of interviews with all of the current and most of the former members of the group, except those who passed away, of course. To my knowledge no séances were held to reach the members that are deceased.

I was very impressed with the book. I was skeptical at first, but after reading it I think Randy did a great job. He was very thorough and the fact that he got viewpoints from every person and every aspect show how complete his research was.

As I said before, Randy is an accomplished musician and an instructor of music history at Eastern Kentucky University and Bluegrass Community and Technical College. He has performed around the country with various groups and his own musical group playing many different types of music.

His book gives a behind the scenes view of a rock and roll band—started by a bunch of young boys (16-21) from a small town in Kentucky—what they went through, how they grew, and what they became.

It's almost like an entity that started as a young inexperienced group that added – subtracted – absorbed – evolved – expanded – and became a talented, respected, popular group with 50 years of history behind them.

I know you will enjoy the journey whether you're familiar with the group, if you have been in a group, thinking of starting a band, or just a fan.

I actually remembered some of it.

Mack Davenport
Drummer and original member of The Exiles

PREFACE

T his is not the story of an individual or a group of individuals. It's the story of a band—Exile. I interviewed a most of the past members and all of the current members in an attempt to trace the band's history from its earliest formation through its rise to fame, decline, reformation, and second phase of fame. And the story isn't over; another wave is cresting as this goes to press.

This book is a "must read" for young musicians who are playing in their first garage bands and cherishing dreams of making it in the music business. It's not easy, but with enough talent, dogged determination, and a generous helping of luck, it's possible.

Randy Westbrook

The Story of a Band in Transition

Chapter One

This Could Be the Start of Something Good

R ICHMOND, KENTUCKY ISN'T THE most practical place to start a band. Richmond is three and a half hours from Nashville, and nowhere close to Los Angeles and New York. Yet somehow, some way, a dream that began in the early 1960s reached levels of success that no one could have predicted. On the flip side, music industry related pressure eventually took a toll on the band, while outside circumstances forced several members to depart before the mainstream commercial success of the group's first major pop hit, "Kiss You All Over," in 1978.

The origin of the band remains murky, but it's clear that the roots can be traced back to a group of high school students attending Madison High School in the early 1960s.

Introducing Mack Davenport

"I went to Madison High," said Mack Davenport, the original Exile drummer. "I started playing drums when I was a freshman in high school. I didn't play anything before then."

His decision to play drums and percussion was due in part to his asthma. He wasn't able to effectively march and play a horn at the same time. (Mack's asthma may have been one of the reasons that he was not drafted later in the 1960s, but that's another part of the story.)

"I had found a pair of drumsticks that one of the drummers in the high school had lost," said Davenport, "and I learned how to play all of the cadences in the band."

His high school influences included Joe Morello, a drummer with The Dave Brubeck Quartet, and an older student at Madison High named John Baker who had been taken under Mr. Morello's wing as a student. Despite this early jazz influence, Davenport found himself drifting into more straightforward, popular styles such as rock and R&B. He would later be influenced by the drummers that he met on tour with The Dick Clark Caravan of Stars such as Dino Danelli of The Rascals and Joe Correro Jr. from Paul Revere and the Raiders.

Mack has a sense of humor that can best be described as dry. Whether talking about the "three or four different times" that he attended Eastern Kentucky University, The Exiles' light show ("that was pre-smoke"), his singing ability ("No, they wouldn't let me"), or his memory ("I don't remember—I'll see if I can contact my spirit guide"), Mack can deliver any line with a straight face.

For instance, after seeing a man get his ear bitten off during a fight Mack responded in his trademark, subdued fashion as described by J.P. Pennington: "Everyone around was pretty upset at seeing this bloody ear lying on the floor except Mack. He said, 'Well, you know what they say—'Ear today, gone tomorrow.'" Mack's steadying presence and humor would be a positive influence on any group.

While Mack was a student at Madison High, he helped start a dance band called The Kings of Rhythm. "I think it was called the Kings of Rhythm—it was a very common name for a high school dance band." Saxophonist Doug Begley was one of the musicians who formed the group. "I think it was Doug Begley who was a saxophone player who came up and said, 'Hey, I'm going to start a band,'" said Davenport. At that time bands with horns tended to specialize in jazz, but the members of this group were open to instrumental soul and blues based material. Accounts of the early rehearsals differ, but it's clear that this early lineup would bear little resemblance to the late 1960s Exiles lineup. Mack remembered the high school group:

> Paul (Smith) Jr. played bass, Doug Jones played guitar, Ronnie Hall was singing, and Buzzy (Cornelison) and two or three other guys were there. And then we got this guy...knows how to do this, and this guy knows how to do this, so let's get them. And Billy (Luxon). Let's get Billy to play trumpet.

Buzz Cornelison confirms that he was at the early rehearsals due to an invitation from Billy Luxon, but at that time his involvement with the group was short lived:

> The year that I was a freshman, Billy (Luxon), and I think it was Mack...and I remember a guy named Doug Begley...and there was a Jones guy, and I think it may have even been Paul Smith, too...wanting to put together a little jazz band that actually read music. Ironically, Paul didn't read, but I think he was going to play bass and thought that he didn't have to.

We had a couple of rehearsals at Doug Begley's house in Richmond, and then that was it. We were reading the big band stuff and all that, and it was very nice to do the rehearsal for a couple of times, but no more than that.

Evolving from this was The Fascinations, a group consisting of Paul, Mack, Stokley, Billy, Ronnie Hall, Doug Jones, and percussionist Ernie Rhodus. The Fascinations spent most of their short existence practicing, but they occasionally played gigs. Their shows included a home birthday party and a gig at the auction ring located in the local stockyard. By the time Buzz rejoined on keyboards, The Fascinations had changed their name to The Exiles and Rhodus, Jones, and Hall were no longer involved. Rhodus was later killed in a car accident, and members of The Exiles served as pallbearers.

Introducing Billy Luxon

Billy Luxon was the first chair trumpet player and drum major of the marching band at Madison High School in 1961. He played in the school dance band with Mack. He explains:

When I was up there we had a dance band and actually played a few jobs, a few gigs. It was pretty typically a big band jazz type dance band. No vocalist or anything like that, all instrumental.

Billy was persuaded to transfer to Madison Central for his last two years of high school. The band director at Central, trumpeter Larry Looney, had gotten to know Billy while student teaching at Madison High. Billy:

He actually came to see me one summer, and he said, 'would you consider transferring to Central?' I didn't know much about Central, and I'd gone to Madison High for the first ten years. He said, 'If you decide to come, I think we're going to go to the Orange Bowl and march in the Orange Bowl Parade in Miami next year.' I said, 'Okay, count me in.' I was a junior when I transferred, yeah, and we actually went and marched in the Orange Bowl Parade that year. I really went because of him, but that was all it took to convince me.

Despite the transfer, Luxon would soon find himself working in The Fascinations, a band with students from both high schools.

The Fascinations

Paul Smith Jr. and Doug Jones formed The Fascinations. Unlike the dance band at Madison High, this group had vocalists. "There were some members that actually kind of had that band going," said Billy. "One of them was named Ronnie Hall, and he was a singer."

Hall was The Fascination's primary vocalist, and Jimmy Stokley had to take a backseat at first. "Jimmy was kind of the second lead singer," explains Billy. "Ronnie was actually in before Stokley."

Paul, another student at Madison Central, recruited some of the members. "Paul Smith recruited me into the group," said Billy. "I think he also encouraged Stokley to join."

Mack was with the band, at least sporadically. "Mack came in right about this time or a little after, but I don't think Mack was playing drums right at that time, and honestly I don't know," said Billy. "And it's very possible there wasn't a drummer." Nevertheless, it's clear that Mack had played with the group prior to Billy's first rehearsal. It's also likely that Mack was either involved with the group consistently at the time or returned soon after Billy joined.

The Fascinations developed a core membership of Paul, Mack, Billy, Ronnie, and Stokley in the months before they changed their name to The Exiles in 1963. One of their early performances was at a band contest at the stockyards in Richmond, in which they lost to another local band called The Digits. The prize was recording time and copies of the finished product. "You got to go record a couple of songs, and they gave you, I don't know, 500 records or...I don't know exactly how many," said Mack. "It could have been three."

Introducing Mike Howard

The Digits featured a young guitarist named Mike Howard. Mike's playing sufficiently impressed the members of The Fascinations, and, after the departure of Doug Jones, they invited him to become their lead guitarist. Mack suggested that the group change their name to The Exiles, and the others agreed. This name change coincided with a newfound dedication, as they strived to improve. "At a certain point we kind of made some conscious decisions that we needed to go in a certain direction, and I guess we were looking that if somebody wasn't musically talented enough or if we knew somebody that was more musically endowed, than we tried to go with them," said Billy.

Mike Howard came from a musical family. He started playing music at age of 11 after his mother bought him a guitar for Christmas. Unlike the other guitar players to pass though Exile, Howard was never particularly interested in becoming a lead vocalist. Nevertheless, he possesses a pleasant singing voice when he is inclined to use it, and he is capable of providing harmony vocals. "There are some songs I can sing, you know, and do a decent job on," says Mike.

Mike is generally associated with the group's rock and roll period, but he was also inspired by country and jazz musicians such as Chet Atkins and Wes Montgomery. As the 1960s progressed he began to assimilate the sounds of rock bands such as Cream and The Jimi Hendrix Experience into his playing. "Clapton's probably my fave," said Mike. "I love the blues, but I never really had an opportunity to play much blues. Most of it was either rock or country-rock."

His skillful guitar playing proved to be the main difference between The Fascinations and The Exiles, and he would be an influence on J.P. Pennington, who has been the group's lead guitarist from 1973 to the present. "I was in awe of him," said J.P. "He could play all of The Kinks' solos note for note."

Mike's laid-back personality helped to balance some of the stronger personalities in the band, and he helped to encourage J.P. early on. J.P. explains:

> Mike seemed to be the one that was most aware of the fact that I was nervous because I was younger and didn't know anyone. He made things easy for me with his good humor. He also had a Gibson Firebird, which was unbelievably cool! He showed me some Kinks licks, too! It made me feel like I was really a part of things right from the start.

Mike's guitar playing has continued to evolve over the years, and he remains an inspiring, easy-to-work-with musician. Unlike many prima donna lead guitar players, Mike doesn't particularly crave the spotlight. "He was always deferring to someone else, but he could play," said J.P.

The group was still using two vocalists by mid-1963, and it became apparent that the secondary vocalist, Jimmy Stokley, was a much better entertainer than Ronnie Hall. Hall's voice was suited for country music, but the band wanted to move in a soul/rock direction. Stokley's powerful, sometimes screaming vocals and his occasionally wild stage antics and dancing fit the rock/soul direction the group was taking better than Hall's more subdued approach. "Jimmy handled the screaming, Wilson Pickett kind of songs while Ronnie sang the mellower Motown stuff," said J.P.

Introducing Jimmy Stokley

According to his first cousin, Nancy Stokley Gulley, Jimmy Stokley was raised next to Shallow Ford Creek in Richmond, Kentucky. Located in the woods on the outskirts of town, Shallow Ford Creek is about as isolated an area as one could expect in Madison County. The creek, wooded areas, and tobacco fields down Shallow Ford Road create an alternate reality free of any outside influences. It is easy to see how a boy growing up in that area would have time to dream and imagine possibilities.

Stokley's father was a tobacco farmer and his mother worked at Westinghouse, a light bulb factory across from Madison Central. They later separated. Nancy recalls: "We lived on one side of the creek and he lived on the other. He was just a little bit younger than I and he wanted somebody to be with, so he always came to our house and stayed with us." Jimmy was a hyperactive child, but he was also prone to illness. "He was sick a lot when he was a kid," said Nancy. "Growing up he had colds and pneumonia and different things like that a lot."

Stokley's emergence as the lead vocalist and driving force behind the band quickly worked to push Hall out of the lineup. Hall was in the group before Stokley, and it's likely that he didn't appreciate being removed from a band that he helped to create. "There were some kind of uncomfortable moments, because what you're doing…you're replacing some people that actually brought you in, and I remember there were some really hard feelings when we replaced Ronnie Hall," said Billy.

This move was the first in a series of personnel decisions that would affect the future of the band and the friendships of those involved in the Exile saga. From the start, the members of the group were committed to making the hard decisions that would allow the band to thrive. "Jimmy was a much better performer," said Billy. "Ronnie had a decent voice for what he did, but Jimmy was much more dynamic." Hall played one gig at a club called The Jolly Roger after they became The Exiles, but by 1964 he was no longer involved. "That was the only gig I played with Ronnie, and they fired him, basically, for lack of a better word," said Mike.

With the exception of the brief experiment with adding a female singer, Jimmy Stokley would be the lead vocalist for the next fifteen years. Interestingly, her departure may have been related to Stokley. "I don't want to mention any names, but I think she got tired of her skirt being chased by a certain individual in the band (*Jimmy Stokley*)," said J.P. Ultimately, Stokley won the job due to his charisma and drive, and he was a singer who was not afraid of the spotlight or important situations. In fact, he relished challenging situations.

In many respects, Jimmy Stokley became the leader of the group. After Hall's departure he became the driving force behind the band. He quickly developed a reputation as a consummate showman, and he was the type of courageous performer who could inspire. Like many young white performers in the 1960s, he was influenced by American soul music, and he looked to push the music in an R&B direction. "That was probably THE influence," says Mike.

The group's set list included covers of songs by James Brown and The Temptations, and they turned away from rock influences in favor of soul. "I don't know that we ever did an Elvis song," says Mike. This move in a Stax/ southern soul-influenced soul direction provided an opportunity for horn players. "Back then we listened to a lot of soul: Sam and Dave, Otis Redding, and James Brown," explains Billy.

With the addition of keyboardist/trumpeter Buzz Cornelison in 1964 and keyboardist/saxophonist Bernie Faulkner in 1967 the band had a built-in three-piece horn section. The soul influence would remain throughout the 1960s even as they branched out into more rock-oriented material and Young Rascals covers.

Jimmy Stokley didn't have a smooth, polished voice, but he had a passionate delivery and he wasn't opposed to screaming. The screaming would eventually contribute to the deterioration of his voice, but it served him well in the early years. "Probably not the best singer in the world, but again, what he lacked in singing ability he certainly made up for in showmanship and energy on stage," asserts Mike.

Stokley gained the respect of his band mates and audiences through his relentless energy and passion, and young ladies were particularly impressed. "He was a mover and a screamer, and he could get the girls going," says Mike.

Stokley performed the classic role of a front man to perfection, and his onstage persona reflected his personal life. "Jim was a hound, for want of a better term," continues Mike. Described as a nice, laid-back person offstage, Stokley was not shy when it came to meeting women before or after he was in the band. "He loved the ladies and the ladies loved him," explains Billy diplomatically. J.P. talks about his first meeting with Stokley:

I had seen him at various dances around the area a few times. He was always the center of attention on the dance floor because of all of his wild moves. All the girls loved him—or hated him, depending on whether or not they'd been out with him.

Stokley certainly wasn't the first or the last front man to gain this type of reputation, and his rock and roll lifestyle, whether real or perceived, only worked to enhance The Exiles' status as the real deal. By the late 1960s he was wearing costumes to gigs in Richmond, Kentucky that would fit comfortably in Mick Jagger's wardrobe, and he successfully incorporated the dance moves from his high school years into The Exiles' stage show.

Despite his wild onstage persona, Stokley was a driven behind-the-scenes businessman. He and Billy handled most of the business for the group. Mike: "(Stokley) certainly took the band seriously, and if you weren't prepared to take it seriously, then, you know, you don't want to go there with him." Stokley was the member of the band most responsible for booking the gigs, and he worked tirelessly to promote the band. "He constantly day in and day out from start to finish was on the phone," said Billy. "He was trying to make connections. He was always trying to branch us out."

Billy helped out with the behind the scenes activities and business arrangements, but Stokley was the contact person for the group. "I really credit him as really the responsible person for where the group wound up, because I don't know that had it not been for him that we would have enjoyed a lot of the contacts and the success that we had," said Billy. "I was more of the behind the scenes kind of guy, and he was more of the main contact."

Other members of the group didn't have to deal with the responsibility of booking gigs for the most part. "I was too shy to even try to call somebody on the phone anyway…try to sell them something," said J.P.

Billy's role included negotiating with club owners, and his strong business sense would bring him success after he left the group. "He was always real good with the money and the business," said J.P. "He was a tough negotiator for us." Billy eventually opened up a successful club called J. Sutter's Mill in Richmond after he left the group in 1975, and his experiences with Exile likely sharpened his business skills.

Introducing J.P. Pennington

The addition of Mike Howard and the subtraction of Ronnie Hall were important moves, but the inclusion of a talented young bass player would prove to be the most important personnel decision in terms of the continuity of the band. For many outside of the Richmond/Madison County area, the name J.P. Pennington is synonymous with Exile. The reasons for this include his lead vocals on eight of the group's ten No. 1 country hits in the 1980s, his co-lead vocal on "Kiss You All Over," and the fact that he was a major contributor to almost every phase of the group's development from 1963 to the present.

His skills as a musician and a songwriter (often collaborating with Sonny Lemaire) have contributed to the group's success, and his determination to keep the group alive after the departure of Jimmy Stokley in 1979 was a critical factor in the longevity of the band. Nevertheless, J.P. was not the founder of the group, nor does he claim to be. J.P. described the springtime day in 1963 when he noticed a '59 Pontiac backing into the driveway of his parents' house while he was mowing the lawn:

> Two guys got out and started walking toward me, obviously wanting to talk. I'd seen them around but didn't really know them. In the passenger seat was Billy Luxon, whom I recognized from Madison Central High School in Richmond, where he was a senior and I was a freshman. Billy was a big marching band hero and was known to be the best trumpet player around. I had seen him at school a lot and had always admired his talent, but was always too shy to approach him. With him was the driver of the car, Jimmy Stokley.

J.P. was only 14-years-old at the time, but he already had a bit of a reputation as a guitar player. In addition, his mother was Lily May Ledford of the well-known Coon Creek Girls, an all-female string group that performed on radio shows in the 1940s and 1950s. Surprisingly, Stokley and Billy looked to recruit J.P. as a bass player instead of as a guitarist. "I told them I'd never played bass, but they said it didn't matter, because they'd heard me play guitar somewhere and figured if you could play guitar, you could play bass," said J.P. He had little trouble making the transition. "I mean, he's a wonderful guitar player, but he is a knockout bassist," said Buzz.

J.P.'s bass playing allowed The Exiles to use a two guitar lineup with Paul on rhythm and Mike on lead. Unfortunately, his bass playing isn't documented on any of the LPs, but it can be heard on a 1970 single, "Church Street Revival," on which he doubled on bass and guitar. He also played bass on early singles such as "Come On."

J.P. came from a musical family, but he taught himself how to play. He was influenced by the instrumental hits of the day such as "Walk Don't Run" by The Ventures, "Red River Rock" by Johnny and the Hurricanes, and "Rebel Rouser" and "Detour" by Duane Eddy. This emphasis on instrumentals influenced his writing style. Several of his hits from the 1980s feature a recurring lick, and the instrumental sections of his songs often contain a memorable "hook" in addition to the verse and chorus sections. "I guess it's just a natural part of me due to my roots in instrumental songs," says J.P.

The Exiles were not J.P.'s first band. He joined a group called The Le Sabers as a guitarist when he was eleven years. The name of the band was taken from the car of the same name made by Buick. The other members of the band were his two first cousins, Clyde and C.V. Foley, Billy Wagers, and vocalist Leroy Pullins. Clyde was the standout musician in the group at the time. He was a few years older than J.P., and he proved to be an important influence on the future Exile guitarist. Clyde was able to play Chet Atkins songs note for note, and he liked to play slide guitar with a water glass. C.V. Foley was an adequate rhythm guitar player, but he occasionally forgot the chord changes. This upset Clyde greatly, and he was known to put his guitar down and leave the stage in reaction to C.V.'s mistakes. Pullins was known for his somewhat perverse sense of humor, often making such comments as, "Clyde's gonna play one by Sh-- Atkins for you right now." He also performed a song entitled "Stick out Your Can, Here Comes the Garbage Man." Pullins played the bongos, and during rehearsals he would tighten the heads by holding them over an open flame on the stove. The drum heads developed brown marks from these "tunings." Eventually, he changed his name to Elroy. He went on to have a somewhat nonsensical country music hit as "Leroy Pullins" in the mid-1960s entitled "I'm a Nut," which was nominated for a Grammy. Billy Wagers was the group's drummer. When they changed their name to "Elroy Pullins and the Le Sabers featuring Clyde Foley" he had the name printed on his bass drum. The Le Sabers had no bass player, so it was up to J.P. to play low notes on his guitar in order to fill up the sound. He would sometimes tune his low E and A strings down in order to thicken the sound.

The Le Sabers first paying gig was at the Madison County Fish and Game Club in Waco, Kentucky in 1960. "They passed the hat and came up with $17.00 dollars," said J.P. The Le Sabers went on to play sock-hops, house parties, pool parties, and a variety of gigs. Sometimes the gigs involved pay, but most did not. Nevertheless, J.P. earned a reputation as a musician through his involvement with The Le Sabers, and it prepared him to join The Exiles.

J.P. remembers that his first rehearsal with the Exiles may have been in early 1964 after a long period of trying to decide where everyone could meet. "I remember being pretty nervous when I walked in the house where everyone was gathered," remembers J.P.

Adding to his anxiety was the fact that they were recruiting him to play bass instead of guitar. J.P. brought a Silvertone bass that someone had borrowed for him, and he had to plug it into an outlet on another member's amp. It was the first time that he had ever held a bass. He wasn't particularly impressed with the sound of the group, but he enjoyed the energy of the rock and roll music. "All out of time and tune, but fun nonetheless," said J.P. He was immediately attracted to the sound of the bass. The group was impressed with his playing, and he was thrilled to be playing with older musicians.

Introducing Paul Smith Jr.

Pennington's involvement as a bass player for The Exiles allowed Paul to fill the rhythm guitar spot, a role that was important due to the lack of a keyboardist. Paul's involvement during the early years was considerable, but he would be the first core member to leave courtesy of the draft board. Like Mack, he was not a lead or background vocalist, but he was a songwriter and he came up with some choreographed dance moves for the band. These were not the type of dance moves that one would expect from Motown.

"It must have been pretty funny to see us little country boys trying to do these soul steps and getting all tangled up in our guitar cords," said J.P. Mike: "We used to do little cheesy steps and moves and stuff with the guitar when it was kind of cool to do that." Smith penned early songs for the group including "The Answer to Her Prayers," the A-side of an early single.

As a guitarist, Smith was not as skilled as Howard or Pennington, but his versatility and personality were seen as positive contributing factors to the band. "He wasn't a great player, but he got the job done and had the kind of engaging personality that can have its advantages within a band," said J.P. Mack described Paul as a "country boy like us."

By the beginning of 1964, a core group of Mike, Paul, Mack, J.P., Billy, and Stokley were calling themselves The Exiles and rehearsing. Davenport suggested the new name based on the wave of Cuban exiles entering the United States at the time. "Mack suggested that since our hair was a little longer than was socially accepted then, that we weren't unlike the Cubans— social outcasts," explains J.P.

The group practiced at various locations including J.P.'s father's used car lot in Berea, but many of the rehearsals were held in Billy's mother's basement on Wallace Court in Richmond. Ruth Luxon was a patient woman, and she was willing to tolerate the sounds being created by the young Exiles. "It's not easy to find a good place to rehearse and thanks to the Ruths of the world, a lot of young musicians could count on a regular place to gather and develop their talents," said J.P.

Despite Lily May Ledford's background as a musician, she was not terribly interested in listening to the band practice at her house in Berea. "While we were growing up in our house in Berea, we'd seen more than one crazed look on our mom's face from being subjected to all the beating and banging on guitars, pianos, and pots and pans," said J.P.

The group practiced for a long time, and they didn't perform publicly until late 1964. The early set list was a bit more rock oriented than it would later become. With the exception of a tune that they played at the end of every set entitled "Hold It," instrumentals were not included. This was due to the fact that there were two lead singers in the group vying for material. Songs such as "Goodnite, Sweetheart, Goodnite" by The Spaniels would later be dropped after Hall's departure. "Goodnite, Sweetheart, Goodnite" was a highlight for Hall, and they closed their early shows with it. As the early rehearsals continued into 1965 and 1966, The Exiles learned songs by The Young Rascals ("I Ain't Gonna Eat Out My Heart Anymore"), The Rolling Stones ("The Last Time," "Time Is on My Side"), and James Brown ("Papa's Got a Brand New Bag," "It's a Man's World"). Stokley did an imitation of Brown's cape routine. It was clear early on that these young men were not short on confidence.

The Exiles soon began playing sock hops, high school dances, and various gigs around the Richmond, Kentucky area. Mack reports:

> Well, we played at the park, the city park. We played at the city swimming pool. We played at a little place called The Paddock, a little bar that's no longer there. It was a little dive. We wanted very badly to play, so we would play for beer. We were not old enough to drink beer. We did that anyway. We forced ourselves, and we learned how to drink beer...while playing.

Other early venues for gigs included The Sportman's Club in Paint Lick, Kentucky and a back-to-school show for Wallace's Bookstore, which was located across the street from Madison High School.

The first Exiles gig was at The Richmond City Park (now known as Irvine McDowell Park) a few months after J.P. joined the band. The park would continue to be a regular venue for the group, a place where they would play for small crowds, especially during the summertime. J.P. showed me the location of the gig, a small shelter in the park. Billy remembered that the shelter was smaller in 1964. "It probably wouldn't hold 35 people," explains Billy.

The first show at the park wasn't particularly memorable, and the band still had a long way to go as a musical unit. J.P. doesn't remember much about the music that they played, but he does remember some members of the audience. "We must have been pretty terrible, because I remember the highlight of the night being a fist fight," said J.P. This wasn't the last fight that the group would witness. A fight at The Richmond City Pool ended up *in* the pool.

Later on, the band played regularly at a youth center in Martin, Kentucky nicknamed "The Gun and Knife Club" where nightly fights were the norm.

Another important club in the group's history was The Jolly Roger, a supper club and bar located just across the river in Fayette County. It was well known among those living in Richmond and other parts of Madison County. The club had an upscale ambiance, and the experience of playing there encouraged the young musicians to consider music as a career. Unfortunately, some of the members were too young to play there. Mike was only 15-years-old when the group started playing at The Jolly Roger, and J.P. was only a few months older. Nevertheless, they worked around those inconvenient technicalities. Billy explains:

> I remember J.P. couldn't play there because his dad didn't think he was old enough, and it seems Mike Howard...I think his dad finally agreed to let him play, but maybe he had to bring him and pick him up, or maybe he had to bring him and stay with him. I can't remember, but we had some age issues. The people at the club said, 'Well, that's okay, we can let them in' even though the alcoholic beverage law said you couldn't. They said, 'Well, you're entertainers, and as long as they don't get around the bar, it's okay.' We just talked the waitresses into bringing us drinks.

Until then, they had played primarily for kids their own age. The Jolly Roger allowed them to flourish in a more adult situation.

Introducing Buzz Cornelison

Buzz joined the group in the fall of 1964. Unlike the other members of the band, he had a background in classical music. He studied piano for twelve years and played trumpet in high school band for four years at Madison Central. His grandaunt was a conservatory graduate, and she encouraged him to play at an early age. He was soon playing by ear. "My aunt was very concerned that if I continued to do so that I would lose any interest for learning to play correctly, or learning to read and all those things," said Buzz.

With his classical aspirations, Buzz never expected to be in a rock and roll band. Nevertheless, Billy remembered Buzz from their dance band experience and the Madison Central High School band. He contacted the young keyboardist soon after the formation of The Exiles, and after a lengthy phone conversation asked him to join the group. Billy and Stokley had strong soul inclinations, and they were keen on the use of a keyboard. Buzz would eventually join the band, but he wasn't The Exiles' first keyboard player. Stokley purchased a cheap organ and managed to learn the changes for The Rolling Stones' "Time Is on My Side," but he wasn't viewed as the long-term solution. "We quickly realized he wasn't the organist we needed," said Luxon.

Despite his technical skill and background in classical music, Buzz wasn't the most practical choice for a rock and roll band. "I was not interested in popular music at all," says Buzz. "And then as I got a little older I was a church pianist." This background in classical music and church music didn't prepare him for life on the road with a rock and roll band. Buzz was a junior in high school when he joined The Exiles, and he didn't expect his parents to allow him to join the band. "When I hung up I remember thinking to myself, 'Well that's the last of that,'" said Buzz. His parents didn't respond to the request immediately, but, to his surprise, they became supportive of the endeavor.

When Buzz first joined the band he didn't have a portable keyboard instrument of his own, and he was forced to play Stokley's organ. It had a volume pedal, but the action was slow. "Jimmy Stokley had bought a Sears Silvertone organ that had two settings—loud and louder," explains Buzz. Glissandos, a common musical device in rock music, weren't playable on the organ. If the performer played a glissando, the listener would hear the first and last note and nothing in between. Buzz eventually purchased a Farfisa organ, which, while slightly dated by today's standards, was an improvement over Stokley's Sears model.

Buzz quickly learned how to play in a rock and roll band, but he had to learn how to play on his own. He didn't know the songs at the first gig, and Paul agreed to call out the chord changes. By the second gig, he began to realize some patterns in the music. "And about the second night I thought, 'Wait a minute. This is just I-IV-V harmony theory. This is basic…what I started studying in the fourth grade,'" said Buzz.

Paul realized that the keyboardist was a quick study, and by the middle of the night he felt comfortable walking away from the organ. Buzz quickly gained a reputation as kind of musical prodigy among other band members. "He was a tremendous musician—far superior to any of the rest of us," said J.P.

Stokley encouraged Buzz to learn the chord changes to Gene Pitney's "Town Without Pity," a feat that no one else in the group had been able to achieve. Gary Edwards and The Maroons, another popular local group, were playing it, and Stokley's desire to perform the song stemmed from his competitive nature. Buzz used a portable keyboard-wind instrument called a melodica and a portable record player to learn the changes. "I typed it all out and then put above the words the chords or the bass note or something like that, and brought it to the next rehearsal," said Buzz. This heroic achievement endeared him to his band mates, and it would not be the last time that he would be called upon to learn chord changes. The stakes would be much greater later.

Gigs came at a reasonable pace for the band, but like many young groups, The Exiles developed a reputation gradually. Gigs were less frequent from 1963–65. One of the early venues they played was The Martin Youth Center in Martin, Kentucky, a small town with less than 1,000 inhabitants. They had to drive 150 miles from Richmond to Martin, but the pay was lucrative. The gigs were on Friday and Saturday nights.

Despite its parent friendly name, The Martin Youth Center could be a dangerous place. Members of the group came to know the venue as "The Martin Gun and Knife Club." Fights were a common occurrence, and there were sometimes two or three on the same night. "One night as we were playing a drunk guy, who was supposed to be thrown out of the place earlier, busted through the front door swinging a hay hook attached to the end of a chain," said J.P. Fortunately, no one was harmed. The efficient, experienced bouncers removed the man quickly, and what they did to him outside of the club is unknown. Mack recalled an incident in which a state cop was severely beaten, only to return with backup.

The Exiles were allowed to stay in a place called The Alpike Motel on Friday nights after their gigs in Martin, an exciting experience for young high school musicians. Nevertheless, they didn't spend much time partying. "We were mostly too scared of the clientele to get into much trouble," said J.P. "I remember a lot of bad-looking characters running in and out of rooms at all hours of the night."

The musicians were also protective of their money, and bootleggers could be difficult to deal with. Often, when stopping at a late night restaurant near the hotel to grab burgers and fries to go, the group was ridiculed because of their long hair and attire. Some of the insults almost led to physical confrontations. The Exiles' early experiences at The Alpike Motel helped to prepare the group for future situations on the road.

Chapter Two

JUST ONE VICTORY

THE EXILES TRAVELED TO their early gigs in a hearse. "A lot of bands that were somewhat solvent had hearses for band cars," explains J.P. "I don't know how we paid for it because nobody ever told me about things like that, and I guess I was too green to ask." Indeed, The Exiles weren't the only band driving a hearse around Kentucky at the time. The Ovations, a band that included future Exile member Les Taylor, also used one. According to J.P., the back window of the Ovations' hearse read, "Don't laugh—your daughter may be in here."

Mike remembers that the Exiles' hearse had a straight-eight, 8-cylinder engine, and that it was a model from the 1950s. Once the group loaded it with equipment, the frame sunk down on the axel. J.P. recalled an incident in Winchester in which an evil-looking man jumped out in front of them, middle finger extended, and insisted they remove their 'hearst' immediately. On another occasion, the band found the back window of the vehicle smashed in after a gig at The Youth Center. "We never knew who did it, but we secretly blamed the old skirt-chaser, Jimmy Stokley, for it," said J.P. "When it came to picking up girls, he could have cared less if there was a possibility they could be attached to some jealous redneck." The history of the hearse came to an end when the engine blew up on the highway about five miles out of Richmond on a return trip from Lexington.

The Youth Center was owned by a tenor saxophone player and high school band director named David Grigsby. His musical background endeared him to The Exiles, and he was known to sit in with the band. He loved to play soul music, especially James Brown covers, and he championed The Exiles. He also provided valuable advice insisting that Mack hit his snare drum harder, and teaching the group about arrangements and tempos. Grigsby fit in well with the group in the days before Bernie Faulkner's arrival, forming a horn section with Billy. Coincidentally, J.P. would end up marrying Grigsby's niece many years later. They're still together.

Grigsby encouraged The Exiles to branch out, and he helped to arrange and finance a performance in Nashville at The Club Steal Away. The clientele at the club was primarily African-American, which provided a unique experience for a group used to playing in Martin, Kentucky. "We were the only white faces there, except for a skimpily-dressed go-go dancer who did nothing but hump on a pole and writhe around on the floor," said J.P.

The Exiles played two nights at the club, but there was low turnout. Surprisingly, they were asked back. "We fared well, because Stokley put on a good show," said Mike. Buzz remembers the gig as a positive experience, perhaps a turning point in the band's career. "I had never had an audience perform back at me," says Buzz. "We actually left that gig thinking we might be able to play something and entertain some people." The Exiles were not able to arrange a return visit to The Club Steal Away, but their initial experience at the club boosted their confidence.

While they were in Nashville, Grigsby introduced The Exiles to DJ John Richbourg, known on Nashville's 50,000 watt AM radio station WLAC as John R. Grigsby had encouraged the band to listen to Richbourg at night, because the DJ played funky soul music. Listeners got most of their music from AM stations in the 1960s, and a group of white DJs at WLAC helped to spread the music of Stax, James Brown, Ray Charles, and others. Many listeners believed that the DJs were black. "We were all big fans and grew up listening through the static to his late night show on WLAC, and I had always thought that he was a black man," said J.P. Grigsby was able to get a demo of The Exiles to John R., and the DJ invited The Exiles back to Nashville to record a single.

The first single that the band recorded was a Paul Smith Jr. composition entitled "The Answer to Her Prayers" (1965). It was recorded at Jimbo Records' studio in Lexington, Kentucky. The sexist, politically incorrect nature of the song was not lost on all of the members. "I thought that was the most self-centered song I'd ever heard in my life," said Buzz. "'Don't you know you're the answer to her prayers,' and I thought 'that is about as misogynist as you can get.'" They recorded the song in one take in a garage studio located on Liberty Road in Lexington. The studio belonged to Jimmy Kincer, who also owned a radio station in Richmond. The single didn't get much radio play at the time, but The Exiles were glad to have a recording out. They also played the song at their live shows. "At the time, girls just thought that was wonderful," explains Buzz. They recorded the B-side, "Come On," in Lexington at a studio on Waller Avenue during the same period, but it also failed to gain music industry attention.

The Exiles continued to play consistently, and several of the members began to lose interest in college in lieu of the band. Billy, who was commuting on weekends between Richmond and Austin Peay University during the fall of 1964 and spring of 1965, eventually dropped out of school and rejected a music scholarship in order to continue his work with The Exiles. He would eventually attend Eastern Kentucky University and Fugazzi Business College, before moving on to a successful career in business.

J.P., Mack, and Mike attended Eastern Kentucky at various times, but none of them finished their degrees. Ironically, one of the band's most important venues at the time was the local hangout for EKU students, a club called Speck's. Speck's has gained a semi-legendary status around Central Kentucky, and as of late there have been annual reunions celebrating the club. Despite the nostalgia, Speck's wasn't a place that the college encouraged students to patronize on a regular basis when it was open. Few clubs in Richmond were open to those under twenty-one in the 1960s, and Speck's was located nearby the campus. Until the mid-1960s, EKU required all females to be in their dorms by 9 p.m. on weekdays. Hard liquor wasn't served at the club, but beer was sold in large quantities.

The downtown college scene in Richmond would eventually spread out to include various clubs on First and Main Street, but in the 1960s Speck's dominated the college scene. This meant that bands such as The Maroons and The Exiles were assured of significant crowds and exposure in the local newspaper, *The Richmond Register*. This atmosphere was enticing for young musicians, but it didn't always encourage scholastic achievement. Various members of the band went back to school after their time in the band. For instance, Mack earned a degree in junior accounting and Buzz earned an undergraduate degree in theater and a master's in English.

Early on, The Exiles were known for their strong vocal-oriented approach. Billy, J.P., Mike, and Buzz added background/harmony vocals to Stokley's powerful lead vocals, and the group could often overwhelm the competition. "They were pretty much a step ahead of all the other bands back then—actually a couple of steps ahead as far as professionalism and that sort of thing," said future Exile member Les Taylor.

The Exiles were aware of doo-wop and groups such as The Beach Boys, and they looked to incorporate advanced vocal arrangements. They held separate vocal rehearsals in addition to full band practices, and they learned Young Rascals hits such as "It's a Beautiful Morning" and "Groovin.'" The soul influence was evident in The Young Rascals' music. Their harmonies and arrangements encouraged The Exiles to move in an R&B direction. "The Rascals were a group favorite in that they were white guys singing black-sounding music," said J.P. The Young Rascals were also quite successful at the time, so The Exiles followed a similar path. Vocal rehearsals were often held at Stokley's house. Buzz helped the group rehearse through the use of his melodica, a small keyboard/reed instrument on which sound is produced by blowing through a mouthpiece.

Soul music is often viewed as danceable, and The Exiles' proficiency in the style led to gigs such as proms and sock-hops. Proms continued to help pay the bills up until the success of "Kiss You all Over." J.P. remembers playing at his future wife's prom in 1978. Proms paid well, but they only lasted for a couple of weekends in the spring. One of The Exiles' most memorable gigs from this period was an "after-prom" on a large riverboat called *The Belle* that cruised down the Ohio River alongside Louisville. The kids attending the prom had raised money for this after-prom all year. It was not chaperoned in the same manner as the traditional prom, and alcohol probably played a role in the after-prom festivities.

Unfortunately, the gig presented a number of problems for the band. They had to drag their equipment across a large parking lot and up a long set of stairs to get to the room inside the boat where they were supposed to play. The electricity on the boat was powered by an old generator that cycled up and down. The band sounded fine when the generator cycled up, but when it went down their instruments sounded weak and distorted. Another interesting prom took place at Johnson Central High School in Paintsville. Some equipment was missing when The Exiles showed up and they had to scour the community for gear. They were able to find some of the necessary equipment, and the locals proved especially helpful by breaking into the school's music room to borrow an upright piano. In their typical "never-give-up" fashion, the band was able to compensate for some of the missing equipment by getting the students involved by inviting them onstage to sing or shake tambourines.

At some point in late 1965, J.P. left the group. There is confusion among band members concerning this incident. It is apparent that J.P. didn't communicate effectively with the others at the time. It should also be pointed out that he turned 16-years-old in 1965, and he was heavily influenced by his parent's decisions. He also seems to have suffered from a bit of confusion concerning what he wanted to do with his life. The Exiles were an intensely driven band from the start, and they did not take kindly to those who didn't seem to share their devotion to the band. "You've got to keep in mind one thing—Pennington was a fair-weather friend back then," said Billy. "He would be gone more than he was there, and he actually left for a couple of years and formed his own band in Berea, so he was kind of in and out of the picture." Billy, Mike, Buzz, and Mack recalled that Pennington left in order to play basketball. Buzz:

I remember that we were having a rehearsal, and we were rehearsing at Speck's. And he walked in with a couple of friends of his, but he didn't walk in with his bass. And he started talking to us I remember—I was up on the stage. And he said, 'I'm gonna have to quit boys.' And he said, 'Well, because I can't do this and do basketball, too, and I really want to play basketball.' He did indeed play basketball. My father was a referee— was a referee at night—and he thought that J.P. was one of the finest natural athletes he'd ever seen.

Soon after he left The Exiles, J.P. decided to form his own band in Berea, a decision that wasn't pleasing to all. Billy:

He lived in Berea, and so while he was at it...I mean we can't wait for him to get through playing basketball. So while he was at it he started his own band in Berea. And they played on their own quite a bit, but at the same time we definitely were heading in the direction that we wanted to go in. And later when it became a compatible situation again, then he joined us. But we made sure we had guarantees from him that he wasn't going to come in and then leave again. 'Cause I think he'd done that a couple of times already, and we wanted stability. The biggest challenge of having a group was keeping it together. And that was one thing I attribute the longevity of our group to the fact that we were able to keep that unit intact.

Ironically, J.P. is now recognized as the lone remaining member of the 1960s version of the group, a role he has held since Buzz's departure in 1980.

J.P. tells a different story concerning his departure, and it is perfectly feasible that his reasons for leaving the band were different from the explanation that he provided in 1965. "Around two years in, my parents announced that I'd have to quit the band," said J.P. "They thought I was too young to be out of the house and on my own."

Other members had graduated from high school by this point, and J.P. was about to enter his junior year in high school. He hoped to rejoin the band when he graduated. Paul switched to bass after J.P.'s departure, leaving Mike as the sole guitarist. The move was a logical one due to the fact that they now had a keyboard player. The six-member band continued to produce a thick sound after J.P.'s departure with their tight vocal harmonies and guitar/keyboard interplay. "I remember packing my gear and saying goodbye to all the guys that day—not knowing whether I'd ever be a part of the band again," said J.P. "I did rejoin them eventually, but a lot happened in the meantime."

The six remaining members continued to perform at The Martin Youth Center, and David Grigsby encouraged them to dig deeper into soul music. Stokley had a raspy voice, and was able to belt out the more aggressive soul standards of the day. He didn't possess a *smooth* voice, and he had a tendency to sound somewhat awkward on ballads. "I think he made up for the fact that he couldn't sing with the feel and the emotion, and that's fine, a lot of people made a big career out of that and so I don't have a problem with it," said Billy. "He couldn't sing a really beautiful song."

Stokley was, however, adept at shouting and imitating the screams that he heard on Wilson Pickett and James Brown records. This style of singing endeared him to audiences in the 1960s, but it caused him problems in the late 1970s. "He wasn't trained, and he wound up just totally blowing his voice because he didn't know how to sing," said Billy. "And he screamed a lot. He had a lot of feel in his voice."

Stokley certainly wasn't the only young white singer trying to sing with an R&B feel in the 1960s, but it is clear that he was interested in soul music before it was particularly fashionable among rock and roll bands. Billy recalls hearing someone claim that Stokley had copied Mick Jagger. "The fact was he'd never seen Mick Jagger, and so he developed that on his own," said Billy. Stokley probably became aware of British Invasion bands at some point during 1964, but he began to develop his aggressive vocal style as early as 1963.

Soon after J.P.'s departure, Grigsby arranged a return trip to Nashville in late 1965. The Exiles had an opportunity to record a single during this return engagement. John R. served as the producer, and he chose the material. The band was anxious, but John R. refused to let them know what they were going to record until after their arrival. The session was held at a Studio called The Red Barn. Buzz talks about the experience:

> It was the Red Barn. All these pictures of Patsy Cline and all this stuff around. Here we are, a little rock and roll group. And not even knowing when they're going to cut. And out comes this gray haired, skinny, white man, who is J.R. Ninety-five percent of his clientele think he's black. And he just started talking about this song, and how it should be done. I don't even remember the session.

Mike remembers that John R. may have been perplexed as well. "I think he was under the impression that most of us were black, especially Stokley," said Mike. "And it was somewhat of a surprise to see a bunch of white boys coming in the door."

One of the songs The Exiles recorded was called "It's Alligator Time." The instrumental prowess of the band had clearly improved since their recording sessions in Lexington, and they were developing a soulful, garage-rock feel. The influence of The Rascals and Stones was still apparent, but Buzz's organ lines and Mike's guitar riffs were equally influenced by Booker T. & the MGs and Stax Records on this one-chord tune. There is a brief saxophone in the song provided by Grigsby. The lyrics were risqué, especially for 1966. "It was kind of one of those 'down in the alley' kind of songs," said Billy.

The lyrics were loaded with double entendre meanings throughout, and the vocals make Stokley's yearning pleas on "Kiss You All Over" sound romantic in comparison. (i.e. "Now get on the floor, and let's do it some more," "Stroke it, 'cause it's alligator time," "Stroke that alligator," etc.) "He'd tell Stokely…he said, 'You've got to imagine that you're on the floor, stroke the alligator, stroke,'" said Buzz. "And I thought, 'Well, that's lurid.'"

Buzz's outspoken nature was well known within the group, and others were afraid that he might voice an opinion that could end the session. "Everybody else was so afraid that I was going to say something that would piss off John R., because he was bankrolling the whole thing," said Buzz. "Every time I'd get ready to open my mouth, Luxon would snap a glare at me, and so I kept my mouth shut."

Stokley's performance was convincing, and at no other time in The Exiles' recorded history did the wilder side of his personality seem as unhinged as it did on "It's Alligator Time." Musically, the song was a one-chord vamp with a few breaks and accents provided by the horn section, and it was up to Stokley to provide much of the interest with his half-spoken narrative. Interestingly, his performance earned him sole songwriter credit, a fact that may not have been lost on the other members of the band.

Despite Stokley's convincing performance and the fact that the song holds up better than much of their material from the 1960s, the single was not a commercial success. The Exiles also recorded a song entitled "A Game Called Hurt" during the session. It features a sultry saxophone solo, a bluesy groove, and raspy vocals provided by Stokley. This funky, soulful track was one of their better recordings from the 1960s. It includes a guitar solo provided by Mike, and is one of the best recorded representations of his playing style during his time in The Exiles.

"It's Alligator Time" provided The Exiles with much needed studio experience, but nothing could have prepared them for what was to come. Package tours were all the rage in the 1960s. Dick Clark's Caravan of Stars tour was one of the most popular. It provided an opportunity for those living in small towns to attend shows by popular entertainers of the day. Buzz was in attendance when the Caravan of Stars arrived in Richmond, Kentucky in 1965. The experience was emotionally draining for the young keyboardist, and he didn't pay much attention to his date. "She wants to talk about this and giggle about that, and all that stuff and I am glued…I am glued to that stage, which is extremely disappointing to her." Buzz wasn't interested in talking on the way home from the show, and when he started to speak he began to cry. "And I said, 'I will never—because I'm from Richmond, Kentucky—I will never, ever have the opportunity to play with people like that and be a part of a wonderful show and all,'" said Buzz. He didn't know that he would soon be on tour with the Caravan of Stars.

The Exiles got their opportunity to play with the Caravan of Stars through another connection via David Grigsby. Grigsby knew Peggy Rogers, Dick Clark's mid-west operating manager. He had assisted her with booking tours in Eastern Kentucky. By this point The Exiles had replaced Gary Edwards and The Maroons as the house band at Speck's, and Grigsby encouraged Rogers to attend a show. As the group anxiously awaited her arrival at Speck's, it seemed as though she wouldn't make it. "When she came down to hear us she was late, and we figured, 'Well hell, she's not comin','" said Mack. "And we found out she hit a deer on the way down."

Buzz remembers that Rogers came across as a sweet, upfront woman, and that she wanted to talk to the members of the band about their careers. A week or two later, she invited the band to travel to Music Hall in Cincinnati to serve as Lou Christie's backing band on a Dick Clark production that also included Roy Orbison. She told The Exiles that Christie was going to bring musical charts, but the band would not know which songs were going to be played until they arrived. She also informed the band that they would be allotted fifteen minutes to perform at the beginning of the show before accompanying Christie. This was the opportunity that The Exiles had been looking for, and Rogers was aware of the stakes. She told them, "Boys, I'm giving you a chance. If you blow it, that's it."

As the band began to learn Lou Christie's repertoire, the young musicians began to worry about how to properly prepare for the show. Buzz called Rogers in the hopes that she might be able to provide some useful information concerning the set list. "And she said, 'Honey, just learn 'em all,'" said Buzz. "So, of course we didn't, because we were so sure that there were charts coming in." Unfortunately for The Exiles, Christie's most challenging song was his biggest hit. "Lightnin' Strikes" topped Billboard's pop chart on February 19, 1966, the week that The Exiles were supposed to accompany him. Buzz reported that he spent a good deal of time working on the song before discovering the right succession of chords.

Lou Christie wasn't there when The Exiles arrived at Music Hall. This gave the band time to rehearse with female background singers hired specifically for the Cincinnati show. They didn't know "Lightnin' Strikes" either, and it was up to Buzz to teach them the notes for the various "puppy-i-woos" heard throughout the hit. "I stopped it, and I said, 'You're singing the wrong notes,'" said Buzz.

The initial shock of Buzz's assertion quickly wore off, and one of the background singers encouraged the others to listen to the young keyboardist. "She came over and patted me on my head," said Buzz. "So they stood around the keyboard, and I taught them that little inversion and they learned it." In the meantime, Lou Christie didn't make his scheduled flight. He didn't arrive until ten minutes before the show, which left no time for rehearsal. The band was told that they would have to "wing it."

Buzz was furious and disheartened. Nevertheless, the group had a job to do, and they soldiered on. The Exiles played their fifteen-minute opening set, and the sellout crowd was appreciative. Lou Christie followed, and, not surprisingly, he opened his set with "Lightnin' Strikes." At one point during the song Christie turned around and looked at the group with what Buzz described as "big open eyes." The group was understandably concerned and worried about Christie's reaction, but they continued to play.

After the performance they returned to a dressing room where Peggy Rogers was waiting for them. As she was talking to the band, Christie suddenly entered the dressing room. He wanted to know who came up with the arrangement for "Lightin' Strikes," and Buzz was quickly pointed out as the guilty party. "And he said, 'Would you please write down those chords, that series of chords, because it isn't even written correctly on my charts,'" said Buzz. Bands had been playing the song incorrectly since it was recorded in the studio, and Buzz had pulled off the most important arrangement of his life. He wrote the chords on the back of a paper sack, impressing Peggy in the process. It was clear that at least one member of The Exiles read music, and Peggy began to consider them as a backing band for future Caravan of Stars tours. "She said, 'Oh boy, we're gonna use you, you did great,' all that, which is, you know, the usual crap you hear," said Mack.

The Exiles were not supposed to be a backing band for the 1966 Caravan of Stars, but they managed to get the gig due to an unexpected event. The equipment truck for the tour broke down somewhere east of Kentucky, and the instruments didn't show up for the Lexington, Kentucky Caravan of Stars performance at Stoll Field. The Exiles had planned to go to the concert, but they had no idea that they would get a call from Peggy on the day of the performance. The Exiles were offered an opening fifteen-minute slot on the show in exchange for the use of their instruments. The band was more than happy to oblige. When they arrived the organ was already set up, because Felix Cavaliere of The Young Rascals rented a Hammond B-3 organ in every city of the tour. Buzz explains:

> And his brother would come ahead and get the organ all set up and everything, and then thank everybody and they would leave. And then he'd take the back off the organ...go in there for the bass pedals and soup them up, because the Rascals didn't have a bass. Felix did it with his left foot, and it would blow Leslies like crazy. And they'd complain every night...'Well you gave us inferior material, you know?' And people would take these Leslies back going, 'I don't know. I thought this was the best one I had.' Because, of course, he would set it back to what it should be before they got it.

Buzz didn't have to set up his equipment that night, and he got the opportunity to play Cavaliere's Hammond B-3 organ. The chance to play an authentic B-3 organ might have thrilled other keyboardists, but Buzz, a pianist at heart, was only playing an organ for practical reasons such as portability and a desire to accurately recreate the sound of radio hits. "I had never played a Hammond organ before, and I didn't know that the black keys were sets," said Buzz. "I had a Farfisa, and on my Farfisa the black keys on the bottom were bass."

Buzz didn't know that the black keys on a Hammond organ were used to change the timbre of the sound, and that they were not used to produce notes. Nevertheless, he quickly figured out the new instrument, and The Exiles went on to have another successful performance. They were asked to finish the 1966 tour as a result, and they were seemingly on their way to the big time on a crowded bus.

The tour started in late October, and lasted throughout most of November. The Exiles were required to back up several acts, often with little or no rehearsal. "Typically on the Dick Clark tours they would give us chord sheets, and just basically—'4/4/ time, here's the chords, good luck,'" said Mike. Luckily, they already knew many of the songs, and they could read chord sheets.

One of the acts on the tour was The Yardbirds, featuring a young Jimmy Page. Page would go on to form Led Zeppelin and achieve large scale success, but at the time he was struggling to keep The Yardbirds afloat after the recent departure of Jeff Beck. "I remember we were in the Holiday Inn restaurant the next morning after the show eating breakfast, and he came over and sat right with us and talked just like we'd known him forever," said Billy.

Jack Nance, the tour manager and a former songwriter ("It's Only Make Believe" with Conway Twitty), took an interest in the group. He became an important contact. John Caldwell, another show business insider involved with The Caravan of Stars tour, wanted to take the group to record in New York City. Things were looking promising for The Exiles.

In January of 1967, The Exiles were given the opportunity to record a few singles in New York City on Date Records, a subsidiary of Columbia. Stokley sang lead on the tracks, and the other members provided background vocals. The instruments were played by session musicians. "Those were actually canned tracks," said Mike. The songs were not composed by The Exiles, and the pop-oriented nature of the songs and the syrupy production was not indicative of their musical style. Not surprisingly, none of the singles were a success.

"What is the Reason" was a more up-tempo and less effective cover of a Young Rascals song. The string heavy arrangement and straight, groove-less rhythm of the track pales in comparison to the original. Mike remembers singing background on it, and Stokley sang lead. "Come Out, Come Out Whoever You Are" was even less impressive. It's not clear whether the track was meant as a kind of double entendre by the songwriters at the time, but the over-produced horn arrangement and cheesy vocal effects at the end of the song ensure that the track will forever be dated. With its Phil Spector inspired wall-of-sound arrangement, "I'd Love to Give My Love Away" represents over-production at its worst. The Exiles would produce much better work in subsequent trips to the studio. These songs represent little more than the exploitation of an unknown band from Kentucky by major label producers. This would prove to be Buzz's last trip to New York for a while, but it certainly made an impression on him. The Exiles' return to Kentucky was postponed due to a blizzard, and Buzz vividly remembers the atmosphere in the city at the time. Buzz:

I mean it completely closed Manhattan—totally. Nothing in, nothing out. Oh, it was wonderful. It was one of the most beautiful things I've ever seen in my life. People were so nice to each other on the street. It sounded like a movie set. The chains on the taxis sounded like bells. The Christmas decorations were all still up. Everything went well on that trip. And then it was at the end of that trip when John (Caldwell) said, "You must move up here." And I could not go back up.

Caldwell's invitation sparked excitement within the group, but it also presented problems for their keyboardist. Buzz started attending Eastern Kentucky University in the fall of 1966. He continued attending EKU in the spring and became active in the theater department. He was the only freshman in the university's production of *Once Upon a Mattress*, and was featured in a show-stopping number called "Very Soft Shoes." The musical ran for three weeks, and the students practiced throughout the semester.

More and more, Buzz found himself drawn to musical theater, a passion that continues to this day. It was during these rehearsals that Caldwell invited The Exiles to live in New York City. Buzz knew that he wanted to perform in the musical that he had worked on all semester, and he was also afraid of being drafted. Student deferment was a way for young people to avoid the draft in the late 1960s, and Buzz certainly wasn't interested in going to Vietnam. "They were taking everybody at that time," said Buzz. Caldwell offered to put Buzz in school in New York, but the young keyboardist was filled with doubt. Buzz opted to stay in Kentucky while his band mates went to New York, and they began looking for a replacement.

Introducing Bernie Faulkner

Buzz's replacement was a young man from Hazard, Kentucky named Bernie Faulkner. Bernie and Buzz were both gifted musicians, but they were also opposites. Buzz was influenced by classical music early on, while Bernie was a self-taught musician. "I learned how to play the boogie-woogie on the piano when I was real young, and beat on pots and pans and all that kind of stuff," said Bernie. His mother played piano, but she took an improvisational approach to the instrument. "My mama played the piano, and played that old style music—the swing kind of stuff," said Bernie.

Bernie learned how to play the piano, but he never stuck with one instrument for very long. His parents bought him a guitar when he was 12, and he took percussion lessons in middle school. "I started taking drum lessons from the band director, Harlan Stone—a big influence on me," said Bernie. "He gave me two drumsticks—didn't have a drum pad, and I learned how to play paradiddles on my knee."

Eventually Bernie found a rubber drum pad, but by that point he was moving on to a different instrument. "I said, 'I'm tired of this, I want something that'll make a melody.'" Bernie switched to saxophone, and he realized that he could quickly learn melodies by ear. He progressed quickly, and was the first chair saxophonist for Harlan High School as an eighth grade middle school student. It was also around this time that he got his first experience playing in clubs on various instruments. His interest in music continued into his high school years. He was offered the position of drum major, but he was reluctant at first. He remembers saying, "Buddy, I ain't wearin' one of them fuzzy hats." The director found a small hat for Bernie to wear, and proceeded to teach him the rudiments of the various band instruments. Bernie was also called upon to direct the group when the director was away.

After graduating from high school, Bernie attended Eastern Kentucky University. He considered majoring in music. To his dismay, they asked him if he wanted to be in marching band or the chamber orchestra. His answer was "neither one." He proceeded to inform the music faculty that he performed music on the weekends. The faculty was not impressed by Bernie's rock and roll chops, and he moved on to other things including The Exiles.

Bernie remembers meeting The Exiles during a practice at Speck's. He saw a white Harley-Davidson Sportster sitting outside as he was driving through downtown Richmond on his motorcycle, and he decided to enter the club. Its owner, Mike Howard, was in the club practicing, and Bernie asked if he could sit in with the band during practice. He was informed that Buzz was protective of his Farfisa. "I said, 'If I break it, I'll buy him another one. I've got a B-3 at the house.'"

Mike and Bernie proceeded to jam for a little while before the other members arrived. Bernie observed the rehearsal. As he sat in the floor and listened to the music, Bernie began to understand the way the group worked. "A little 45 record spinning, and Buzzy is saying that's an F major 7 going to a B-flat major 7 and then to a C, and all that kind of stuff," said Bernie. "I said, 'Right there is the dude putting this music together for them.' He was like the ear."

Bernie appreciated Buzz's arranging skills, but he couldn't relate to him personally. "Buzzy: classically trained, real, real stiff—has to be this way," said Bernie. "Buddy, if I have to do that I'm gonna quit." Bernie's approach was more laid back, and he was a more instinctive, improvisational musician. He was offered a chance to sit in with the group at the rehearsal, and he impressed them immediately. "I think he probably joined the next day," said Billy. "He was just one of those people that was a soul brother…he was right there with us."

Bernie added new dimensions to the group due to his multi-instrumental approach. "I'm not any virtuoso on any of them," said Bernie. "I'm a feel player. I can read, but I don't let it get in my way." Like many musicians, Bernie became familiar with The Nashville Number System, a method designed to help musicians adjust to different keys. In addition to his keyboard skills and occasional rhythm guitar work, Bernie was a skilled saxophone player. Bernie and Billy teamed to create a two-piece horn section. Buzz also played trumpet, which gave the group the option of using a three-piece horn section. Both keyboardists would work together successfully in the group later on, but in 1967 it looked as though Bernie might become Buzz's permanent replacement. During the spring semester of 1967 they ran into each other on the EKU campus. "He said, 'What are you planning to do? I need to know, because I have to make arrangements, and I'm from Hazard,' and, you know…all this," said Buzz. Buzz decided to stay in school and act in *Once Upon a Mattress*, and Bernie traveled with The Exiles to New York City.

Soon after The Exiles arrived in New York, Paul was drafted. This left the group in search of a bass player. Paul returned to Kentucky in 1968. Mike remembers that Smith "went to the service, came back, and he started booking bands with Julie (Steddom)." Steddom would soon become his wife. The Exiles had gotten to know her because she was the personal secretary to Dick Friedberg, the president of Premier Talent in New York City. Premier Talent was one of the largest booking agencies in the U.S. at the time, and Paul used his connections to continue his career in the music industry.

Paul's initial replacement was a young man named Larry Davis. Davis was from Jackson, Tennessee, but he met The Exiles in New York. Davis didn't get along with the other members of the band, and he soon developed the derogatory nickname of "dipsh--." Personality conflicts and musical differences convinced the group that Davis wasn't going to be their bass player of the future. "He was okay, he was just young and kind of a dipsh--," said Mike. Davis' departure opened the door for J.P. Pennington to return, a personnel move that would influence future events dramatically.

J.P. missed out on the group's Dick Clark experience by a few months. He transferred from Madison Central to Berea High School after his freshman year, which made it difficult to communicate with his former band mates in Richmond after he quit the group. He didn't know if he would ever get another chance to rejoin. This created a good deal of envy, and helped instill a drive that would pay off in the long run. "I was so glad for them—and so jealous!" said J.P. Cell phones and the internet were not available in 1966, and J.P. had to rely on second hand information concerning the progress of The Exiles. "I wanted to be a part of it so bad it hurt, but, for now, I'd have to have to settle for hanging around Berea and going to school and wondering what it felt like to be a part of big time show business," said J.P.

While The Exiles were breaking into show business, J.P. founded a group in Berea called The Midnighters. The group included Kenny Todd on Hammond "L" model organ, Bobby Asher on bass, Paul Barker on drums, and J.P. on electric guitar.

One of the group's greatest moments took place at a talent contest in Richmond. They had to work up thirty minutes of material in order to enter, and they decided that J.P. should sing. He wasn't excited about singing at the time, but the experience would prove valuable later on. "We won the contest, but as far as I was concerned my singing days were over," said J.P. "I hated it! Not only did I suck, but singing and playing guitar at the same time was more than I could grasp."

He may not have enjoyed singing, but he certainly enjoyed winning the contest. "It was funny, there was a band that was one of our competitors in that contest that the Exile boys had taken under their wing, and their singer was a Jimmy Stokley clone," said J.P. "They did the same songs and everything, and it did us a lot of good to beat them out." Soon after the contest, J.P. ran into his old friend, former Exiles vocalist Ronnie Hall. J.P. asked Hall to join The Midnighters, and they went on to play several gigs around Madison County. Hall knew several dance-oriented songs, and they soon had enough material to fill out an entire evening. One of their more memorable gigs took place after a Berea High School basketball game. J.P. had played in the game (a loss), and his participation in the after party irritated his coach. The Midnighters were together until J.P. received a phone call from Mike Howard in the spring of 1967. Mike invited J.P. to replace Larry Davis in The Exiles, effectively breaking up The Midnighters in the process. This time J.P.'s parents were supportive of his desire to play with The Exiles, so he traveled to New York City to join the band.

The Exiles' first extended trip to New York lasted about three months. They experienced a good deal of culture shock when they arrived. The new environment took some getting used to. "I'd only seen pictures of New York, but pictures alone couldn't begin to describe what I saw and felt," said J.P. "Everything was coming at me at hyper speed. The traffic, the huge buildings, the smog, the noise." The cab ride through Manhattan was an exhilarating experience for the recent high school graduate from Berea, and he was shocked by the group's living conditions. They stayed in a small two-bedroom apartment on West End Avenue and 96th Street in Manhattan. Each bedroom contained a double bed, and there were two couches in the living room. J.P. and Bernie, the latest additions to the group, were required to sleep on the couches. J.P. and Bernie had never met, but they got to know each other quickly. J.P:

Bernie was a real country character from Hazard, Kentucky the fellows had met while he was a college student back home in Richmond. Like me, Bernie had never been far from home. He was never self-conscious about his country ways, though. One afternoon during rush hour we were all walking down the street when Bernie stopped us. He pointed to a giant loaf of Italian bread in a deli window and said at the top of his lungs, "God a-mighty, lookee yonder, what a loaf of bread!" For those New Yorkers who happened to be passing by, he might as well have been from Mars.

The Exiles had already played several gigs before J.P. arrived, sometimes on bills with bands that would go on to have significant success. "I remember the first job we did in New York City," said Bernie. "The Vanilla Fudge was opening for us." Bernie was astonished by Vanilla Fudge organist Mark Stein's playing ability, and he realized that there would be significant competition in New York. J.P. remembers seeing The Hassles, a group that featured a young vocalist/keyboardist named Billy Joel. Mack remembers that The Exiles opened for The Vanilla Fudge and The Vagrants at a club on Long Island called The Action House. The Vanilla Fudge had not yet broken through to the mainstream with their version of The Supremes' "You Keep Me Hangin' On." The Vagrants featured a young guitar player named Leslie West who would later have success with the group Mountain. "We opened up, and they didn't like us because we were a jukebox band," said Mack.

Interestingly, The Vagrants and The Vanilla Fudge also indulged in covers, but their versions were substantially different from the originals. The Exiles were still trying to emulate the sound of the records they were listening to. "We'd learn stuff and try to imitate the record, which did us well in clubs, and the bars, and the dances," said Mike. The Exiles were still influenced by R&B groups such as The Temptations, The Four Tops, the Impressions, and The Miracles, and they continued to focus on adding tight vocal harmonies to their arrangements. "We liked that sound, and tried to copy it," continues Mike. And unlike The Vanilla Fudge, they didn't turn soul standards into psychedelic workouts for the love generation. Perhaps the most unique thing about The Exiles at this time was the fact that they were from Kentucky, not a region known for its soul music history. "We were a little bit unique, you know, we were a bunch of hicks from Kentucky in the big city," explains Mike. Nevertheless, the competition was stiff and The Exiles were in the middle of a musical scene that would influence the next several decades of music. "It is still to this day the most exciting scene I've ever been a part of," said J.P.

The Exiles were fascinated by their New York experience, but it also proved grueling at times. The most difficult stretch of gigs on their first New York trip took place at a club called Chollie's in the Bronx. They were required to play six sets a night from 9:00 p.m. to 3:00 a.m., seven nights a week, with a three-set matinee on Saturdays. The band would arrive back at their apartment around 7:00 each morning. This arrangement worked to improve their cohesiveness as a band, but it was difficult. "Once you do those gigs for that long you can just about play that stuff in your sleep, so you don't have to worry about rehearsing because you rehearse every night," said Mike.

The Exiles were glad to play their last show at Chollie's, but the excitement was dimmed by the first of several unfortunate events that would plague their New York trips. The van ran out of gas after the last show, and, since there were no gas stations open at that time of night, they had to push the vehicle for what J.P. describes as "100 blocks or so back to the apartment."

Another club that they played was Googie's, an establishment owned by a retired baseball umpire in Waterbury, Connecticut. The Exiles enjoyed playing at Googie's, but they got off to a rough start at the club when an audience member yelled out "Where's the Plug?" after their first song. Pennington remembers another gig at a club in Pittsfield, Massachusetts on a Sunday during a snowstorm. There were two couples in attendance, and response to the band was noticeably light. Pittsfield is at least a three hour drive from New York City, and the trip seemed useless. The mood was lightened when a waitress dropped a tray during a brief pause before Stokley was about to sing the closing line of a ballad. Gigs of this nature didn't justify life away from home, and the group soon returned to Kentucky after three months in the New York City area. "The old adage about New York being a nice place to visit, but I wouldn't want to live there…that's me," said Mike.

The Exiles couldn't wait to get back to Kentucky, and they resumed their regular gig at Speck's. "I could have kissed the ground!" said J.P. By this point the band had developed a substantial reputation, and they packed the club on a regular basis. "These days the fire codes wouldn't allow such a crowd in a place that small," explained J.P.

The Exiles' success at Speck's was also partially due to the fact that the club almost had a monopoly on the EKU student crowd at the time. The other bars in town were considered too rough, and college students weren't particularly welcome. Speck's was divided into two rooms: one side contained the bar and some booths; the stage and a dance floor were on the other side. The drinking age was twenty-one, but those eighteen years of age were allowed to enter. Patrons under twenty-one years of age were stamped on the wrist when they entered, but that hardly ensured that alcohol would not be served to minors.

The police would occasionally make a token bust, but it never affected business in a substantial way. "When we'd play there, man, the people would be backed all the way around the block to get in," said Bernie. "The floor would start shaking, you know, the dancing, and it was a great atmosphere. The fan base was a lot of girls."

One of the more unfortunate incidents at Speck's involved tear gas. "We were playing one night and someone threw an army issued tear gas canister in Speck's," said Mack. This forced the patrons to empty the establishment quickly. "A couple of them jumped out the windows, and sprained ankles and stuff like that," continues Mack. Patrons were lying around vomiting and experiencing painful breathing and burning eyes. The guilty party was never discovered, although there has been some speculation as to who was responsible.

The Exiles learned a good deal about showmanship in New York City, and they were a changed band when they returned to Kentucky. They wore matching blue, striped, double-breasted gangster-like suits early on during the New York trip, which were eventually discarded in favor of light blue Nehru suits. By the time they arrived in Kentucky, The Exiles were wearing mismatched Edwardian suits. Stokley had a penchant for wearing over-the-top outfits. His "cricket" outfit consisted of Speedos over a leotard with knee-high boots. Other outfits included a headdress with large feathers sticking out in all directions and a James Brown cloak. Audiences never knew what outfits or onstage antics to expect from Stokley. He became the focus of The Exiles' stage show.

J.P. recalls a much later gig during which Stokley traded shirts with a woman. Stokley ended up wearing her pink, lacy-top, and she went home in his Exile shirt that she had been requesting throughout the evening. The Exiles also incorporated a light show that was years ahead of its time. Jim Linford, one of the band's roadies, developed the lights by rewiring genuine aircraft strobe lights from the wing of an airplane. "He ordered several boxfuls of parts, and the next thing you know he had some strobe lights that would literally put your eyes out," said Billy.

Linford hotwired the lights so that they would blink rapidly, creating a vibrant effect that would sometimes leave drunks confused. "It was so strong that it would make drunks fall over when we turned them on full blast," said J.P. Audiences weren't used to strobe lights at the time, and the effect must have been staggering in 1967.

One of the songs that The Exiles included in their set during this period was The Vanilla Fudge's version of "You Keep Me Hangin' On." "We played their version of that, and cranked those strobe lights up," said Mike. "People were falling down. It was so disorienting."

Chapter Three

THERE'S BEEN A CHANGE

THE EXILES WERE INVITED to play on The Caravan of Stars tours again in 1967 and 1968. Their job was to open the show with twelve minutes of cover songs and to provide accompaniment for three or four solo acts per show. Once again, there weren't any rehearsals leading up to the tour, and the band had to go over the music with the acts backstage in the dressing room on the day of the first show. The Exiles only had a few minutes to go over the music with each of the solo performers, and this time they had to do it without Buzz. Nevertheless, the young band from Kentucky still featured a solid group of talented musicians, and they pulled through despite the challenging conditions.

The Exiles encountered several interesting personalities on the tour. Freddy Cannon was a singer that they enjoyed working with. Cannon's hits included "Palisades Park," "Tallahassee Lassie," and "Way Down Yonder in New Orleans." J.P. described him as "a dyed-in-the wool Massachusetts Yankee." Cannon wasn't breaking down artistic doors with his material, but the songs were fun to play and he made a point to acknowledge the band during the performances.

Surprisingly, he had a morbid side offstage, sometimes playing practical jokes and making up stories. "He'd always be holding court on the bus about seeing a man running alongside us with a net and a pitchfork, or seeing someone in the audience the night before with the word 'kill' written across his forehead," said J.P. Cannon also liked to develop elaborate tricks designed to scare hotel employees.

Not wanting to be outdone, Stokley would occasionally join in on the fun. In one instance, Cannon and Stokley asked a hotel maintenance man to help them remove a bat from the shower. When the hotel employee pulled the shower curtain back, Stokley jumped out with his partial plate of front teeth removed and let loose with a primal scream while his fangs were showing. The employee was scared out of his mind, but received a tip for his efforts. Cannon's shenanigans were in good fun, and they helped to keep spirits high on the road.

The Exiles also played for Bryan Hyland, an artist known for his hit "Itsy Bitsy Teenie Weenie Yellow Polka Dot Bikini." Hyland had a mellower personality than Cannon. This may have been due to chemical enhancement. "Bryan was the first guy any of us had ever seen that was a pot user," said J.P. Hyland was usually late for every bus call, and was kicked off the show for one date by tour manager Jack Nance. Known for his iron fisted approach to running the tour, Nance once cancelled a show hours before a gig because the stage wasn't set up right. He was The Exiles' first exposure to a big-time road manager.

The Exiles also got to open up for some popular bands on the 1967 and 1968 Caravan of Stars tours. The Young Rascals were now simply The Rascals, and they headlined several shows. The Exiles were thrilled to be opening up for one of their biggest influences. The Rascals were known for their entertaining live act, and drummer Dino Danelli was a particularly impressive performer, tossing drum sticks in the air and hitting the crash cymbals with his hands without sacrificing the groove. Mack was influenced by Danelli's style, as were many other young drummers at the time.

Paul Revere and The Raiders were another popular headliner. The Exiles played on several sold out shows that The Raiders were headlining. Paul Revere and the Raiders were supportive of the young Exiles, and went out of their way to make them feel welcome. For instance, Paul Revere, a former professional barber as well as organist, used to give the Exiles free trims. Raiders drummer Joe Jr. was also a jazz flute player. He and J.P. occasionally stayed up late working on music for flute and guitar. Freddy Weller, the guitarist, entered the field of country music while he was working with The Raiders. His transition may have influenced J.P.'s decision to make a similar move in the 1980s. "They showed us the ropes at a time when we could really take advantage of it by being exposed to a lot of people in a fairly short period of time," said J.P.

Nevertheless, The Exiles may have been a little too comfortable around The Raiders. Stokley was detained at a show in El Dorado, Arkansas for mooning Paul Revere from the wings during a performance. Fortunately, Nance was able to convince the officers to refrain from arresting the young singer.

The Exiles returned to Kentucky after their last Caravan of Stars tour in 1968, and they proceeded to play at regional venues and events; Speck's, dances, proms, etc. Before returning to Kentucky, The Exiles met and were managed by a New Yorker, Mark Alan. Alan started his management company after having worked for the New-York based Premier Talent Agency. Premier was a major talent agency for rock musicians at the time, and Alan would prove to be an important connection. He insisted that the group needed to move to New York again to capitalize on the exposure that they had received from the Dick Clark tours. Alan arranged for them to stay at The Broadway Central Hotel in Lower Manhattan, so The Exiles moved back to New York City in the fall of 1968. "It turned out to be the sleaziest place you could imagine," said J.P. "There were winos sleeping in the stairwells, and pimps and prostitutes working the lobby and the front entrance."

The Exiles requested better living conditions, but Alan talked them into staying. The decision would prove particularly devastating for Bernie. His beloved red Corvette was stolen soon after the band arrived. It was never recovered. Mike remembers that Bernie "put it in a parking garage and was paying, at that time, what we considered an outrageous price to keep it there." "I think it lasted about a week, and somebody got it," continued Mike.

The Exiles were given another chance to record on Date Records during the trip. The band was allowed to play their instruments on this session. One of the songs they recorded was "Mary on the Beach." The session was engineered by Roy Halee, a well-known producer known especially for his work on Simon and Garfunkel's *Bridge over Troubled Water* album. "I'm not sure how he ended up doing our session, but we felt that it was a feather in our caps," said J.P. The single didn't generate success on a national level, but it was popular in Central Kentucky. "To this day, I still have long-time fans mention that song," said J.P.

The second extended stay in New York proved to be a waste of time. They played in several bars and recorded a single, but the handwriting for the first phase of the group was on the wall. Their living conditions were less than desirable, and as a result they didn't take care of the place. "It's just that young guys are typically pigs at that time, and I was right there with the rest of the pigs," said Mike. The Exiles decided to leave New York City in early 1969, but not before leaving behind an indication of how they felt about their apartment. J.P. described it:

There was a winter storm howling as we were loading our belongings into our cars in front of the hotel. There was also a fire somewhere inside the hotel as several fire trucks were parked out front. Although we weren't supposed to be going back inside, several of us snuck back into our room and destroyed the place—turning over beds, knocking lamps over and throwing left-behind food all over the floors. It was our way of saying goodbye to a dismal place none of us wanted to live in to begin with. It felt good.

Billy was more hesitant in recalling this situation, and may not have been involved. "Gosh, I don't know," said Billy. "I don't know. I don't remember trashing the hotel room, but I'm not going to deny it."

Soon after the group returned to Kentucky, Mike was drafted on February 2nd, 1969. The draft ended his career with The Exiles. "I didn't want to go, but I'm glad I did at this point," said Mike in 2010. Mike was in Vietnam for eleven months and four days, and he received a 27-day drop on his tour. It's unlikely that he was thrilled by the prospect of traveling to Vietnam after a frustrating trip to New York City, but the young 19-year-old guitarist made the best of it.

Mike never rejoined The Exiles after he returned from Vietnam. He was glad to be back in Kentucky. He didn't possess the same constant drive to make it that burned inside of Jimmy Stokley at the time, and he certainly had not enjoyed his last trip to New York. "Maybe some of the other guys liked it better," said Mike. "Stokley probably didn't care—wherever he could make the band work is where he would go." At this point the group was still basically a cover band, and the lack of original music made the prospect of future success look somewhat bleak. "If we had had opportunities and original material and blah, blah, blah, I would have gone wherever it took, too," continued Mike. At that time no one in the group had stepped forward as a motivated songwriter, which forced the band to record material that wasn't geared toward their live sound. "Nobody really was interested in writing anything," says Mike. "Stokley would write words and stuff occasionally, and J.P. obviously had the ability to write stuff, but we didn't place a priority on it at that time."

Mike held various jobs outside of music after he left The Exiles, but he continued to play guitar in bands. He worked on a boat dock at Boonesboro, worked construction from 1972-75, sold cars in Lexington from 1975-82, returned to construction from 1982-87, and worked at the post office in Richmond from 1987-2009 before retiring at the age of 60. The Exiles went without a guitar player from 1969 until J.P. switched over to that instrument in mid-1973. Mike was a tough act to follow, and it took a skilled guitarist to fill the void left after his departure. He was the lead guitarist for The Exiles throughout their first phase, and his blues-rock sound had been what the group needed as they were breaking into the music business. "What I played probably was a little more suited lead-wise for what we were doing at the time," said Mike. "J.P. is and always was a better guitar player, but again, what I played was probably more of what the band needed at that particular time." Mike and J.P. continue to admire each other's playing to this day, and both are quick to compliment the other.

Mike's departure almost coincided with Buzz's return to the band. Buzz's time away had not been uneventful. Peggy instructed him to contact Bea Donaldson, the mother of Bo, about playing with The Heywoods, a band that was fulfilling duties on The Caravan of Stars tour for which The Exiles had previously been responsible. Buzz was familiar with Bea Donaldson. "We had done some jobs that she had set up in Cincinnati, and she'd always have her little crew around and wanted us to stay at her house," said Buzz.

He had already decided that he was going to attend Northern Kentucky University in the fall instead of EKU, and planned on playing cocktail piano to help finance his way through school. Buzz wasn't excited about working with the Heywoods, so he took a gig playing at a nightclub called The Lookout House in Northern Kentucky. "And then Bea decided that I really ought to be a part of her band," said Buzz. "To this day I've always thought that she did something to sabotage it."

At the last minute, Buzz received a telephone call from the owners of The Lookout House informing him that he would not have the job. The owners opted to hire a female cocktail pianist. They reportedly worried that a male cocktail pianist might encourage stag women to enter the club, which would, in turn, encourage single men to patronize the establishment. "This would cause The Lockout House to become a brothel, so I lost that gig," said Buzz sarcastically. Soon after hearing this unusual explanation, he received a phone call from Bea. She had spoken with one of the owners at The Lookout House, and she offered Buzz her sympathy. He also offered him a gig with The Heywoods. Buzz had signed a lease, so he agreed to take her offer in order to pay the bills. The Heywoods later achieved a good deal of commercial success in the mid-1970s scoring a No. 1 hit with "Billy Don't Be Hero," but they were relatively unknown during Buzz's short stint with them.

Buzz was with The Heywoods for eighteen months, but he left when he received an offer to rejoin The Exiles in early 1969. At the time, Northern Kentucky University was a two-year school. Buzz returned to Richmond after a year. Billy Luxon contacted him shortly after The Exiles returned from New York. Buzz had just rekindled friendships with his former band mates when everything came to a halt courtesy of the draft. Mike, Mack, and Buzz were called for the draft at the same time in early 1969. "You went up twice," explains Buzz. "You went up first for the test and the physical, and then they called you again and gave you another test." Mack and Buzz only went once, but it was Mike's second trip. "Well it was Mike's second time, and we got up there and he was gone...gone," said Buzz in a stark tone. Mack's asthma led to his deferment. Buzz was deferred because of his severe allergy to wool. Mack and Buzz rode back to Richmond on the bus without Mike.

The Exiles were left without a lead guitarist after Mike's departure. They did not try to replace him. They responded by asking Buzz to return to the group to form a two-keyboard lineup. Buzz: "Stokley calls me one night and he says, 'Buzz, we've got some friends that we got to know in New York who are in a play called *The Drunkard* that's being done at The Barn Dinner Theater in Winchester. They sent us some tickets. Would you like to go, too?'" This gave Buzz an opportunity to get to know Bernie and to spend some time with his old friends, Mack, J.P., Stokley, and Billy. A few days later The Exiles invited Buzz to rejoin the group on piano/electric piano. Bernie continued to play organ, saxophone, and occasional rhythm guitar parts, and J.P. remained the bassist. The Exiles used the two-keyboard lineup from 1969 through the end of 1972. "We did some really nice things without a lead guitar," said Buzz. Bernie and Buzz had differing styles, but they were able to work together. J.P. had little trouble following along with the keyboard players. "He just knows…I mean, his inversions and things are wonderful," said Buzz. "That comes from being a very good guitar player."

Billy continued to add trumpet lines, and Bernie added saxophone on various tunes. The horn arrangements continued to develop and become more complex. Billy provided background vocals and percussion (cowbell, tambourine, etc.) when he wasn't playing trumpet. The band also continued to grow as a vocal group. All of the group members sang except for Mack. The Exiles were capable of singing unconventional harmonies, sometimes stretching into chords commonly found in jazz. "We could do all the major 7s and all the four note chords," said Bernie. "Sometimes I would double on the lead with Stokley on the choruses and this and that, but we had harmonies and that was the thing."

One of their most important venues during this era was Club 68, located in Lebanon, Kentucky. Club 68 hosted concerts by national acts, as well as shows by well-known regional performers. Regional acts sometimes got the chance to perform with national acts. "One night, I never will forget this, B.J. Thomas had just released 'Raindrops Keep Falling on My Head,' and we had toured with him, so we knew him," said Billy. "He was in Louisville and one of the DJs at WAKY mentioned that we were down at Club 68 and he got somebody to bring him…one of the DJs, I believe…and they brought him down there to see us and just kind of party on." The Exiles had developed a loyal fan base by that time, and were able to bring a crowd with them that would rival or outdo the national acts. J.P. explains:

We've been told that we still hold the all-time attendance record there that was previously held by Ike and Tina Turner. I don't know if that's true or not, but I remember the night we supposedly broke the record. You couldn't have squeezed one more person into that joint. We were told that there were over 1,500 people there that night. I'd estimate that eight or nine hundred was probably the listed capacity with the local fire marshal. What fire marshal?

Part of Club 68's popularity was due to the fact that Marion County was adjacent to several dry counties. One could purchase alcohol at Club 68, and people came from the surrounding counties to party, have a good time, and, unfortunately, to start fights. "One of the worst fights I saw was on Christmas Eve when about 50 people were going at it," said J.P. "I actually saw a guy punch a girl in the face during the fracas." The Exiles rarely stopped playing during fights, but this was an exception because it threatened to spill over to the stage. Despite its flaws, Club 68 was an important venue for live music in the 1960s and 1970s, and is sorely missed in that region today. It's now a parking lot.

The Exiles were able to take advantage of the exposure that they gained on the Dick Clark tours. They often drew large crowds. They continued to play proms and dances, but they also booked shows in other parts of the country due to Mark Alan's continued involvement. Through the connection with Alan, The Exiles were invited to a reception at the Louisiana governor's mansion in Baton Rouge before a Tommy James and the Shondells show in early 1969. After skepticism from the security and an extended question and answer session, they were finally allowed to enter the reception. James got along well with The Exiles, and invited them to open up for his band at another show that evening. James was looking for a group to produce, and he watched the Exiles' set intently. He invited The Exiles to New York to record a song he had written entitled "Church St. Soul Revival," and they quickly agreed.

Recording "Church St. Soul Revival" was an unusual experience for The Exiles. They noticed that Tommy James was acting differently when they arrived. "All wiry and aggressive," said J.P. The Exiles spent thirty-six straight hours recording "Church St. Soul Revival" and a B-side that was composed by Stokley and J.P. entitled "John Weatherman." Band members noticed that James had a lot of energy, and he wasn't having any trouble staying awake. "Him and…I can't think of his manager…the guy who was always with him…they had ways and means of staying up a long, long time," said Mack. "And they taught us how to do that, too, to some extent."

James seemed oblivious to anything other than creating a hit record, and he wasn't going to stop until it was finished. "We didn't even stop to eat," said J.P. "It never occurred to him that we weren't taking amphetamines like he was." Mack's drums are prominently featured during the breakdown in the middle of the song. The song also includes a horn arrangement and intricate background vocals. It is the best recorded representation of the band during the 1969-1972 period. The use of guitar was the most notable difference between the recording and the group's live show at the time. J.P. doubled on bass and guitar, and James added guitar to the song as well.

"Church St. Soul Revival" was released on Columbia Records in the spring of 1969. Contrary to popular belief, The Exiles' version of "Church St. Soul Revival" did not chart reaching 101 nationally on Billboard's Hot 100. Tommy James re-recorded the song in 1970 in a similar fashion, and it peaked at No. 62. Billy believes that the success of the single was hindered by James' irresponsibility. "It was good, but Tommy James didn't have the wherewithal to support the song," said Billy. James may have missed an important meeting, killing the progress of the single. "One Monday he was supposed to go down to CBS and get on the phone and Clive Davis was going to support us as well, and they were going to call the key radio stations, the key program directors and try to get everybody on the same page with that song because simultaneous impact was our problem," said Billy. "And the very day he was supposed to go he was so wild…."

Despite the lack of commercial success, "Church St. Soul Revival" provided The Exiles with another gig opportunity. Washington D.C. promoter Charlie Tompkey became a fan of the record, and he invited the group to play a summer gig at a club called Lucky Pierre's, an upscale club inside a new shopping mall. Lucky Pierre's was located near the downtown area of Washington D.C., but the band stayed in a desirable apartment in affluent Silver Springs, Maryland. It was a forty-minute drive from their apartment to the gig, but the apartment was much nicer than the one they lived in during their New York excursion.

The Exiles hoped to develop a following at Lucky Pierre's, but audiences were usually small. "We played five nights a week, and I don't think there was ever more than thirty or forty people there on any night," said J.P. The area had been a slum for years, and the owners of the club knew that it would take a while for the venue to catch on with the public. The owners wanted The Exiles to play five nights a week regardless of how many people were in the audience. J.P. remembers a night when there were no customers. "We expected the manager to give us the night off, but he had us play our five sets anyway," said J.P.

There were some advantages to the gig. The pay was good, and the band could enjoy movies in a laid back atmosphere at the multiplex before their performances. Buzz made up for the New York trips that he missed earlier. He traveled on the newly opened Metroliner from Washington to New York on his days off in order to watch musicals. "I had some friends there, and I saw every show worth seeing," said Buzz. The Exiles saw posters for Woodstock in Washington during the summer, and considered making the trip to the festival. They didn't go because their road manager ended up with bad hemorrhoids, and they didn't want to leave him. "He was the most fun-loving of us all and it seemed a shame that his summer had been ruined by a bad rear end," said J.P.

The Exiles returned to Kentucky at the end of the summer of 1969, and their next significant recording opportunity took place in 1970. They got a chance to record with producer Buddy Buie through their connections with Paul Revere and The Raiders guitarist Freddy Weller and Billy Joe Royal. This was the last time that The Exiles were backed by session musicians, in this case members of The Atlanta Rhythm Section. This was disappointing after the experience of playing their instruments on "Church St. Soul Revival." Bernie:

On 'Put Your Hands Together' we were in New York, and we had cut some stuff on CBS and they said, 'Well, you all from the south, we gonna send you to Atlanta to this producer down there and maybe he can hook up with you.' His name was Buddy Buie, and he did all the Classics IV Records and all that stuff. Pulled up and said, 'Where are we puttin' our equipment?' Said 'Leave it in the truck. We gonna use these boys right'chere. They're gonna play on the record. Y'all just gonna sing.' 'What?' 'Yeah.' Walked in this little office, and he played us three songs, and he said, 'Which one do you like the best?' We said, 'Put Your Hands Together.' He said, 'That's gonna be the single. Anybody in here write?' And I'm the only one who wrote. 'You got the B-side.' I said 'You ain't heard it yet.' 'Don't need to, you got the B-side.'

"Put Your Hands Together" features a stinging guitar riff and a funky arrangement that was much better suited for The Exiles than the songs that they had recorded on Date Records. The opening riff was created during a break as the guitarist was randomly playing his guitar. "He got that on tape," said Buzz. "And he actually formed the track around that." The guitar and electric piano provided by The Atlanta Rhythm Section drove the track in a way that was representative of the tight, funky band that The Exiles were. The atmosphere at the studio (located just northeast of Atlanta in Doraville) also differed from the New York sessions on Date. Buzz remembers musicians walking around in stage costumes, and union people standing around throughout the session. The bass player was legally blind, and he recorded his part in the control booth because he didn't like going into the studio.

By 1970, The Exiles started to lose faith in their New York management, and they decided to focus on writing their own material. "Put Your Hands Together" worked musically, but that didn't translate to any commercial success. Despite his connections, Mark Alan had not been able to help The Exiles break through to the big time. Billy explained:

> While he was doing a good job for us—he hooked us up with Tommy James and he was making a lot of things happen—in the process of all that he and his partners just kind of got all strung out. The next thing you know he's really not functioning and not performing and not doing much for us. It was pretty much evident that he wasn't going to be able to progress our career as we had hoped, so that's when we kind of started heading in other directions from him, and from New York.

J.P. became interested in writing music at this time. Inspired by bands with horns such as Chicago and Sly and the Family Stone, he looked to find ways to blend funk and rock in new and original ways. This was the age of album rock, and groups were expected to provide full-length albums. Bands such as Led Zeppelin were achieving great success without releasing any singles from their albums. Glamorous solo acts were more likely to be created in the studio, but bands were more likely to gain respect as self-contained units.

Stokley's efforts to compose original material never amounted to much, and J.P. realized that it would be up to him to write music and lyrics. Stokley and J.P. tried writing together, but they never developed a significant creative partnership. Buzz described working with Stokley: "You've got to realize that writing with Stokley…He'd give you a hundred sentences, possibilities, and if you used a word from one of 'em, he was co-writer. I never ever felt that was fair to J.P. It wasn't."

This encouraged J.P. to compose on his own, and to refrain from writing with others. He had all of the necessary tools to become a successful songwriter. He composed on guitar and piano, was a skilled bassist, and had a strong sense of melody. His keyboard compositions weren't always particularly pianistic, but he wrote what he heard in his mind. "You could tell some of J.P.'s songs were written by a guitarist, because they are non-pianistic when you tried to play them," said Buzz.

J.P. was the only member of the band who seems to have been serious about writing at this time. Buzz was not interested in writing. "My attitude has been, for as long as I can remember, that I really don't have anything that sterling to say that everybody else in the world needs to hear or read." Buzz was quite the arranger, however, and he could be critical when J.P. brought in compositions that did not impress him. "He'd bring something in or we'd be talking about a line or something, and I'd go, 'Wait a minute—that's a direct line from so and so or this and that,'" said Buzz. "And he'd go 'Purist.'"

This initiation process helped to mold J.P. into an exceptional songwriter, and he was eventually bringing in a couple of songs a month. "Sometimes we'd say, 'Nope, don't like it,'" continues Buzz. "And I think that probably some of those songs were 'Nope, don't like it' simply because they didn't want J.P. to have another song." Nevertheless, J.P.'s focus on songwriting would pay off later when the group was required to provide original material to fill up albums built around the songs that Mike Chapman and Nicky Chinn were writing for them in the late 1970s. In the 1980s, J.P. would become one of the more successful songwriters in country music.

The focus on original material changed the band's live show, lifestyle, and rehearsals. Half of their live show now included original songs, and they began to lose gigs due to disinterest from fans who wanted to hear covers. The crowds began to dwindle, and they had a period of six years where they each pocketed $75 a week. "We were poor as hell, man," said J.P. "None of us had any money."

The Exiles were living in Richmond before credit checks were as common. "I must have lived in twenty different apartments around here," states J.P. "I knew how to play the system. Rent came two months overdue—I'd move out and find a new place." J.P. did try to make amends years later at the local music store, Currier's Music World. "I bought a Fender Champ amp from them when they were at the other location, and it wasn't until years after they were here that I finally finished making payment on it," admits J.P. The band began to hold intensive rehearsals in Bybee, Kentucky, an unincorporated community just outside of Richmond. The rehearsals were held in a garage owned by Buzz's Aunt Franky. Buzz continued to live in Bybee in order to help out with the family business, Bybee Pottery.

The new direction led to the end of Mack's involvement with the group. "We weren't playing much—we weren't doing anything," said Mack. He missed the good time rock and roll and soul the band had been performing in the 1960s, but his departure from the band was also related to his heavy consumption of alcohol. Mack: "I actually figured out a way to get drunk twice a day." He had developed a dependency during his life on the road, and his lifestyle wasn't compatible with the rigorous creative process required to work on new compositions. "I would get up and take my wife to work, get drunk, go to bed, wake up and then go play, get drunk and go to bed, wake up, take my wife to work, get drunk, go to bed, wake up, go play...," explains Mack.

Mack's last performance with the group was a Toys for Tots show at Madison High School in late 1971 or early 1972. It's not clear whether he was let go from the group or if he left. "Well, I think it was kind of a mutual thing," said Mack. "They were kind of glad to see me go." Despite his absence from any of Exile's full length LPs, Mack's contribution to the band should not be overlooked. He paid dues on The Caravan of Stars tours and all of the New York trips, was a co-founder of the group, and played on early songs such as "The Answer to Her Prayers," "Come On," "It's Alligator Time," and "Church St. Soul Revival."

In addition, his laid-back personality was a stabilizing factor during the group's first eight years of existence. "I'm kind of like the Peter Best of Richmond," said Mack. "I left about the time they became famous." The Exiles wouldn't become famous until 1978, and it's unlikely that Mack's loose, feel-based approach to drumming would have worked well within the strict studio demands that Mike Chapman later imposed upon the group. Nevertheless, the disappointment must have affected Mack. He went almost forty years without touching a drumstick.

After he left the band he became a bartender, and worked at the first mixed drink bar in Richmond, The Library Lounge. He currently works in sales (floor covering). Fortunately, Mack has recently started playing again, sometimes in collaboration with Mike Howard. This author had the pleasure of performing with Mack and Mike at a Speck's reunion in 2011. Mack sums up his time with The Exiles: "Seventeen-year-old kids out taking on the world, running around learning things. It was an education."

The Exiles quickly replaced Mack with drummer Bobby Johns, but they soon faced another personnel change when J.P. left the band in early 1972. J.P. was focusing on his songwriting and guitar playing at the time, and he was beginning to lose faith in The Exiles. He decided to move to California with his cousin to pursue opportunities. The future of The Exiles was suddenly in jeopardy. "The day that J.P. left, he came to a rehearsal and announced that he was leaving, and said, 'I don't have any faith in the way the group is going,'" remembers Buzz. "'I have an opportunity to do something with my own music.'" The other members were understandably concerned about the future of the band. "So then he leaves, and Bernie says, 'Boys, I don't know whether we ought to go on or not,'" continues Buzz. "We started talking about it, and then Stokley goes, 'We can't quit.'" This was a crucial moment in the group's history, and it was a time when Stokley's dogged determination shone through in a big way. He had been the front man for The Exiles for almost a decade, and he didn't know anything else. He wouldn't stop; he couldn't stop. Bobby Johns, the most explosive rock-based drummer the group ever had, suggested that the group add guitarist Kenny Weir and bass player Bill Kennon. The new members came on board, but didn't have long to learn the material. The band had to cancel a gig on a Saturday in order to rehearse intensely, but they were ready to play by the next Wednesday. "And nobody could believe it," said Buzz.

J.P.'s trip to California was short lived. He returned to Kentucky after a few months, and was ready to rejoin The Exiles. The group released Kennon, and J.P. was allowed to return. This time J.P. joined the group as lead guitarist while Weir moved to bass. This marked the first time that J.P. played guitar in The Exiles, and it is a position that he has held to this day. Many fans have no idea that J.P. was ever the bass player for the group.

J.P.'s skilled, versatile playing and songwriting helped to move the group to a new level of cohesiveness and creativity. The trio of J.P., Kenny Weir, and Bobby Johns pushed the group into a new hard-rock direction. They would never rock this hard later on, and comparisons to bands such as Aerosmith and Led Zeppelin are apt. Despite the new hard rock sound, the group retained its more subtle elements (advanced vocal harmonies, horn arrangements, dynamics, etc.). Their arrangements of covers such as The Beatles' "We Can Work It Out," The Rascals' "A Beautiful Morning," and The 5th Dimension's "Up, Up, and Away," were showstoppers featuring vocal arrangements that were much more intricate than what was expected from the average bar band. "We'd work the vocals first, and then we'd come and get our instruments, and that really increased the sound," said Bernie. The increase to seven members also allowed Bernie, Buzz, and Billy to form a three-piece horn section. By this point The Exiles had the personnel to pull off any style of popular music. They turned into a powerhouse band. "We had two trumpets and a sax, man—we could kick it," continued Bernie.

In 1972, The Exiles were offered a record deal by a label out of Chicago called Wooden Nickel. Wooden Nickel had some regional success with Styx's first two albums, and The Exiles were excited to have an opportunity to record their first full length LP. It was at this time that the band changed its name from The Exiles to Exile. They felt that "The Exiles" sounded dated.

The group was allowed to play all of the instruments on the album, and they created their own arrangements. All of the instruments were recorded live in the same take, with overdubs being limited to vocals. Bill Traut, Styx's producer, was hired by the label to produce Exile. He also took credit for the horn arrangements. The self-titled LP offers a glimpse of how The Exiles sounded live in a way that had only been hinted at in previous recordings, but Bernie insists that some of the onstage magic was lost in the recording process. "The live sound and what I experienced from my perspective on stage was unbelievable, and then you go in and cut it and you just can't capture that energy—all of it—it seems like," said Bernie. Nevertheless, the album shows the band at the peak of its powers, instrumentally and vocally. This was clearly a seasoned rock and roll band.

The only setback facing the band on the *Exile* album was that they were still required to perform mostly covers selected by the producer. Only two of the album's ten songs were written or co-written by members of the band, while the other eight selections were covers by artists such as Todd Rundgren, Van Morrison, and Seals and Crofts. "I didn't realize they were covers," said Buzz. "I thought that Bill Traut was sending us all this wonderful new music that nobody had ever heard."

Buzz, never a record collector or intense fan of rock music in general, didn't realize that Traut was trying to mold Exile into a "blue-eyed soul" band, blending Stokley's vocal approach and the band's rock and roll sound. The album opens with a Stones-like take on Todd Rundgren's "Devil's Bite." J.P.'s guitar and Bernie's organ are upfront in the mix. Hard rock influences are immediately apparent. The fiery guitar solo worked to demonstrate J.P.'s abilities, and it was clear that Exile had a guitarist who could hold his own with the rock guitar heroes of the day.

Exile's funky version of Seals and Crofts "Ridin' Thumb," is also driven by Bernie's deep organ groove and J.P.'s guitar, while the rhythm section provides a rock solid groove. Buzz's RMI piano is somewhat buried in the mix on the first two tracks, but his gospel-inspired acoustic piano works to drive the Van Morrison cover, "You're My Woman." Another funky tune, "Mabel," features some impressive interplay between J.P. and Kenny. Exile's version of Rundgren's "Just One Victory" includes intricate vocal harmonies, a thick horn arrangement, and closes with Bernie's relentless organ passage. Their version of Art Reid Reynolds' "Jesus is Just Alright" was released after versions recorded by The Byrds (1969) and The Doobie Brothers (1972), but Exile's keyboard dominated arrangement was recorded without knowledge of previous recordings of the song. Buzz's RMI piano is much more prominent in the mix. It blends with Bernie's organ passages to create an atmospheric, ethereal backdrop for the vocal harmonies. Orleans' "Please Be There" is a soul tune that would have fit in with Exile's set list from the late 1960s. "Believe" is built around an acoustic guitar pattern played by Bernie and acoustic piano arpeggios from by Buzz. "Do What You Think You Should" was composed by J.P. It features the most prominent horn lines on the album. The horns were played by Billy, Buzz and Bernie, along with four additional players. "I came up with that lick, and Bill Traut took credit for it on the album," said Bernie. The song features a rare slide guitar solo from J.P. He sounds comfortable on slide guitar, and his solo blends seamlessly with the horn lines. "Hold Tight, Woman," credited to Stokley-Pennington-McGuire-Traut, is a showcase for Stokley's screaming vocals. It demonstrates the power of his voice. The lyrics celebrate a monogamous relationship, even in the midst of a rock and roll lifestyle. Once again, J.P. plays a slide guitar solo; an additional solo is played by Bernie on alto saxophone. Unfortunately, *Exile* failed to sell in significant quantities when it was released in 1973.

The group's stay on Wooden Nickel was short-lived, but they learned a few more show business lessons while they were on the label. The label flew them out to L.A. to play at the well-known Whiskey a Go-Go, but no influential music industry insiders showed up. As a result, the trip felt like a waste of time. Soon after, the group was introduced to Jerry Weintraub, the head of Wooden Nickel. "We were up there at Paragon Studios and we're recording and all this stuff, and all of a sudden the world comes to a screeching halt," said Buzz. "Women are coming out of their offices and all, and whispering to one another, running from one cubicle to another and all this stuff…'Mr. Weintraub is here!'"

Jerry Weintraub was known for his authoritarian presence, and the meeting was not a pleasant experience. "Someone said, 'Nice to meet you, Jerry,'" said J.P. "He responded by announcing that he would prefer to be called Mr. Weintraub." Things weren't going well with Wooden Nickel at the time, and Weintraub, later a successful film producer, was not in a particularly good mood.

It looked as though Exile would not be a priority on the label, and the group was disheartened by the meeting. "On our way out of the office Kenny Weir asked the assistant to please tell Mr. Weintraub to kiss our asses," said J.P. Kenny was known for his brutal honesty, but his timing was unfortunate in this circumstance. "Kenny would let you know exactly how he felt about something," said Buzz. It may have seemed funny at the time, but the group began to worry about the possible repercussions. It's likely that the assistant refrained from relaying Kenny's message to Mr. Weintraub, since the group was allowed to create another album on the label.

The second album on Wooden Nickel was entitled *Stage Pass*. It was released in late 1973. This would be the last Exile album to include contributions from Billy, Bernie, Kenny, and Bobby. Three of the album's nine songs were composed by group members—two by J.P. and one by Bobby. The first side consisted of studio recordings, while side two consisted of songs taken from a live performance at a Cincinnati club called Reflections. The album includes covers of songs by The Beatles, Jeff Beck, and others. Like the band's debut, the album did not sell. The group was dropped from the label soon after it was released.

Stage Pass continues in the hard rocking guitar-driven direction of Exile's debut album. Horns are noticeably absent. The album opens with "Sing a Song," a joyous, hard rocking song composed by J.P. It's driven by J.P.'s guitar, Buzz's electric piano, and Stokley's intense vocals. Bernie is either absent from the track or buried low in the mix. Cowbell and percussion, played by Billy and possibly Stokley, are used to create an interesting rhythmic texture on "Whatever Mood You're In." J.P. uses a wah-wah pedal on "Rock N' Roll Woman" and "Whatever Mood You're In." "Rock 'N Roll Woman" is a hard rocking song featuring guitar overdubs, and the keyboards are low in the mix. Keyboards are much more prevalent on J.P.'s "Leave Me Standing." It includes Bernie's only organ solo on the album, and Buzz's RMI electric piano is heard throughout.

Exile's cover of The Beatles' "We Can Work It Out" is a highlight. Buzz's arranging skills are on full display throughout this creative version of the well-known song. J.P. wanted the band to do a version of the song, but he faced resistance at first. "For years he'd been saying I want to do, 'We Can Work It Out,'" said Buzz. Buzz felt as though too many groups were playing the song, and he didn't want to play it unless they completely rearranged it. "I said, 'let's do it, but let's redo it,'" said Buzz. "And he said, 'How?' And I said, 'I don't know. Next rehearsal, I promise you.'" "We Can Work It Out" opens with an acoustic piano introduction developed and played by Buzz. "They put that through some kind of filters," said Buzz. The vocal arrangement is thick, with most of the band members contributing to the background harmonies. This was one of the few times that Buzz was asked to sing a lead vocal line. Buzz:

Early Exiles promotional shot at rehearsal: (seated on floor) Paul Smith Jr., (middle row, seated) Buzz Cornelison, Billy Luxon, (back row) Mike Howard, Jimmy Stokley, Mack Davenport (with leash and dog food). Courtesy Mack Davenport.

Early Exiles promotional shot with Dale Wright and the Wright Guys: (front row) Dale Wright and the Wright Guys (middle row) Mack Davenport, Jimmy Stokley, Paul Smith Jr., (back row) Mike Howard, Buzz Cornelison, Billy Luxon. Courtesy Mack Davenport.

Promotional shot circa 1964: (front row) Mack Davenport, Paul Smith Jr., (middle row) Billy Luxon, Jimmy Stokley, (back row) Buzz Cornelison, Mike Howard. Courtesy Mack Davenport.

THE EXILES . . . This popular music combo, composed of Madison County boys, is kept busy with out-of-town as well as local bookings. Composed of B u z z y Cornelison, Bill Luxon, Mack Davenport, Jimmy Stokley, Mike Howard, J i m m y Pennington and Paul Smith, the groups latest playdate will be at the Richmond Pool Saturday evening.
—Daily Register Photo

Bold New Sound Emits
From Septet—The Exiles

By TOM CARTER

An exile: a person expelled or separated f r o m his own kind. The Exiles: a septet of juvenile musicians who emanate the mad, new sound of the teen set.

Surely there is a difference

Newspaper article detailing The Exiles as a septet during J.P.'s first phase with the band. Courtesy Mack Davenport.

for the members of the group: Mike Howard, Jimmy Pennington, Buzzy Cornelison, Paul Smith, Mack Davenport, Bill Luxon and Jimmy Stockley — have been widely accepted by the adolescent advocaters of such rhythmic calisthenics as the 'frug' and the 'jerk'.

The combo utilizes an organ, a set of drums and a vocalist, who the other members of the group encourage by supplementing his tonal lamenting with various forms of positive affirmations like 'Yeah! Yeah!'

Several members were formerly in the ranks of the "Fascinations". The present group has been together for nearly a year. The ages of the seven male counterparts range from 16 to 21.

The Exiles are primarily a rock 'n' roll group, but they can conform to most any occasion with the appropriate sounds. At club dances a n d parties for adults their repertoire includes slow popular ballads and old standards.

The non-mopped top group

Appeared In Lexington

have appeared at several Lexington night spots although bookings have included stints in Oxford and Hamilton, Ohio. Clarksville, Tenn., Middlesboro and other spots in Central Kentucky. The Exiles have several engagements in the Dayton area and throughout Kentucky this summer, including a one night stand each week in Williamstown.

The Exiles h a v e a record which is creeping up the Lexington popularity charts called "Answer to Her Prayers", the flip side being "Come On." They have mailed the disc to various radio stations in t h e United States and abroad hoping for a wide acceptance. Recently an individual in Americus, Georgia, after hearing the record, contacted the group to check on their terms and traveling facilities.

Their first record, "Stay With Me" was on the Rem label while the recent recording is on the Jimbo label.

The Exiles play for the Lexington Park and Recreation Department when they are requested for dances and their next job will be tomorrow night at the Richmond Pool. The Jaycees, who have recently taken over the pool, have hired the group for a teen pool party.

Left: *The Exiles in the early 1970s: (left to right, circular) Billy Luxon, Buzz Cornelison, Mack Davenport, Jimmy Stokley, J.P. Pennington, Bernie Faulkner. Courtesy Mack Davenport.*

Below: *Promotional photo circa 1966 for Premier Talent after The Exiles were discovered at Speck's: (left to right) Paul Smith Jr., Buzz Cornelison, Billy Luxon, Mike Howard, Jimmy Stokley, Mack Davenport. Courtesy Mack Davenport.*

THE EXILES

Manager
Masser–Caulfield
1697 Broadway
New York N.Y

PREMIER TALENT ASSOCIATES, INC.
200 WEST 57TH STREET
New York, N.Y. 10019 · 757-4300

Climbing a ladder: (on deck) Billy Luxon, Paul Smith Jr., (bottom to top) Buzz Cornelison, Mike Howard, Mack Davenport, Jimmy Stokley. Courtesy Mack Davenport.

Above: *Circa 1966: (seated) Jimmy Stokley, (left to right) Mack Davenport, Mike Howard, Billy Luxon, Buzz Cornelison, Paul Smith Jr. Courtesy Mack Davenport.*

Left: *Early gig in front of Wallace's Bookstore located across the street from Madison High School. Courtesy Mack Davenport.*

One of the last promotional photos with Paul Smith Jr. in the band. Courtesy Mack Davenport.

A new lineup for 1967: (left to right) Bernie Faulkner, Mike Howard, Mack Davenport, J.P. Pennington, Billy Luxon, Jimmy Stokley. Courtesy Mack Davenport.

Above: Mack Davenport circa 1967. Courtesy Mack Davenport.

Left: The Exiles around the time of their first New York trip: (front row) Bernie Faulkner, Jimmy Stokley, Mike Howard, (back row) J.P. Pennington, Mack Davenport, Billy Luxon. Courtesy Mack Davenport.

More pinstripes: (left to right) Mack Davenport, Jimmy Stokley, J.P. Pennington, Bernie Faulkner, Billy Luxon, Mike Howard. Courtesy Mack Davenport.

Promotional poster, mid-1960s. Courtesy Mack Davenport.

ENTER THE **EXILES!**

HOPE YOU were all lucky enough to see the Exiles when they toured with Mark, Paul and the Raiders and introduced their Date single, Come Out, Come Out, Whoever You Are. They are six of the most charming Southern gentlemen you could ever hope to know. Come along and let the Exiles introduce themselves to you one by one —

JIMMY

My full name is James Carr Stokley, but you can call me Jimmy. I was born in Richmond, Ky., on October 18, 1945. I'm five feet and eleven inches tall, weigh 148 pounds and have dark brown hair and blue eyes. I'm lead singer with the Exiles and handle most of the business matters for our group — which is a full-time job in itself. However, I always find time for girls! — especially ones with pleasant personalities (neatness is very important to me too). On dates, I enjoy going out to dinner and dancing (I like to be up on all the latest steps, so I can use them in our show). However, I must warn you — I'm unpredictable and can't sit still for long. So when you're with me, you'll never know what to expect next!

BILLY

I was born William Hoffman Luxon on March 19, 1946, in Lexington, Ky., but I now live in Richmond. I attend Eastern Kentucky University there and live in a three-room trailer with Jim Marr, our road manager, who is a real groovy guy. I have dark blond hair, blue eyes, stand six feet tall and weigh 175 pounds. I like girls who are understanding and easy to have a good time with — whether we go out to a good club, spend a day at the beach or just stay home and watch TV. I play trumpet with the Exiles and sing harmony. My secret ambition is to be a lawyer.

MIKE

My name is Michael Gordon Howard. I was born in Richmond, Ky., on March 9, 1949 — which means I'm the youngest. The boys don't tease me about being the "baby" cos I'm also the tallest. I'm six feet and one inch tall, weight 170 pounds and have dark brown hair and brown eyes. I attend Eastern Kentucky University and am studying to be a veterinarian, but I love playing lead guitar and singing harmony with the Exiles. Another thing I love are girls who are witty and personable. I won't tell what my favorite dates are — you'll just have to wait and see for yourself! I'm the quiet, secretive type!

MACK

My real name is Ronnie Mack Davenport, but everyone calls me "Mack." I was born on September 24, 1946, in Detroit, Mich., but I now live in Richmond, Ky., where I attend Eastern Kentucky University. I'm majoring in Business and Accounting and some day I would like to be a CPA (Certified Public Accountant) — or maybe just keep the books for the Exiles. Right now, I'm happy being the drummer for our group. I like girls — each and every one of you — and the only thing I look for on a date is that we both have a very good time!

BERNIE

My entire handle is Bernard Edwin Faulkner, Jr. I am six feet tall, weigh 170 pounds and have blonde hair and blue eyes. My birthdate is September 30, 1947, and I was born in Hazard, Ky., which is still my real home — although I now stay in Richmond, where I attend Eastern Kentucky University. I am majoring in girls! — I mean music! With the Exiles, I play organ, bass, guitar, sax, trumpet and drums (not all at the same time, though!) and sing harmony. We all truly love entertaining you!

JIMMY

My entire name is James Preston Pennington. I was born in Berea, Ky., on January 22, 1949, but I now live in Lexington. I too attend Eastern Kentucky University. I have blond hair, brown eyes, and I'm five feet and ten inches tall and weigh 145 pounds. I play bass guitar and sing harmony with our group. I like girls (don't we all?) who are sincere, cos I don't like phonies. On dates, I enjoy going somewhere different than where everyone else goes, so that we can be alone and I can really get to know you. By the way, all six of us love reading your letters — thanks!!

Write to the Exiles c/o Date Records, 51 West 52nd Street, New York, N.Y.   67

Bios circa 1967. Courtesy Mack Davenport.

Revere's Raiders, Exiles Provide Thrills For Dick Clark Productions

BY DONNA FOUST
PROGRESS FEATURE EDITOR

The 1968 version of the Paul Revere and the Raiders Show came to Eastern on Monday night. But, when the crowd of over 3,000 came to their feet cheering and applauding for nearly ten minutes; it wasn't Paul Revere and his famed Raiders' or lead singer Mark Lindsay who had earned these laudits. It was simply a well-deserved welcome home for the evening's show stoppers--Richmond's own Exiles.

And it wasn't the first time the Exiles have shared billing with the Raiders and Lindsay. Including this trip, the Exiles have toured with the Dick Clark Tour Production Group four times.

When questioned later about this lead singer, Jimmy Stokley commented, "Yes, our reception hs been good, but we are really worried about tonight. Everyone on the tour knows this is our hometown, and if we don't bring the house down we aren't going to look too good."

The first time they had the opportunity to play a Raiders date was as a local group in 1966 when T.V.'s "Where The Action Is" played a concert appearance at Eastern.

Then in 1967 the Exiles did their first tour with a Raiders show. Since that time Revere has used them frequently.

Keith Allison, a show headliner and fellow performer from the "Action" series said, "The Exiles are a good band with a lot of talent. Too often a single act like myself suffers on the road from a bad back up band, but Paul usually tres to find some group like the Exiles to tour. He knows that they are going to do a good job."

Allison was not the only member of the show that had good things to say about the Exiles. The four members of The Napolenic Wars gave the group a rave review. Joey James, the lead singer and organ player said backstage, "The Exiles have had a tremendous reception everywhere we've played on the tour the crowds have really liked them."

Jim and the rest of the band needlessly worried. The audience gave them a standing ovation at the end of their last number.

One of the songs in their act was their newly released single "Come On Out, Come On Out;; which appears on the Date label, a Columbia subsidiary. The song is currently number one in Oklahoma City and on the charts in Memphis and Nashville.

When asked about their future plans, Stokley ran down the summer schedule. Through May they will be playing at Speck's in Richmond; June will be a two week club date in the Bahamas and a two-week date in New York. Then starting in July, and running through August, will be another road tour.

What's Goin on Here?

That seems to be what the Exiles' lead guitarist, Mike Howard is saying to vocalist Jimmy Stokley as the local group performed with the Paul Revere and the Raiders' show Monday night in Alumni Coliseum. The group seemingly stole the show from some of the 'name' acts, receiving a standing ovation on one occasion.
(Progress Photo by Bobby Whitlock)

Above: *Newspaper article detailing a 1968 performance on The Caravan of Stars tour. Courtesy Mack Davenport.*

Left: *Mike Howard and Jimmy Stokley on the Caravan of Stars tour. Courtesy Mack Davenport.*

The Exiles two-keyboard lineup in 1969 after Mike Howard's departure: (front row) Billy Luxon, Bernie Faulkner, (back row) Mack Davenport, J.P. Pennington, Buzz Cornelison, Jimmy Stokley. Courtesy Mack Davenport.

Public Relations:
NEW BEAT TIMES LTD.
300 West 55th Street
New York, N.Y. 10019
(212) 765-1540

THE EXILES
DATE RECORDS

Direction:
NEW BEAT MANAGEMENT LTD.
300 West 55th Street
New York, N.Y. 10019
(212) 765-1540

One of the last promotional photos before Mike Howard was drafted. (top) J.P. Pennington, Billy Luxon, Bernie Faulkner, (bottom) Mack Davenport, Jimmy Stokley, Mike Howard. Courtesy Mack Davenport.

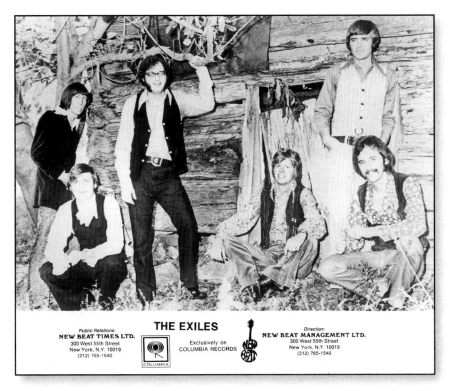

The Exiles just before they released "Church Street Soul Revival:" (left to right) Jimmy Stokley, Buzz Cornelison, Mack Davenport, Bernie Faulkner, Billy Luxon, J.P. Pennington. Courtesy Mack Davenport.

Another promotional shot for Columbia Records: (standing in back) Bernie Faulkner, (left to right) Buzz Cornelison, Jimmy Stokley, J.P. Pennington, Mack Davenport, Billy Luxon. Courtesy Mack Davenport.

Promotional photo for Triangle Talent circa 1971: (left to right) Mack Davenport, Jimmy Stokley,
Billy Luxon, J.P. Pennington, Buzz Cornelison, Bernie Faulkner. Courtesy Mack Davenport.

EXILES

Exclusive Booking
Triangle Talent
9912 Taylorsville Rd.
Louisville, Kentucky
Phone (502), 267-5466

Another promotional photo for Triangle Talent: (standing) Buzz Cornelison, (left to right) J.P. Pennington, Bernie Faulkner, Mack Davenport, Billy Luxon, Jimmy Stokley. Courtesy Mack Davenport.

Under a bridge: (front row) Buzz Cornelison, Bernie Faulkner, (back row) Mack Davenport, Jimmy Stokley, J.P. Pennington, Billy Luxon. Courtesy Mack Davenport.

Flyer for Club 68. Courtesy Mack Davenport.

EXILES
Next Wednesday
(JUNE 9)
CLUB 68
9:00 till 1:00
Admission Only $2.00

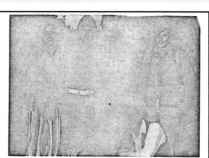

TUNE IN

The Exiles Look For a Big Hit

"What we want now is to get a national single."

Jimmy Stokley, lead singer for The Exiles, isn't alone in that wish. There are probably several hundred thousand rock-and-roll bands in the United States working and hoping for a nationwide hit record. But The Exiles have a head start—"Put Your Hands Together," this week's Tune In.

The six-member group from Richmond, Ky., has been one of the busiest bands in the area for a couple of years, playing frequently in Louisville and throughout the Midwest.

The band came painfully close to having that big national hit with their last record, "Church Street Soul Revival." That song was No. 1 on the local charts in Washington, D.C., Jacksonville, Fla., and Louisville. It made No. 101 in national ratings.

The Exiles started out as a quartet of high school boys in the early '60s—Stokley, drummer Mack Davenport, guitarist Jimmy Pennington, and Billy Luxon, who sings and plays trumpet.

Dick Clark Tours

"We really got started at Speck's Restaurant, a college hangout," says Stokley. Richmond is the home of Eastern Kentucky University. "One night a lady from the Dick Clark organization's office in Cincinnati dropped in and heard us, and after the dance she came up to talk to us. This was approximately three and a half years ago. As a result of that we did a national tour with Paul Revere and The Raiders and a couple of other Dick Clark tours."

Between high school and the post-graduate course with Dick Clark, the band added Buzzy Cornelison on piano and Bernie Faulkner on sax and organ.

And as a result of the tours The Exiles were signed by Columbia Records. Three singles on a Columbia subsidiary, Date Records—"What Is the Reason," "Come Out, Come Out," and "Mary on the Beach"—demonstrated to the Columbia people that

The Exiles, from Richmond, Ky., are, (standing from left) Buzzy Cornelison, Bernie Faulkner, Jimmy Pennington and Bill Luxon. Kneeling are Jimmy Stokley and Mack Davenport.

The Exiles had potential, and they were moved to the Columbia label for "Church Street."

"We did 'Church Street' with Tommy James of Tommy James and the Shondells." (James wrote the song and produced The Exiles' recording.) "After that, we decided to change the sound a little," says Stokley. The group's decision led it, through Columbia, to Atlanta and current producer Buddy Buie, an established hit-maker with tunes such as "Traces," performed by The Classics IV, to his credit.

Newspaper article following the release of "Put Your Hands Together." Courtesy Mack Davenport.

84

"THE EXILES" will soon head for New York to record with Paramount Records, Inc., some new and old rock music. In front are Jimmy Stokley and Mack Davenport; standing, from left, are Buzzy Cornelison, Bernie Faulkner, Jimmy Pennington and Billy Luxon.

Newspaper article from 1972. Courtesy Mack Davenport.

Jimmy Stokley after the group moved into more of a hard rock direction. Courtesy Kim Gulley Owens.

Jimmy Stokley singing intensely. Courtesy Kim Gulley Owens.

Playing at a festival circa 1974. Courtesy Kim Gulley Owens.

Performance in front of Wallace's Bookstore in Richmond, KY: (left to right) Bernie Faulkner, J.P. Pennington, Jimmy Stokley, Bobby Johns, Billy Luxon, Kenny Weir. Courtesy Kim Gulley Owens.

Another shot from Wallace's Bookstore. Courtesy Kim Gulley Owens.

Stokley in full-fledged rock and roll mode: (left to right) Bobby Johns, Jimmy Stokley, Kenny Weir. Courtesy Kim Gulley Owens.

Stokley releasing his trademark scream. Courtesy Kim Gulley Owens.

Jimmy Stokley and J.P. Pennington in the mid-1970s. Courtesy Kim Gulley Owens.

Exile around the time that Billy Luxon and Bernie Faulkner left the group: (left to right) J.P. Pennington, Kenny Weir, Bobby Johns, Buzz Cornelison, Jimmy Stokley. Courtesy Kim Gulley Owens.

Exile in late 1974 with new member, Marlon Hargis: (front row) Jimmy Stokley, Kenny Weir, (back row) Marlon Hargis, Bobby Johns, J.P. Pennington, Buzz Cornelison. Courtesy Kim Gulley Owens.

Right: *Bobby Johns with a friend in the mid-1970s. Courtesy Kim Gulley Owens.*

Below: *J.P. Pennington and Jimmy Stokley in the air. Courtesy Kim Gulley Owens.*

Above: *Stokley rocking out in the mid-1970s. Courtesy Kim Gulley Owens.*

Left: *Stokley in the mid-1970s. Courtesy Kim Gulley Owens.*

*Stokley and J.P. circa 1975.
Courtesy Kim Gulley Owens.*

Stokley entertaining the crowd: (left to right) J.P. Pennington, Jimmy Stokley, Bobby Johns. Courtesy Kim Gulley Owens.

Exile with new bass player, Danny Williams: (front row) Marlon Hargis, Danny Williams, Jimmy Stokley, (back row) Buzz Cornelison, Bobby Johns, J.P. Pennington. Courtesy Kim Gulley Owens.

Exile circa 1976: (left to right) Marlon Hargis, Danny Williams, J.P. Pennington, Bobby Johns, Jimmy Stokley, Buzz Cornelison. Courtesy Kim Gulley Owens.

Exile circa 1976: (front) Bobby Johns, (back, left to right) Danny Williams, Buzz Cornelison, Marlon Hargis, J.P. Pennington, Jimmy Stokley. Courtesy Kim Gulley Owens.

Stokley in 1976. Courtesy Kim Gulley Owens. *Danny Williams. Courtesy Kim Gulley Owens.*

J.P. in the mid-1970s. Courtesy Kim Gulley Owens. *Danny Williams staring into the distance. Courtesy Kim Gulley Owens.*

J.P. and Marlon in 1977. Courtesy Kim Gulley Owens.

Stokley before a gig. Courtesy Kim Gulley Owens.

J.P. after hours. Courtesy Kim Gulley Owens.

Marlon and Danny in 1977. Courtesy Kim Gulley Owens.

J.P. with two guitars, two basses, and new shoes. Courtesy Kim Gulley Owens.

The first time we did it...'Life is very short and there's no time'...just like The Beatles had done it. The second time we did it, I said, 'We need to change that. We need to do some kind of variation on a theme.' And I sang it, and I said, 'This is what we need to do,' and I sang the part. And J.P. said, 'Then you ought to sing that.' I'd never, ever sang a lead line. And I said, 'Me?' And he said, 'Yes, you should start it – Life is very short...' And the next voice comes in....

Buzz's reluctance to sing in a rock setting is surprising, since he didn't have any trouble performing in a musical theater context. "Scared me to death every night, but I did it," continues Buzz. The original version of "We Can Work It Out" alternates between 3/4 and 4/4 time, and the Exile version emphasizes the different sections through changes in timbre and dynamics. The intense, carnival-esque waltz-like section is almost psychedelic. 1973 represented the peak of the progressive rock era, and Exile's ambitious arrangement of "We Can Work It Out" fit the times. "One of the things that I'll have to say about the boys that always, always I'm so proud of was that they could do it," says Buzz. "Just because they didn't think of it was no indication that they couldn't do it."

The live performances on side two of *Stage Pass* demonstrate the ways in which the band was being influenced by hard rock styles. J.P.'s performance is exemplary, but the keyboards are pushed deep into the background. "Goin' Down," the opening track on side two, has no relation to the well-known song associated with blues guitarist Freddie King. Kenny trades soaring, high vocal lines with Stokley during the verses, and J.P. provides one of the most intense solos of his recording career.

"The Bobber," a drum solo, shows Bobby to be a creative rock musician capable of holding his own with the famous hard rock drummers of the time. Exile's version of Jeff Beck's "New Ways-Train, Train" clocks in at 11:02, and includes bluesy unison riffing and an extended guitar solo/jam. The keyboard players seem to drop out in the middle of the song while J.P., Kenny, and Bobby move deep into blues-based/funky improvisational territory.

Exile would never include an instrumental section of this length on subsequent albums, and the successful country version of the group was not known for moving into lengthy jam sections. Nevertheless, "New Ways-Train, Train" shows the depth of J.P.'s rock and roll roots, and it offers an interesting snapshot into Exile's glory days as a club band. "Don't It Feel Good" closes the album with a funky, soulful groove that showcases the band's rhythm and blues roots.

Exile's association with Wooden Nickel ended after *Stage Pass* failed to sell, and members began to leave the band shortly thereafter. Bernie left after the release of the album in late 1973. He informed the group of his intentions after a gig in New York City with Richie Havens. "We drove from New York to Richmond and there wasn't hardly a word said, and I got out and I said, 'Boys, it's been nice. Love y'all, I'll see you,'" said Bernie. "So I went back to Hazard and helped run that car dealership for twenty-five years. I was a dealer. Raised a family and all that."

Bernie missed his opportunity to play on a No. 1 hit by a few years, but it's important to remember that his instrumental skills helped the group progress. His soulful organ playing provided an element that Buzz didn't bring to the band, and it made the group more versatile allowing them to move effectively into hard rock territory.

Ironically, Bernie was writing country songs in the 1970s, a move that anticipated Exile's direction in the 1980s. He was also working at Lemco during the mid-1970s, a Lexington studio owned by Cecil Jones that would play a major role in Exile's later success. Lemco stood for "Lexington Music Company." "Walked in, Cecil gave me a roll of tape and the key to the studio, and he said, 'When it's empty you can have it,'" explained Bernie. "I slept in the floor, wrote commercials and cut them for him for free. He showed me how to run the studio and I helped engineer and all that stuff."

Bernie has owned and operator a studio for several years and has contributed as a songwriter to some high profile albums. He co-wrote "April's Fool" (1991) for Tracy Lawrence, "Rain on the Roof" (with J.P.) for Dale Ann Bradley, "Old Man and His Fiddle" for Bobby Osborne, and "The Porchlight" for Les Taylor. Bernie has never quit playing music. He is still active as a multi-instrumentalist. The success of "Kiss You All Over" in 1978 affected Bernie in a negative manner, but he came to terms with the situation. Bernie:

> For years and years I was an ex-Exile, and I gathered my self-esteem from that. Well, after going to rehab about three years ago they said, 'Man, you got one foot in the past and one in the future—anything but showing up for the now. Who are you?' I said, 'I'm Bernie Faulkner, I'm a songwriter.' 'No, who are you?' 'I'm Bernie Faulkner, I'm a musician.' 'Who are you?' 'Buddy, I done told you twice.' He said 'People come out here—they say I'm a doctor, I'm a lawyer—that ain't who you are, that's what you do. What are you going to do if you get your hands cut off, and can't play or can't sing?' I said, 'I see where you're going.' Now I'm a child of God. I'm

perfectly imperfect. My imperfections make me special. Therefore, I have the right to be here on the Earth. There's only one of me that will ever be mixed up just like me, thank goodness. And there's where I get my strength, and I rely on that instead of anything else I was or might even be. And when I stay in the now, I am perfectly fine.

It's not clear when Kenny Weir left the band, but group photos indicate that he had left the band by the end of 1974. "He was there and then he was gone, but I can't remember why," said Buzz. "I don't remember why Kenny left," adds J.P.

Kenny moved back to West Virginia to work with his father. His replacement in Exile was Danny Williams, another talented bass player with a high tenor voice. Kenny passed away in a car wreck years later after leaving the band. The wreck occurred at a time when he was trying to get back into music. "He called me up one day—said, 'Bernie, I'm going to produce a record on me, now I want you to produce it,'" explains Bernie. Kenny had a significant amount of money saved for the project, and he was willing to get some high profile musicians on the session. His car wreck occurred on I-64 in West Virginia during the sessions. Buzz:

> And he drove down there and it snowed, and his father said, 'Why don't you spend the night here?' And he said, 'No I'm going to go on home.' It was a new section of 64, which had almost nobody or nothing on it, and he slipped off the road. It was my understanding that the jeep flipped, but that this was a very survivable accident. He bled to death. It was cold and nobody came along, and they had straw on the sides where they had put grass, and all that stuff, so I guess it didn't look like anybody had gone off the road until much, much later.

One is left to wonder what Kenny's project would have sounded like. He was a multi-talented bassist/guitarist/vocalist, and the music may have reflected his strong rock and roll background.

Billy Luxon wasn't happy with Exile's new hard rock musical direction. His role as a trumpeter/percussionist/background vocalist was being obscured underneath the guitar-driven direction in which the band was heading. He began to feel as though the group had moved away from its original soul-based direction. "When Kenny and Bobby Johns joined, it really changed the musical direction of the group quite drastically," said Billy. "The type music that they were wanting to go to kind of really took the brass out of it."

Billy's trumpet is only heard during two songs on the *Exile* LP, and there are no horns on *Stage Pass*. He decided to leave the group at the beginning of 1975, and was not replaced. Billy had been in the group for almost twelve years, and he was ready to do something else. He missed out on the "Kiss You All Over" experience, but he went on to have a good deal of success in business.

Soon after leaving Exile, he opened up a successful club/bar called J. Sutter's Mill in Richmond with his brother. J. Sutter's Mill opened at a time when Richmond's downtown area was gaining a reputation all over Central Kentucky as a major hub for partying/entertainment. "We really did well when we were there, yeah," said Billy. Customers over eighteen years of age were allowed to enter the club, but, as in Speck's, they could not drink unless they were twenty-one. This began to change in the 1990s. "At one point the town kind of became twenty-one only, and then it was back to eighteen, and then it was back to twenty-one," said Billy. He began to tire of the drinking age issue, so he sold the club in 1993. It has since been demolished.

Billy kept in touch with Buzz and Stokley, but not J.P. "We don't stay in touch," said J.P. "Every now and then something will come up and we'll end up spending our afternoon together." Billy wasn't the only member of the band to leave in the mid-1970s, but he was the one who had been in the group longest. His tenure with the band dated back to his time in The Fascinations. "He wasn't there long enough to see the real culmination of a lot of the hard work that he was a part of," said J.P. "I don't blame him. I really like Billy."

Billy kept up with the band's progress after he left. He invited them to play at his club in the 1970s. Billy was also active in the arrangement of a benefit for Jimmy Stokley in 1984, after the singer became deathly ill. He was somewhat irritated by the group's decision to become a country band in the 1980s. Billy:

> Well, it really wasn't the same group that I had been affiliated with. And J.P., I love him and wish him the best, but it really wasn't Exile. I mean, it's fine—he kind of inherited the name. And we kind of had a deal all throughout, kind of 'last man standing.' And he was the last man standing. He inherited everything about it. So, that's fine, but it really wasn't Exile. And I think it kind of clouds a little bit the Exile that other people knew. It's like two different Exiles, but that's fine—I mean, it's one of those things. But still, it might have been nice if he'd called it "Country Exile" or something else, you know—"Nashville Exile" or something.

Billy is currently living in Richmond, and is the director of marketing at Performance Food Service in Somerset.

Introducing Marlon Hargis

Bernie's replacement on keyboards was Marlon Hargis, a talented keyboardist who was also an experienced studio engineer. Hargis grew up in Somerset, Kentucky, and earned a degree from the University of Kentucky. He majored in music during his first two years at UK, but he switched degree programs after his sophomore year. "My degree was not in music, it was in…I think it was called Communications Technology," explains Marlon. He changed his major because he wasn't interested in becoming a band director or a concert pianist. "That was back when quote 'serious musicians'—they kind of looked down their noses at people who played rock and roll or any kind of music," said Marlon. "They kind of laughed at it. However, I realized while they were laughing I was out making three or four hundred dollars a week working on the weekends while they were broke."

Marlon worked at a couple of radio stations after finishing school, and he spent some time as a newspaper reporter before going to work with at Lemco studio. Marlon's abilities as an engineer would prove to be an essential key to Exile's success, because the group was able to record high quality demos at a time when it was difficult for a band to make their own recordings. Marlon's situation at the studio was somewhat similar to Bernie's, and he spent a good deal of time working as a musician and engineer.

Marlon credits the owner of the studio, Cecil Jones, as a major contributor to Exile's success. "We would never have made it without him," explained Marlon. Lemco session musician and future Exile drummer Steve Goetzman also remembers Jones in a positive light. "He was really loved by everybody in the Lexington music business," said Steve. "He had played snare drum with the Ringling Bros. Circus—played in the service, and then started his little studio business and he became the most successful studio in Lexington."

Marlon remembers Bernie coming to the studio to work on country music, but the two never became close. "I wouldn't say we're friends, but we were acquaintances over the years, basically," explains Marlon. Marlon recalls musicians such as J.D. Crowe, Keith Whitley, Ricky Skaggs, and Jerry Douglas passing through the studio. Musicians trusted Cecil Jones, and they felt at home recording at Lemco. "He had no ulterior motives," said Marlon. "He just wanted to help musicians." The studio where these demos were created was located in the garage of a house on Longview Drive in Lexington, not the most luxurious of locations. "He had converted his garage into a studio, so he used to call it a two car studio," recalls Steve. There weren't many recording studios in Lexington, and Lemco was able to thrive until Jones passed away in the 1980s. The house was later sold.

Like many members of Exile, Marlon Hargis began playing professionally in high school. His first band was called The Savages. He didn't own a keyboard instrument, so he borrowed a Hammond organ from another kid in the band. They played high school gigs, but he considers a 1965 gig at Renfro Valley in Mount Vernon, Kentucky to be his first professional experience. "I got paid two dollars for it," said Marlon. He also played piano for southern gospel quartets while he lived in Somerset. Those experiences proved useful when J.P. started penning hits with Southern gospel chord progressions in the 1980s. Marlon spent a lot of time listening to the radio in the 1960s, and he remembers a time when the airwaves were more diverse: "Radio was really interesting back then, because you could have someone play a Four Tops songs, then you might hear a Frank Sinatra song next. And then something totally different. It wasn't such a narrow format like it is today."

Like many musicians from his generation, he was particularly influenced by American R&B and British Invasion rock and roll bands such as The Beatles and The Rolling Stones. He was also influenced by jazz and soul-jazz artists such as Dave Brubeck, Jimmy Smith, and Groove Holmes. In addition to keyboards, Marlon played guitar early in his musical career. Steve Cropper from Booker T. & the MGs was an influence. "I played organ on some Booker T. stuff, but I played guitar on most of that stuff 'cause I was playing guitar with a band at that time," says Marlon.

Marlon was a skilled keyboard player, but his prowess in the studio and his connection to Lemco were probably the major considerations when the group decided to hire him. Exile's use of two keyboard players was somewhat unique for a rock and roll band. Bernie and Buzz had played together as a quick fix when Mike Howard was drafted. Bernie didn't necessarily need to be replaced. Nevertheless, adding Marlon as a keyboardist turned out to be a good choice, because, like Bernie, his style fit well with Buzz's classical approach. Marlon explains:

> We were so different. Buzz came from a real heavy classical, Broadway type background. And he had a certain style of playing—totally different than me, even though I did have a classical background. I just had more of a funky, R&B style. And Buzz had more of a...I don't know what you'd call it. I guess you'd say a Broadway style of playing—just a lot of flourishy type playing, a lot of open chords, arpeggios, that sort of stuff. And I had

more of a funk feel, so it just kind of worked. We would just normally play two different things. It just kind of worked out that way. We didn't even have to really work at it.

Unlike Buzz, Marlon took to electric/electronic keyboards. He played Fender Rhodes piano or Hammond organ while he was working in the clubs in Lexington, and he eventually added monophonic analog synthesizers to his set-up.

In addition to his skilled keyboard work, Marlon was able to get the band into Lemco on a regular basis to make demos. "That's really what got us our break is just the fact that we were able to go in there and spend hours and hours, days and weeks, just working on material," explains Marlon. Many of the demos still exist, many of which were retrieved by future Exile bassist Sonny Lemaire when the studio closed.

In addition to working on their own demos, various members of Exile also participated in session work at Lemco. "They did commercials or studio work, and it was for almost all country people," said Buzz. Many of the commercials were local jingles. A good deal of country music and bluegrass was recorded at the studio, by artists such as Ricky Skaggs. "I just remember people saying, 'Watch your language—Ricky's in there,'" reports Buzz. Virtuoso banjo player Bela Fleck worked at the studio early in his career. Some early sessions were experimental. Steve Goetzman was Jones' first call drummer. He occasionally broke the mold by applying his drums to traditional bluegrass sounds. J.P. and Danny Williams started visiting the studio on a regular basis through their association with Marlon, and they were soon playing on sessions, often with Steve.

Steve was known for his rock solid drumming, and his willingness to adhere to somewhat meager circumstances. "I worked cheap, too," said Steve. "That was another reason I was first call drummer." During the zenith of the studio Steve was working several days a week, every week. He remembers playing on several country albums recorded at the studio. Many of the "performers" couldn't sing very well, and some of the sessions were a struggle. The session musicians were occasionally relied upon to direct the sessions, and they continued to get tight as a unit. While J.P., Danny, and Marlon were breaking into session work, they continued to perform regularly with Exile. Bobby, Buzz, and Stokley remained with Exile, but they were not regularly involved with Lemco.

It was during this period that Exile began to shift their attention away from Richmond, Kentucky. "I never was in Richmond a lot personally," said

Marlon. By this point the club previously known as Speck's and The Steak-out, was called The Family Dog. This would be the name of the club until it closed. "Family Dog" is still painted on the side of the abandoned building. Exile continued to draw a substantial crowd for their shows at The Family Dog in the mid-1970s. "The only thing I remember about them is they were always packed," said Marlon. "You couldn't even move. It was hot."

Richmond was developing a reputation as a major party location for college students. Young people were flocking to Richmond from all directions on Thursday nights and the weekends. The Family Dog had competition from J. Sutter's Mill and a new club called O'Riley's Grill & Bar. The downtown party scene was beginning to spread out. Eighteen-years-olds were still allowed to enter the clubs, and the alcohol flowed relatively freely. "I don't know that they were there to hear us," said Marlon. "They were just there because it was a place to be, and get drunk." Marlon also remembers playing at the EKU campus bookstore, but since he never lived in Richmond his familiarity with the town was limited.

Chapter Four
COME ON OVER

J.P. MADE THE DECISION TO move to Lexington in the mid-1970s. There he and Steve Goetzman shared an apartment, which enhanced their friendship. Steve introduced J.P. to albums by Bob James and other funk-jazz artists, broadening the young guitarist's listening interests in the process. "I was playing albums at the apartment all the time, and he'd run and get his guitar and play along as he was listening," said Steve. Steve became impressed by J.P.'s dedication to music. J.P. was still struggling financially during this period, and Steve often had to pay more than his fair share of the rent. "He helped me pay my half of the rent on many occasions," admits J.P. Steve and J.P. lived together in Lexington for a year-and-a-half, and would continue to share hotel rooms on the road.

Stokley continued to book Exile throughout the mid-1970s, but gigs were sometimes hard to come by as the group continued to focus on original material. The group, now consisting of Stokley, J.P., Buzz, Marlon, Danny Williams, and Bobby Johns, was invited to Daytona Beach, Florida several times to play spring breaks during the mid-1970s. Buzz had quit school by this point, and none of the other members were taking classes. This allowed the band to play the six-week stretch that was spring break in Daytona.

They were invited to Florida by Bud Asher, the owner of a club called The Safari. Asher would later become the mayor of Daytona Beach. Exile was hired to play on the large outdoor patio behind the building. Asher did not pay them during their first visit other than room and board, but the band was excited to spend time on the beach, so they accepted his offer. Exile had been a top-notch live act for several years, and they immediately made an impression at their first performance. "We started playing, and it started rocking," said Buzz. "It was bursting at the seams. He was very, very pleased." The band was required to play every night, and they dined in a small cafeteria located in the club. They were able to negotiate a better pay situation the second time around, and they continued to play spring breaks until the success of "Kiss You All Over." In addition to the gigs at The Safari, Asher started booking Exile to play on a band shell just off the beach. A local radio station sponsored events at the shell, and Exile was able to consistently draw large crowds. Asher was delighted. "We were his hero," said Buzz.

An Exile demo came to the attention of well-known producer Mike Chapman in 1975. Chapman's work as a producer and songwriter (often with Nicky Chinn) with groups such as Sweet, Suzi Quatro, Mud, Smokie, and others had resulted in numerous hits. Nevertheless, Chapman wanted to make more of an impression on the American market. He was looking for a talented American group that was well established, but had not been able to achieve mainstream success.

The Exile demo got to Chapman through a series of connections. A DJ named Dane Eric became a fan of the group, and he passed the demo on to his friend Ed Leffler, a Los Angeles based manager who went on to work with Van Halen, The Osmonds, and several popular artists. Leffler had also worked with Sweet, and he developed a working relationship with Chapman. He had a feeling that the Exile demo might appeal to Chapman, and his instincts proved correct. Exile's high quality demo tape impressed Chapman, and he arranged for a meeting with the group in Lexington at a room in an apartment complex called Kirklevington.

The small room wasn't ideal for the band's thick sound. "We couldn't even get both speakers in for our PA," said Buzz. Despite a room with acoustics that were less than favorable, Chapman was impressed with Exile. He took the band out to eat after the gig, and they arranged to work together. It soon became clear that Chapman had the resources and the influence to make things happen for the group. "Here was a man willing to put up his own money to take us to California, put us up—and not in a hole—but in the Hyatt House," continues Buzz. "And—make sure we were fed and had money, and paid for all the recording and everything else UP FRONT."

Chapman did not have immediate success with Exile, and Bobby Johns left the group in 1977. Chapman and Chinn tried to write hit songs for the group in order to secure a record deal, but the first singles recorded for Atco failed. "Try It On," a disco-oriented tune with a string arrangement and high falsetto background vocals probably provided by Danny Williams, was the group's biggest hit up to that point, reaching No. 97 on Billboard's pop chart in 1977. Still, the group was not having the success they anticipated. "We tried to push it and we did all this stuff, and it just seemed like the end of the world," said Buzz.

The stress may have taken its toll on Bobby Johns. "Bobby Johns left the group simply because we just weren't getting along anymore," said Buzz. "Well, we need to remember that Steve Goetzman and J.P. were roommates, so he had kind of a push there for Steve." Bobby had been a solid, dynamic rock drummer for the group, but Steve's extensive studio experience prepared him for the rigorous timekeeping associated with pop/rock material tailor-made for radio play and, later, country music.

Buzz doesn't remember an unpleasant situation when Bobby left, and no one that I interviewed said much about it. "I never was quite sure exactly what was going on," said Buzz. "There was tension, musical tension, that concerned Bobby and maybe J.P., I don't know." Bobby soon joined the hard rock band Roadmaster. Roadmaster was signed to Village Records, a subsidiary of Mercury, at the time. They were about to record their second album. Roadmaster opened up for artists such as Pat Travers, Ted Nugent, and Blue Oyster Cult before breaking up in 1980 after the release of their fourth album. In the midst of the drummer situation and failed attempts at a hit single, Mike Chapman decided to sever his relationship with the band. "He called us and he said 'Boys, I'm sorry, but we just can't go on like this,'" explained Buzz.

Steve Goetzman

Steve Goetzman joined Exile in late 1977 following Bobby John's departure. He remained the drummer until 1995. Steve was born in Louisville but moved to Lexington for his middle and high school years, graduating from Tates Creek High School. Around the age of two or three he decided that he wanted to be a star.

Several years later, he bought a microphone from a friend for fifty cents and decided to join a garage band. "The drummer and the guitar player and I were the only ones who showed up," said Steve. Steve plugged his microphone into the guitar amp, and proceeded to demonstrate his "skills." "Finally the drummer said, 'Man I hate your singing,'" relays Steve. "Not wanting to lay down I said, 'Well, I hate your drumming!'" Surprisingly, the young drummer was happy to stop playing the drums, opting to jam away on the piano. This left the drum stool open to Steve, and a new drummer was in the making.

Steve never took any lessons and he didn't join the high school band, but he continued drumming in various groups. His drumming was influenced by Motown and Stax musicians early on. Steve moved to Atlanta in 1974, and he gained an appreciation for R&B-based jazz. "I was off to the races with the new funk-jazz kind of stuff," explains Steve. He didn't live in Atlanta for very long, and soon returned to Lexington. He was broke when he returned from Atlanta, and he felt dejected by the fact that he was moving back in with his parents. "I had lost everything I had," said Steve. "My drums, a nice stereo, my clothes and stuff like that, an album collection, and a Honda 350 motorcycle, and everything else was gone."

He lived with his parents for six months when he returned. It was during this time that Steve started playing sessions at Lemco, and he became close friends with Danny Williams. "Danny told me that J.P. was living with his mom, and he was looking for a roommate," said Steve. Steve enjoyed playing in the studio, but he was still interested in more progressive styles of music. He played by ear, and realized that he would need some musical training if he wanted to play jazz-oriented material. Steve enrolled at the University of Kentucky where he studied piano, percussion, and theory from 1977-78. He joined Exile during that year, and his activities with the band forced him to withdraw from school. "UK—classical training—everything was along those lines," said Steve. "What I took away from there that was most valuable was tuning. The percussion teacher at UK was a timpanist so he was very knowledgeable about tuning and drawing tones out of drums."

Steve remembers playing several gigs with Exile prior to the success of "Kiss You All Over" including a show at a club in Lexington called The Fireplace, the band's last performance at Club 68, and all of the dates on the last spring break trip. He remembers driving to gigs in Stokley's Winnebago. "Usually we'd bring girls along and wives and girlfriends and just friends of the band," recalls Steve. The engine was between the front seats, and Steve remembers Stokley playing a trick on the other members of the band by acting as though he had passed out on the protruding mound. "And then he would sit up and grab the wheel," said Steve. Steve also remembers being impressed by Stokley's showmanship and ability to entertain a crowd. During a performance at The Fireplace in Lexington the Exile singer pulled off one of his more impressive stunts. The club was built around a huge stone fireplace with a mantle, which Stokley proceeded to use a large prop. "During the show I saw Stokley one time climb up on that mantle and walk out to the center of the fireplace...and he's standing over the drummer...and he jumped over the drummer and landed on the front of the stage in a splits," exclaims Steve. "He could hook his feet behind his head and walk around on his hands."

A couple of weeks after severing his ties with Exile, Mike Chapman had a change of heart. "About two weeks later we got a call from Mike...well I got a call from him," said Buzz. Chapman's wife Connie was a fan of Exile, and it was through her efforts that he was persuaded to give the band another chance. Connie loved the group and their southern charm. Chapman had worked with disrespectful musicians in the past, and the guys in Exile represented a breath of fresh air. He asked Buzz to call a studio called The Forum in Covington, Kentucky. "He said, 'I want you to find out what you can about it, and let me know something,'" said Buzz.

Buzz contacted the studio the next day, and asked them about their set-up. He refrained from mentioning money. Buzz relayed the information to Chapman, and arrangements were made for Exile to record at the studio. Covington is located just outside of Cincinnati in northern Kentucky. It was much easier and cheaper for the band to drive to The Forum rather than fly to California. They stayed at The Drawbridge Inn during the sessions. The group didn't understand why a world class studio would be located in northern Kentucky, especially since they were one of the few bands recording there. "We heard rumors that it was front for illegal activities of some sort, but it didn't distract us from accomplishing our goal of making the best possible recording of 'Kiss,'" said J.P.

Before flying to Kentucky, Chapman sent the group some new songs that he had written for them. One of the songs was a sexually suggestive ditty entitled "Kiss You All Over." The group was somewhat shocked by the sensual lyrical content, but it's important to remember that this was the same band that recorded "It's Alligator Time" in 1966. Stokley wasn't shy, and he certainly wasn't afraid of suggestive lyrics.

The band listened to Chapman's version of the song and completely rearranged it to suit their more progressive tendencies. The band was proud of their arrangement, and they were excited to play it for Chapman when he arrived at one of their rehearsals in Bybee. Chapman acknowledged that their version was a "nice variation," but he insisted that they play it exactly like he recorded in on the demo. "I thought, 'Nobody is going to listen to those straight eights like that,'" exclaimed Buzz. He felt as though Chapman's arrangement was boring, and that no one would want to listen to it. "And he said, 'There's your song, right there,'" continues Buzz.

The basic skeleton of the song was simple, but some of the more interesting features of the tune were related to sound and timbre. Chapman was influenced by the music of Barry White at the time, and he looked to incorporate string synthesizers and sensual elements in the lead vocals. Marlon played a Fender Rhodes electric piano on the song, but he was also asked to play an ARP String Ensemble. Chapman owned several electronic keyboards at the time, and he was interested in futuristic sounds. Neither Buzz nor Marlon had played an ARP String Ensemble before. "Marlon says to me, 'Can you play that thing?'" said Buzz. Buzz opted to play grand piano on the song, leaving Marlon to deal with the synthesizer.

The string ensemble gave the tune an interesting sound, one that suggested strings but was futuristic sounding at the same time. The sound of the synthesizer was enhanced by a phasing sound provided by a guitar pedal. "It's actually routed through an MX-R Phase 90," explains Marlon. They discovered the sound by accident. "I think J.P. had been doing some overdubs, and I just plugged in the same line he was using," explains Marlon. Marlon was experimenting with the string sounds, but he couldn't find the sound he wanted. "By accident someone stepped on the phase unit, and it was still hooked in line," said Marlon. "Then we all of a sudden heard…I don't think anyone had used that sound before." Chapman told Steve to listen to a Barry White record and to try to emulate the sound. "A little slower, disco tempo, and a deep groove," said Steve. The music they were creating was a far cry from the country and bluegrass sessions at Lemco.

Chapman had a reputation for being a taskmaster in the studio. He was the most demanding producer that Exile ever worked with. Chapman expected perfection from all members of the band, and would spend hours trying to get the exact sound that he heard in his mind. Steve was required to come into the studio hours before the rest of the band on the day that they were recording the instrumental track in order to bang on his drums while Peter Coleman, the engineer, tried to get the sound that Chapman desired. Next, the band was called in, and they also spent hours working on the sonic details related to their instruments.

The band worked all day into the night, and comic relief was limited to a belch courtesy of Steve that J.P. described as "one that was so loud that we could hear it even above the ear splitting level of the band." They were relieved when they discovered that Chapman was pleased with the musical results at the end of the session. After several attempts at large-scale success, they knew that the future of Exile was at a crossroads. "I believe that everyone sensed this might be our last go-around, not only with Mike, but maybe our last go-around period," said J.P. Still, the band believed that they had a hit in the making, and excitement levels were high. "We all knew it was the best thing we had ever recorded," continued J.P.

The group needed to let off some steam after the session, and they decided to pull a prank on Steve. He was the latest addition to the group, and clearly the top choice for pranks at the time. After years of saving, Steve had just purchased a new car, a Volvo. The other band members were tired of hearing about it, and they asked Jeff Hunt, a roadie, to fill Steve's hubcaps with gravel. "When it came time to leave, we all gathered in the parking lot to watch him take off," remembers J.P. "When the car started rolling, the noise coming from those hubcaps was tremendous!" Every time Steve got out of his car to see what was going on, the noise would stop. "The look on his face was priceless," said J.P. The other members of the band tried to fake concern, but they eventually cracked. Steve's predicament provided some much needed laughter.

The band proceeded to let off additional steam in the bar at The Drawbridge Inn. This wasn't a great idea, as they were supposed to lay down vocals the next day. Nevertheless, they slept in, had a large breakfast, and drank a significant amount of coffee the next morning before returning to the studio for another long day.

The events surrounding the group's second day in the studio mark a significant turning point in the history of Exile. As pleased as Chapman had been with the instrumentalists, he was equally displeased with the lead vocal that Stokley was providing. "He and Mike had a history of butting heads in the studio," said J.P. "We had always felt that he had done a good job on other lead vocals for Mike, but Mike was a taskmaster, and it never seemed to be good enough."

Chapman knew what Stokley sounded like, but he was trying to mold the rock and roll veteran into a more polished vocalist. The results were often disheartening for all involved. Stokley's vocal problems wouldn't be an issue in the studio today, as Auto-Tune and other programs can readily correct pitch in an instant. In 1979, however, it was up to the vocalist to perform effectively in the studio, and Stokley couldn't provide what Chapman was looking for. The tension between Chapman and Stokley hit a new high during the "Kiss You All Over" session. "Mike really believed in this song, and nothing was going to stop him from making every aspect of it perfect," said J.P. Stokley, the strong leader and businessman, was now being put through an experience that was excruciating, and possibly uncalled for. J.P.:

It was hard to watch. Here was a man who had put his heart and soul into the band for all these years, suffering an embarrassment that no one should deserve. Since 1963, Jimmy Stokley was Exile. He was the one they all came to see. And now he was being humiliated in front of his best friends. One by one, we filtered out of the studio and left them alone, praying that a light would come on for Jimmy, that he would be able to rise to Mike's expectations.

Surprisingly, Stokley's gruff singing voice contributed to Chapman's interest in the band early on, but it was a completely different situation in the studio. "Mike did indeed have a golden ear, and could not abide anything be-ing the slightest bit off pitch," explained Buzz. One thing that never seems to come into question was Stokley's effort during this trying situation. "He tried so hard," said Buzz. "It was heartbreaking." Stokley was committed to giving his all, but he simply did not have a voice for the material that Chinn and Chapman were penning for the group. "So Jimmy being the fighter that he was, he would just give Chapman whatever he wanted no matter how much it hurt," said Steve. "I've seen Stokley in the studio for eight to ten hours straight trying to sing a song and do it exactly the way Chapman would want him to do it note for note."

Chapman was looking to turn Exile into a slick, pop-disco/Anglo-funk band, and Stokley didn't fit in well with that sound. It's also clear that years of screaming in the clubs affected Stokley's vocal range. J.P.:

It was very seldom that any of us were actually in the studio when they were doing vocals. I think probably the biggest reason for that was because we knew it was gonna be hard for Jimmy. And so we just stayed away. I remember times sitting in a hotel room and calling every couple of hours to see how it was going, and it wasn't going good. I remember one day, one whole day of like, them being in there together for like eight or nine hours or something like that trying to get one vocal. Mike had real specific things about what he heard. I guess he just found that Jimmy sang like Jimmy. He just either didn't want to or couldn't sing like someone else. Like whoever, whatever kind of voice it was that Mike was envisioning.

Stokley was a rock and roll singer at heart, and he didn't fit the mold of a polished, romantic pop/R&B singer. "Ultimately that was his demise, because the band was evolving more into pop," said Steve. After spending several hours trying to get a successful lead vocal from Stokley, Chapman called the rest of the band into the studio. He asked if anyone else in the band could sing. After an awkward silence, J.P. raised his hand and agreed to give it a try. With the exception of the first verse and a section where the vocalists trade lines, J.P. provided the lead vocal.

It was the first time that J.P. had provided lead vocals on an Exile record-ing, and it was an intimidating experience for him. "I never considered myself much of a singer," said J.P. "I just try to sell it, what I've got." J.P. was able to finish the vocals without much grief from Chapman. His vocal is strong and convincing, and he was able to sing the higher notes on pitch.

The low background vocal on the chorus sections was provided by Danny Williams. Williams had a strong falsetto, but he could also work his voice effectively in a low register.

Stokley handled the situation professionally, and the band moved on. "Interestingly, there was never any awkwardness that occurred between Jimmy and me," said J.P. Stokley was committed fully to the band, and he was willing to do whatever was best for Exile. The band returned to the hotel after the lead vocals were complete, and J.P. remembers that Stokley and Chapman seemed to be in a good mood. Background vocals, Marlon's synthesizer part, and guitar overdubs were added the next day, and Chapman flew back to L.A. in order to try to secure a record deal for the band.

Finding a record deal for Exile was difficult. "He was told 'Forget it' by a lot of labels," says Buzz. "He wanted us to be with Chrysalis, because he had Blondie with Chrysalis." Chapman was also turned down by Warner Brothers, but as he was leaving he noticed that Mike Curb's record label was located downstairs in the same building. Upon entering the label office, Chapman ran into a woman named Nola Leone whom The Exiles had met on one of their New York trips. She had worked for a magazine in the 1960s, and was now an influential player in the music industry. Leone was able to get Chapman in to see Mike Curb. "Mike Curb listened to it the first time and he said, 'It is a solid, monster hit,' and signed him right there," said Buzz. Such was Curb's belief in "Kiss You All Over" that he quickly signed Exile to a four-album deal on Curb Records. The records were to be distributed by Warner Brothers. This was quite an achievement for a band that was yet to hire a manager. Chapman informed the band that he would be returning to Kentucky, and that they needed to get enough material together for an album.

The ensuing weeks were spent writing and rehearsing songs for an album that was to be called *Mixed Emotions*. Chapman sent them another Mike Chapman/Nicky Chinn composition entitled "You Thrill Me." J.P. contributed six songs, and Danny Williams provided a song entitled "Ain't Got No Time." Due to their association with Lemco, the group was able to make demos and send them to Chapman during this stretch. Marlon explained: "What we would do a lot of times before we would go to L.A to work on an album is we would actually kind of pre-record the songs in Lexington to send to our producer to listen to." This saved the band time, and it also allowed them to preserve the feel of the original version of the songs before Mike rearranged them. "Listening back, I think we all agree we actually like the sound and the feel of some of those demo tapes better than some of the masters that ended up," said Marlon.

When Exile returned to the studio to record the album it became clear that bassist/vocalist Danny Williams was having a difficult time working with the rest of the band. "Ain't Got No Time" was one of the first songs that the group recorded when they returned to the studio, and Danny was not happy with the way that things were going. "At one point, in a fit of rage, he threw his bass across the room and stalked out," explains J.P. "After a cooling off for a while, he came back in and we finished the song to his satisfaction." For reasons that none of the members seem thrilled to talk about, Danny had been unhappy for some time. Marlon tried to remember: "It was just... You know something—it's been so long I don't really remember. Seems like he kind of wanted to start his own band or something." Buzz put it this way:

> He just started not liking us very much anymore. He didn't like what Mike was doing. It had nothing to do with Jimmy. He didn't like that way that Mike was leading the group. Danny Williams was one of the sweetest guys I've ever known. When he turned...I even asked him one day, I said, 'Danny, you've done a complete 180.' And he said, 'Let me tell you something. When everything's going okay, I'm the nicest guy in the world. I work hard to be it, Buzz.' But he said, 'If it's not, I can be the biggest SOB there is.' And it just kind of became intolerable. He didn't like us. Lord, okay. That's it.

The group decided to ask Danny to step down. J.P. was elected to convey the message. "Danny took it surprisingly well, though," said J.P. "It was as if he was relieved to be out of it." Danny's departure was particularly hard on Steve. Steve and Danny were close friends, and their shared experiences dated back to sessions at Lemco. "Finally, it was so unproductive that we had no choice but to ask him to leave," remembers Steve. "At the time I was calling him my best friend, and it was very difficult emotionally for me. It was for all of us, but you can imagine firing your best friend."

Danny was officially fired from the band near the end of 1977. Despite his departure, Danny's presence on *Mixed Emotions* is strong. He performed on seven of the nine songs, and "Ain't Got No Time" was included on the album. In addition to his versatile background vocals, Danny was a fluid bass player capable of driving the band in an exciting manner. His versatility had allowed the band to incorporate a number of popular styles including funk, rock, soul, and disco. Musicians like Danny Williams don't come along every day, and it was going to take a talented bass player to fill the void.

Introducing Sonny Lemaire

Danny's replacement was Sonny Lemaire. Sonny is originally from Jeffersonville, Indiana, located just across the river from Louisville. He never took bass lessons, but he played along with records and taught himself. "Paul McCartney and James Jamerson taught me how to play bass," explains Sonny. He joined his first band, The Sceptors, while in high school during 1964. They told him that he could join the band if he would agree to play bass. He didn't know what a bass was at the time, but he agreed because he wanted to be in the band. His mother supported his ambitions, and bought him a Kent bass at a Louisville pawn shop. He played along with Beatles records, picking out individual notes without knowing what to call them. "In those early days, of course, I didn't even know the notes I was playing," explains Sonny. "I had no clue. I was just mimicking where they were on the neck."

Sonny continued to progress on the bass, and played with a number of cover bands in his twenties. He became well-versed in popular music styles playing "whatever was on the charts in those days that you had to work up to play in clubs." Marlon was among the musicians who Sonny played with during the 1970s. Sonny was working a steady gig at a bowling alley bar in Lexington called The Terrace Room located in Eastland Lanes with a band led by Doug Breeding when he was asked to join Exile near the end of 1977. He was reluctant to join Exile at first, because he was making better money with Breeding. He had a family to support, and he initially turned Exile's offer down.

It was when Chapman agreed to float him additional funds from his own pocket that Sonny agreed to join. This proved to be a great time to join the band as they would have a No. 1 pop hit less than a year after he replaced Danny. Seven of the nine songs for *Mixed Emotions* were complete when Sonny joined. He contributed bass and background vocals to the two remaining selections, "Never Gonna Stop" and "Stay with Me." Sonny was introduced to the band's excursions at The Drawbridge Inn the night before his first studio session, and he was worried that his subsequent hangover might affect his performance. "He went in and proved himself beyond the shadow of a doubt," said J.P. The band now had a record contract, and there was peace and harmony within their ranks.

Mixed Emotions, produced by Chapman and engineered by Peter Coleman, presents Exile as an Anglo-funk/disco/R&B/pop band, and the sound of the record is drastically different from their records on Wooden Nickel. This was romantic music, not hard-driving rock and roll. That isn't to say that the album lacks diversity; a number of divergent styles are present.

Chapman and Chinn's "You Thrill Me" opens side one, making the pop inclinations of the record clear from the start. This is more of a straight ahead pop-rock song, and it fails to measure up to the funky swagger of "Kiss You All Over." The record buying public agreed. "You Thrill Me" would prove to be a disappointing follow-up only reaching No. 40 on the Billboard chart in late 1978. The lead vocal was provided by J.P.

"Never Gonna Stop" introduces the slick, funky music associated with this era in the band's history. Once again, J.P. is the lead vocalist. Chapman's decision to open the album with two songs featuring J.P. on lead vocals suggests that he was trying to push Stokley to the background. Sonny's bass playing drives the song, thus demonstrating that he would be able to effectively replicate the feel that Danny Williams had been providing. J.P.'s slightly extended guitar solo works to show that he had not abandoned his rock and roll roots, and that the band could still jam effectively. Disco/R&B artist Linda Clifford later covered "Never Gonna Stop," and her version was sampled by rap artist 2Pac on his song "All Eyez on Me." Disco-influenced sounds are present on this song and others, and it should be noted that several rock and roll bands were experimenting with the new dance styles at the time.

The Rolling Stones, a band often held up as the epitome of rock and roll, had a disco-influenced hit in 1978 with "Miss You," and the backlash against the style had not yet taken hold of the record buying public. "So it was just kind of part of the landscape of music at that time," explains Sonny. Stokley provides the lead vocal on "There's Been a Change," the most overt disco workout on the album. Danny's bass line sounds like it was ready made for a 1970s dance club or a skating rink. Stokley's vocal performance is confident yet substantially understated compared to his earlier work. "You and Me," also featuring a lead vocal by Stokley, is a memorable side closing track. The thick vocal harmonies show the skill with which Stokley, J.P., Danny, Buzz, and Marlon could blend their voices. J.P.'s guitar solo adds bite to this skillfully crafted slice of pop/funk.

Side two opens with "Kiss You All Over," before moving into Danny's "Ain't Got No Time." Stokley is the lead vocalist on the track. His presence is felt more strongly on side two as he also provides vocals on "Don't Do It" and "One Step at a Time." "Ain't Got No Time" opens with a quirky synthesizer solo provided by Marlon that unfortunately works to date the track. The song deals with the difficulties between love/commitment and life on the road as a musician, a theme that runs through side two after "Kiss You All Over." "Don't Do It," one of the more effective funk oriented tunes on the album, directly addresses an intense devotion to music as a lifestyle. "One Step at a

Time" is a pleasing, if not particularly memorable pop-oriented track that was wisely placed near the end of the album. It makes way for the much more interesting closing track, "Stay with Me." "Stay with Me" is a country song, and it must have surprised listeners at the time. It's hard to believe that it was cut during the same sessions as "Never Gonna Stop." The fact that the band could pull off both styles effectively is a testament to their strong musicianship. J.P. sings the lead vocal, and his guitar solo is stylistically suited for the country based tune incorporating "chicken-picking" elements that show the influence of James Burton. The song was a sign of the direction in which the band would soon be moving. "It already shows even right then and there how naturally the band could flow into that side of music," said Sonny.

Sonny was interested in songwriting, and he liked to play his songs for Chapman. He knew that he would get an honest opinion from the demanding producer. This was an important period of growth, both for Sonny and the future of Exile. Chapman listened to the songs, patiently critiquing them and suggesting ways in which they could be improved. Sonny remembers Chapman as patient, and willing to work with those who wanted to learn. Despite these sessions, Sonny's songwriting didn't impress Chapman at first. Sonny had no songwriting credits on *Mixed Emotions*. Nevertheless, the hard work would pay off. Sonny is listed as a co-writer on four songs on Exile's fourth Warner-Curb album, *Heart and Soul*, and he would form a songwriting partnership with J.P. during Exile's country years that would be responsible for the bulk of the band's material from 1983-1987. "It was a real eye-opener for me because I had never been around anybody at that point that had his talent or expertise," said Sonny. "So when you're just starting out and you can hook up with somebody that really is way ahead of the game and learn from that, that's a big help."

Exile returned to the Central Kentucky area after recording the *Mixed Emotions* LP, and continued to play the club circuit. They immediately added "Kiss You All Over" to the set list after they recorded it, and it was met in the clubs with what J.P. describes as "apathetic response." "This was always interesting to me because after it became a hit, we'd go back to the same place with the same crowd, play and -sing it the exact same exact way, and they all went apesh--," exclaims J.P.

The band started getting reports that "Kiss You All Over" was being played at radio stations across the country, and there was a sense that the single would be more successful than previous recordings. Steve and Sonny had taken jobs at a landscaping company in order to help make ends meet, and they remember hearing a radio station play "Kiss You All Over" while they were working. The song eventually charted in *Billboard Magazine*. The single continued to gain recognition, and by the summer of 1978 it was a major hit, reaching the top of the charts and staying there for four weeks. Exile had finally broken through to the mainstream, and in a big way. Part of the reason for the single's success was the controversy surrounding it. "Kiss You All Over" was considered risqué in 1978, a fact that seems unthinkable in the postmodern internet age. "There were politicians making comments on national television regarding the sexual nature of the lyrics, and how it was a symptom of the moral degradation of our country," said J.P. A disc jockey in Illinois became so irate by having to play the single that he quit his job. Popular music artists such as The Rolling Stones, Led Zeppelin, John Lennon, and Marvin Gaye had set the stage for more sexually suggestive material to enter the musical mainstream, and the success of "Kiss You All Over" was simply a reflection of how things were changing in the music industry and American culture. The controversy only served to make the song much more popular.

Once "Kiss You All Over" reached the top ten, Exile was booked to play *The Midnight Special* in Los Angeles. The show was popular at the time, and it featured performances by the most successful bands in the industry. They arrived at the show in a limo. "None of us had ever been in a limo before; we could see that people were trying to figure out who we were," said J.P. "We were met with blank stares when we said 'Exile.'" The band's excitement was somewhat stilted when they discovered that they were going to have to perform the song live. "We only had about half of our stuff, and we had no monitors," remembers Buzz. They met the well-known announcer, Wolfman Jack, during the taping. "I believe he sensed that we were a bit shy and out of our element, and was doing what he could to make us feel accepted," remembers J.P.

As a rock band from Kentucky, Exile was always a bit of an underdog. The Wolfman's acceptance was a big deal. "Being accepted by your peers was important to us," said J.P. "We hadn't grown up in a music town like L.A., New York, or Nashville, and there were instances where people treated us badly or talked down to us because they sensed an innocence about us." Still, Exile knew that they had a cheering section back home in Kentucky, and several of their friends told them that they were going to have *Midnight Special* parties when the show aired the following week.

Exile taped additional video performances of "Kiss You All Over" in 1978. They recorded for the BBC's *Top of the Pops*, but the show never aired. Groups had to have the No. 1 single to appear on the show. "Kiss You All Over" seemed destined to reach the No. 1 spot that week, so they went ahead and taped the show. Unfortunately, *Saturday Night Fever* was released that week, and The Bee Gees' "Stayin' Alive" moved into the No. 1 spot.

Exile also recorded a video of the song in Holland. "We did it about ten times, so that camera angles and all could get all of us at different times," said Buzz. "I don't remember doing that, but there I sit." Buzz's blank mental state during the shooting was due to the valiums that he took that day to try to overcome his fear of the band's traveling situation. The group was forced to fly to Holland and back in the same day in the midst of harsh weather, and Buzz had to get himself in a comatose state in order to deal with it. He has faint recollections of the trip. Buzz:

> I remember being outside the studio and there was a forest and these straight...it looked like The Black Forest of Germany. Walking through that forest before we had to tape the video...and I wasn't dressed yet. But walking around that forest and thinking, 'This is some of the most beautiful country I've ever seen in my life.' And it was in Holland. My family's from Holland, so I wondered, 'Am I feeling any kind of DNA jerk around here?'"

The success of "Kiss You All Over" quickly changed Exile in several respects. They were booked to do a short tour through Texas with Eddie Money and Dave Mason. Mason had been a member of the British group Traffic with Steve Winwood, and a song that he wrote for that group, "Feelin' Alright," was turned into a hit by Joe Cocker. At the time he was riding the success of a 1977 single entitled "We Just Disagree." "Dave seemed a little shy, as none of us had the chance to meet him that I know of," said J.P. Eddie Money was much more willing to socialize with Exile. Money had been a New York City police officer, and he lacked some of the more arrogant personality traits associated with rock stardom. Two singles from his 1977 debut album, "Baby Hold On" and "Two Tickets to Paradise," had enjoyed considerable success. "He was a real singer and entertainer who put every ounce of energy into his show," said J.P.

Interestingly, Buzz doesn't remember Eddie Money or Dave Mason, but he does remember being in Houston, Texas when Exile met their future manager. Peggy Rogers was still in touch with the group at this time, and she told them to contact Jim Morey, a successful manager who had worked with big names in the industry. Buzz remembers that Morey had worked with The Osmonds, The Jacksons, and other well-known artists. Despite Morey's impressive credentials, Exile wasn't interested in working with a manager. Their early experiences in the business led to a healthy skepticism of music industry operations, and they were content to handle their own affairs. "Nobody, including me wanted to hire a manager," remembers Buzz.

Morey flew to Texas in order to meet the group, and he introduced himself as a partner in a company out of Los Angeles called Katz-Gallin Associates. Morey was aware that Exile had no manager, and he wanted the job. The band didn't take him up on his offer at first, but they began to change their opinion about this when their instruments were accidentally destroyed on an airplane shortly before a gig in Anaheim, California. Buzz remembered that he still had Morey's card, and he decided to phone the manager. "In about forty-five minutes a truck pulled up with all those instruments in it," said Buzz. Exile was able to make the gig, and they had a new perspective on the value of a high profile manager. Buzz arranged for Morey fly to Kentucky in order to meet all of the members of the band. Morey met with each member of the band for thirty minutes, and when the meetings were over the band had a manager. "He was unlike any manager we'd ever talked to," said Buzz. Morey was a major player in the music industry, and he was an effective manager for Exile. He also refrained from taking the group's publishing.

Morey signed Exile to the William Morris Agency, and their touring situation improved considerably. Their first tour after signing with the agency was opening up for Aerosmith. Aerosmith had developed a reputation as an exciting live act throughout the 1970s with albums such as *Toys in the Attic*, *Rocks*, and *Draw the Line*. They were drawing large crowds at the time, and Exile gained significant exposure as the opening act. Exile and Aerosmith aren't compatible by the more rigid genre music industry definitions that developed later, but audiences in the 1970s were more accustomed to eclectic lineups. The Aerosmith tour was a southern tour, and Exile was well received, especially when they played their hit.

J.P. remembers being an Aerosmith fan at the time, but he couldn't take the loud volume of their stage show. "It was probably the single loudest thing I'd ever heard, and my ears couldn't take it for more than about sixty seconds," remembers J.P. Exile didn't get to spend much time with the members of Aerosmith. Aerosmith flew into the gigs on a jet, and arrived at the shows in a limo just in time to hit the stage. Steven Tyler introduced himself to Exile one evening, and J.P. and Buzz remember the meeting as a pleasant experience.

The next arrangement was a northern tour with Heart. Buzz remembers a particularly harsh experience in the northern portion of the Midwest. "The audience was rude to us, just rude," remembers Buzz. "Now they weren't rude during 'Kiss You All Over.' They cheered that, but they hated everything else." Once again, Exile didn't get to spend much time with the opening act. Nancy Wilson was the only member of Heart to introduce herself to Exile. J.P. described her as a "very nice person who complimented us on our music."

Exile also headlined some gigs during this period. J.P. remembers returning to Frankfort, Kentucky as a national act. They had previously played dances, proms, and school functions in Frankfort providing background music. Now audiences were coming to the show to hear the music. The fans reacted ecstatically to "Kiss You All Over" at the show in Frankfort. "It once again reminded us that a little over a year ago before the song was a radio hit the reaction would have been tepid at best," said J.P.

The success of "Kiss You All Over" and *Mixed Emotions* (No. 14 on the album chart) gave the members of Exile some financial security. J.P started getting royalty checks for his songwriting contributions on the album, and he was able to buy his first new vehicle, a white Toyota pickup truck. He was also able to purchase a house, and he got married. "I married Linda Hicks in 1979, but didn't really see much of her, the truck, or the house," said J.P. The marriage would only last about a year and a half. Hopes were still high for the band, but they didn't reach this level of mainstream pop success again. "I remember we went out to L.A. and we were called over to the label, Warner Brothers," said Steve. "They announced to us that our single had gone number one and our album had gone gold all in the same breath. As we were leaving the building we were telling people, you know…in the hallway people would be coming towards us, and we'd say 'We're No.1'…kind of a party mode." A somewhat jaded, yet honest Warner Brothers employee took the opportunity to let the band know that it was just the beginning, and that they would now have to work even harder. He is reported to have replied "Oh good…that means now you have to work your ass off." "It really caught me off guard, but that WAS true," remembers Steve.

Morey suggested that the band travel to L.A. to do interviews and socialize. J.P. was already in California writing songs, but the other members had to fly in from Kentucky. Nicky Chinn was in Los Angeles at the time, and he invited Stokley and Buzz to the premiere party for *Sgt. Pepper's Lonely Hearts Club Band*, a musical film featuring new versions of songs composed by The Beatles. Chinn wanted the band to meet Warner Brothers executives. "I remember thinking 'I don't have a suit,'" said Buzz. Not sure of what to do, Buzz and Stokley purchased suits at McAlpins, a local department store in Lexington. They looked terribly out of place when they arrived at a record company board meeting in Los Angeles dressed in their suits. "Here we were in suits like nice little southern boys getting ready to go to church," continues Buzz.

They knew that they didn't want to wear suits to the *Sgt. Pepper* party that evening, so they contacted one of Chapman's assistants. She helped them find suitable attire. Clothes were less expensive in 1978, and Buzz was surprised to find out that he would be wearing a $150 dollar shirt. "I said, 'It's not even permanent press,'" exclaimed Buzz. Buzz and Stokley showed up to the party appropriately dressed, and Chinn proceeded to introduce them to some well-known figures in the music industry including The Bee Gees and George Burns. Buzz was especially excited about meeting Burns, but he claimed that the comedian "wanted to get the hell out, and he did." Chinn introduced them to the president of Chrysalis Records, one of the executives who regretfully turned down "Kiss You All Over." He is reported to have said, "I don't know what was wrong with me that day."

The tension between Chapman and Stokley came to a head during the sessions for the band's second album for Warner-Curb, *All There Is*. Chapman is reported to have thought highly of Stokley personally, but he could not deal with the singer's vocal difficulties. The producer reluctantly agreed to work with the struggling vocalist, but the sessions were unbearable. Chapman wanted to turn Stokley into another type of singer, but by this point the Exile vocalist was having a difficult time sounding like himself. As a result of several years of untreated illness, life in the clubs, and screaming, Stokley was losing his voice. "Jimmy started having to have nodes taken off of his vocal chords," said Buzz. "We didn't know about the first few times." Singers aren't supposed to sing, speak, or whisper when dealing with vocal cord nodules, but Stokley never stopped working. Buzz didn't find out about the nodes until Stokley's last operation, and J.P. was never aware of the physical realities of the situation.

In addition to his vocal problems, Stokley suffered from health issues. He struggled with hepatitis in the late 1960s or early 1970s, and his skin would at times appear yellowish. "It was so bad that he wore dark glasses while on stage, so that people would not see how jaundiced he was," remembers Buzz. Billy Luxon's mother was a nurse, and she warned about the seriousness of Stokley's condition. "She said, 'he is destroying his liver,'" said Buzz. Stokley seemingly recovered from this early illness, but he had suffered massive liver damage in the process. "Jimmy was extremely self-destructive," continues Buzz. "The only thing in his life that he cared about was the group, was performing." By *All There Is* Stokley's health problems were affecting his performances dramatically. "Jimmy was having problems with his voice at that point," said Sonny. "I mean really, really struggling."

In a shocking turn of events, Chapman refused to work with Stokley after the recording of *All There Is*. "It sort of came down to, and I don't know if it was actually ever said, but it came down to…we were gonna lose our gig with Chapman if we retained, you know, Jimmy," said J.P. "We just, you know… As a result of that we had to let him go—a tough time."

Steve remembers that Chapman was adamant about Stokley's departure after *All There Is*. "That was the album where Chapman had had him in the studio all day, and then turned around to us and said, 'I'll never make another album with him,'" says Steve. "That was the end of Jimmy right there—total obscurity." The move to release Stokley undoubtedly seems harsh to those who remember the band's roots, but the game changed entirely for the band when they started making significant money. Chapman was one of the most successful producers in the music business on an international level, and he wasn't particularly concerned about the legacy of a rock and roll singer who flourished in the bars of Kentucky. "Chapman's word was God," laments Steve. "He was our link."

The move to release Stokley was difficult for the band, because they liked him personally and he had devoted much of his life to the group. "It was heartbreaking to have to part ways with him, but we really didn't have any choice," said Marlon. Marlon remembers Stokley as a "really good guy," and a "nice good 'ol boy." "Jimmy and I came from kind of different backgrounds, and I don't remember ever spending huge amounts of time in deep conversation," continues Marlon.

No one that I interviewed recalled Stokley in a negative light personally. "I loved him," said Steve. "I mean, he and I never got sideways on any issue." Chapman was responsible for firing Stokley, but his reasons were apparently musical, not personal. "Mike thought the world of Jimmy," said J.P.

The move to release Jimmy was controversial among their longtime fans, and some of the newer members felt a bit uncomfortable during this period. "Jimmy is still so revered, and honest to God rightly so," said Sonny. "I really, really like Stokley, and for any number of years the band was referred to as Jimmy Stokley and Exile." Stokley had served as the backbone and the leader of the group for many years, and his departure marked a major shift in the band as J.P. continued to develop as a songwriter/vocalist. "When he left the band there was a, kind of a…you know, in Richmond, Lexington, Central Kentucky area…kind of a shock," said Sonny.

All There Is was the last Exile album to include contributions from Jimmy Stokley. The responsibility for informing Stokley of his firing fell on Marlon and Buzz. They invited Stokley to Buzz's house, and the singer knew what was happening as soon as he entered the room. "We talked, and he got up and walked to each one of us and said, 'Well, you know, you two guys had the guts to tell me, and that took a lot of guts,'" remembers Buzz. Buzz started crying as soon as Stokley left. "Marlon said, 'You know, Buzz, it does no good to react like this,'" said Buzz. Buzz pulled himself together, and the group moved on.

Chapter Five
How Could Disco Wrong

T HE *ALL THERE IS* sessions were loaded with problems in addition to the
Stokley situation. There were equipment issues as soon as the band
showed up for the sessions at The Forum. The Stephens 24-track machine
they were recording with was not working properly, and they had to wait
for the inventor of the machine to fly in to fix it. This led to downtime, and
Chapman was not happy.

In addition to his problems with Stokley, the producer's marriage was
also falling apart. "There was another situation going on that was not very
helpful, and that was that Mike and Connie were getting a divorce," said
Buzz. "Mike did not want that divorce."

The group was also losing its direction musically. The influence of disco
was obvious on *Mixed Emotions*, but Chapman was plunging the group head-
first into the style on *All There Is*, especially on side one. "We didn't really
know what we wanted to do at that point," remembers Marlon.

Side one features a couple of extended dance tracks, ready-made for the
disco dance floors. Anyone familiar with the various personalities and tastes of
the band members would quickly understand that these disco-based tracks were
not representative of what Exile was about. "I can just remember spending a lot
of hours in the studio, and just kind of beating ourselves to death," said Marlon.

The album certainly lacked cohesiveness. The rock elements were absent
by this point, replaced by pop-friendly sounds and ethereal synthesizers. *All
There Is* was recorded at the height of the disco era, and many bands were
forced to incorporate the style at the time. This would ultimately lead to
anti-disco sentiment throughout the music industry, which would only serve
to make albums such as *All There Is* sound severely dated. "I mean, we hated
disco," explains Steve.

Stokley is on a number of tracks, but Chapman called on J.P. and Sonny
to cover a high percentage of the lead vocals. The producer expected something close to perfection from them as well. "He just demanded that you get
it right, and do it his way," says J.P. "And if you had to do fifty takes on one
line, then that's what it was gonna take." As the newest member of the band,
Sonny was particularly troubled when he discovered that Chapman wanted

him to provide lead vocals on the album. "Chapman enlisted me to sing some lead vocals on that project, which was never...I joined the band as a bass player and harmony singer," explains Sonny. "There was never an intention or a thought on my part to sing lead."

Perhaps the most underlying stress came from the fact that the band was looking for an adequate follow-up to "Kiss You All Over." "You Thrill Me" had proven to be a major disappointment, and the band turned to disco in a panic. "We were just trying to get ourselves back on the radio, and that seemed to be what was working," remembers J.P. "If you'd call it falling victim to a trend, then we were guilty." Sonny remembers a "dark cloud" over the project. The band largely ignores the album to this day. None of the songs are currently included in their live show, and the album didn't spawn any major hits for the band or other artists.

Side one consists of three songs. The opening song is "How Could This Go Wrong," a dance track that clocks in at 8:09. It was composed by Chinn, Chapman, J.P., and Lynda Lawley. Lawley was a member of Thieves, a Chapman-produced band featuring three female singers with a backing band. The extended instrumental sections suggest that the producer was trying to avoid the use of vocals for prolonged sections of the album on purpose due to Stokley's deteriorating vocal cords. Chapman hoped that the song would catch on as part of the disco craze, with the song title being a play on words. The producer realized that "How can this go wrong" sounded remarkably like "How can disco wrong" when sung, and he was always looking for some kind of hook. "He said, 'Now when you say it, you have to really kind of make it sound like 'How can disco wrong,'" said Buzz.

Synthesizers and drum machines were becoming more prominent in the late 1970s, and there was a feeling among the music industry that detached, futuristic, dance-oriented music was going to be the way forward. Chapman embraced the new trends. "Mike kind of thought that was going to be not only the coming thing, but the permanent thing," continues Buzz. Acoustic piano was abandoned in favor of synthesizers on tracks such as "How Could This Go Wrong" and "Too Proud to Cry." It wasn't as though the band completely opposed the direction Chapman was leading them in. "I guess we felt like we could write those kinds of things, and I can't really blame that on anybody but just all of us in the studio working together," admits J.P.

The title track, sung by J.P., is the strongest song on the album, and it sits uncomfortably between the two longer dance tracks. The song was composed by J.P. and Lawley. Lawley's input was primarily lyrical. J.P. was developing into a first class songwriter, one who was willing to utilize unusual chord progressions and melodies. Musicians might note that the main hook or melody is drawn from the Lydian mode, a scale uncommon in popular music. J.P. discovered the unconventional melody by accident while playing the piano. "Mistakenly, I hit a root note with my left hand, and I mistakenly hit a two chord with my right hand meaning to hit a one chord," explains J.P. Musicians may recognize that J.P. had discovered something resembling a #11 chord, but non-musicians will simply hear a pleasant, unconventional melody in a song that should probably have been released as a single.

"Too Proud to Cry," another extended dance track (8:19) closes side one. It was composed by Marlon, Sonny, and Stokley. "J.P. usually wrote by himself or with somebody out of Mike Chapman's office, and then it would be me and Marlon, or me and Stokley, or all three of us to write together," remembers Sonny. "Too Proud to Cry" represents the only time that Marlon received a songwriting credit on an Exile album. In retrospect, Stokley's strained vocal is haunting and a bit autobiographical. The song includes instrumental passages and "woo-oos" sung by the entire band, while Stokley's lead vocals are kept to a minimum.

Side two is more song-oriented. It opens with "The Part of Me That Needs You Most," a pop-rock Chinn/Chapman composition with shared lead vocals from J.P. and Stokley. "Destiny," another Pennington/Lawley collaboration, is a pleasing pop song, but unlike "All There Is", the polished arrangement sounds forced and ready-made for a fern bar. J.P.'s "Being in Love with You" examines a lyrical theme that would run through his country songs, romantic relationships that seem to progress naturally. Stokley sings the last two songs on the album. "Let's Do It Again," penned by Sonny and Stokley, includes a clavinet solo and comical closing vocal sounds from Steve. This is the only time that Steve was allowed to "sing" on an Exile album. "Come on Over," composed by J.P., is the hardest rocking tune on this release. Its interlocking guitar and synthesizer riffs demonstrate how tight the band could be. J.P.'s fiery solo represents one of the few times that he "rocked out" on the album.

All There Is failed to chart, and "How Could This Go Wrong" peaked at No. 88 on the singles chart. "Let's Do It Again" and "Too Proud to Cry," both songs with writing contributions from Stokley, were released, but failed to chart. "How Could This Go Wrong" was prophetically titled, and its chart performance was particularly troubling to Chapman. "He thought, 'How Could This Go Wrong' was going to be the one that brought us back," said J.P. Exile and their embattled producer were on edge during this period and the outside distractions weren't helping. Chapman didn't produce their next album, leaving the producer chair to his engineer, Peter Coleman.

Stokley's replacement was a young singer/guitarist named Randy Rickman, or as Buzz refers to him, "Randy whatever it was." Rickman was suggested by Peggy Rogers. He may have been brought in for his appearance as much as for his musical abilities. Buzz remembers that Rickman turned the group "bubblegum as hell," a fact that was not lost on their management.

Jim Morey wasn't sure how to handle the new lineup. "He looked at me, and he said 'You know, I'm going to have to start marketing the group differently,'" remembers Buzz. Exile's fan base was getting younger, and Rickman was serving as a kind of teen idol. "Because these little girls, prepubescent girls and all that, were running to the edge of the stage where RANDY was," continued Buzz. "We're kind of looking at each other like 'What on earth is going on?'" The band quickly realized that Rickman wasn't working out, and he only lasted a couple of months.

Rickman's work ethic was adequate, but he simply didn't fit in with the other members of the band. "Randy did nothing but try to help the group," said Buzz. "That boy was solid, and there was nothing else wrong except that he was the wrong type for us." Rickman appeared in a lip-synched performance of "You Thrill Me" on a German television show entitled *Disco* in mid-1979. His long blonde hair and black leather jacket with no shirt stand out among the Kentucky music veterans, but he doesn't seem to be vying for any extra attention otherwise. "In all honesty, he wasn't a real major player in the overall picture of things," said Marlon. Rickman passed away in 2004, at the age of fifty.

Exile was experiencing success in the late 1970s, but it was small in scale compared to Chapman's achievements as a producer. In addition to his work producing Exile, Chapman experienced success with Nick Gilder's *City Nights* album and Blondie's *Parallel Lines*. He also managed to convince The Knack, a highly sought after band at the time, to let him produce their debut album. All of this success brought the attention of the mainstream press, and Chapman was asked to conduct an interview with *Rolling Stone* magazine. *Rolling Stone* exerted a much greater influence in early 1980 than it does in the internet age, and this was a great opportunity for the producer. He didn't make the most of it.

Chapman took the opportunity to criticize Journey, a popular group at the time, and to discuss the state of radio. "If you look at a band like Journey, you've got the epitome of trash in American music," said Chapman.[1] The interview was being taped in the studio, and the members of Exile sat stunned in the control room as it was taking place. "He was not stoned, he was not drunk, he was not incapacitated by time or anything, it was in the afternoon, everything's fine, he was fresh, he was congenial, and he started in on this," continues Buzz.

Stokley encouraging the crowd to put their hands together. Courtesy Kim Gulley Owens.

Marlon in 1977. Courtesy Kim Gulley Owens.

Stokley relaxing. Courtesy Kim Gulley Owens.

J.P. at a live show circa 1976. Courtesy Kim Gulley Owens.

Exile in 1976 around the time that they were discovered by Mike Chapman: (front) Jimmy Stokley, (back row) Marlon Hargis, J.P. Pennington, Danny Williams, Bobby Johns, Buzz Cornelison. Courtesy Kim Gulley Owens.

J.P., Stokley, and Danny at a show in 1976. Courtesy Kim Gulley Owens.

Promotional shot, 1976: (left to right) Jimmy Stokley, Marlon Hargis, Bobby Johns, Danny Williams, Buzz Cornelison, J.P. Pennington. Courtesy Kim Gulley Owens.

Buzz, Stokley, and a young lady enjoying some downtime. Courtesy Kim Gulley Owens.

Just after Steve Goetzman joined the band in 1977: (left to right) Buzz Cornelison, Danny Williams, Steve Goetzman. Courtesy Kim Gulley Owens.

Promotional shot following the success of "Kiss You All Over" and Danny Williams' departure from the band: (left to right) Marlon Hargis, J.P. Pennington, Jimmy Stokley, Buzz Cornelison, Steve Goetzman, Sonny Lemaire. Courtesy Kim Gulley Owens.

Another photo taken after Sonny joined the band: (seated on floor) J.P. Pennington, (seated on couch) Marlon Hargis, (back row) Sonny Lemaire, Steve Goetzman, Buzz Cornelison, Jimmy Stokley. Courtesy Kim Gulley Owens.

One of Stokley's last photos with Exile, which appeared on the back of the All There Is *album: (front row) Marlon Hargis, Sonny Lemaire, (back row) Buzz Cornelison, Jimmy Stokley, Steve Goetzman, J.P. Pennington.*

Exile following Stokley's departure and one of Buzz's last photos with the band: (front) Steve Goetzman, (middle row) Mark Gray, Buzz Cornelison, Les Taylor, Sonny Lemaire, Marlon Hargis, (back) J.P. Pennington. This photo appeared on the back of the Don't Leave Me This Way *album cover.*

The Knack's …but the little girls understand *album.*

Showcase at Stockyard (Bullpen Lounge), Buddy Killen, producer (dark sport jacket), August 2, 1983. Courtesy Steve Goetzman.

Showcase at the Exit/In, Nashville, October 11, 1983. Courtesy Steve Goetzman.

Last 1983 showcase at Stockyard restaurant with Epic Records staff, the group's agents, and manager, Jim Morey (left to right): Roy Wunsch, Jim Morey, Rick Blackburn, Marlon Hargis, Joe Casey, Steve Goetzman, Scott (?), J.P. Pennington, Lane Cross, Les Taylor, Susan Burns, Rich Sehwan. Courtesy Steve Goetzman.

One of five showcases in 1983 across the U.S. Epic Records used to introduce the "country" version of Exile to radio. Janie Fricke attended. Courtesy Steve Goetzman.

Left: Pat McMakin, engineer, with Sonny and Steve. McMakin engineered all of the group's albums on Epic, 1983. Courtesy Steve Goetzman.

Below: Taken right before Exile left for their first tour as a country band, 1984. Courtesy Steve Goetzman.

Steve playing a gig on August 13, 1984 in Ashland, KY. Courtesy Steve Goetzman.

Marlon, J.P., Sonny, and Steve with Kris Kristofferson in 1984. Courtesy Steve Goetzman.

Steve and Sonny with Roger Miller and Willie Nelson. Courtesy Steve Goetzman.

Exile enjoying their success after the release of the first album: (left to right) Les Taylor, Marlon Hargis, J.P. Pennington, Sonny Lemaire, Steve Goetzman. Courtesy Kentucky Music Hall of Fame.

A victory cake. Courtesy Kentucky Music Hall of Fame.

The victory cake ended up in Steve's face. Courtesy Kentucky Music Hall of Fame.

Country Awards Dinner 1984 – Left to right: (seated in floor) Kris Kristofferson, Roger Miller, Frances Preston, Randy Owen, J.P. Pennington, John Hartford, (seated on sofa) Mort Shuman, Lewis Anderson, David Allen Coe, (leaning behind Owen and Pennington) Don Gant, (standing) Dan Bourgoise, Karen Brooks, Del Shannon, (behind Shannon) Fred Bourgoise, Marlon Hargis, Sonny Lemaire, Steve Goetzman, Del Bryant. Courtesy Steve Goetzman.

Exile on Austin City Limits *television show in 1985. Courtesy Kentucky Music Hall of Fame.*

Billy Moore, Jeff Hunt, Steve, J.P., and Les in Pennsylvania after the tour bus broke down in 1985. They finished the trip in the merchandise truck. Cold! Courtesy Steve Goetzman.

Sheet music cover for "She's a Miracle." Courtesy Kentucky Music Hall of Fame.

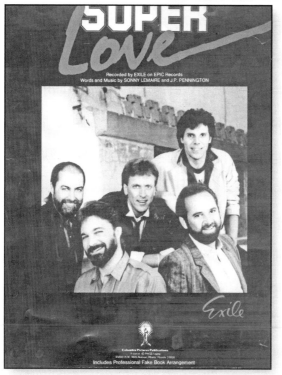

Sheet music cover for "Super Love." Courtesy Kentucky Music Hall of Fame.

Pacific Amphitheater, July 11, 1985 – Costa Mesa, CA. Courtesy Marlon Hargis.

Music City News Awards, June 1986, with Danny Cooksey – Nashville, Opry House. Courtesy Marlon Hargis.

Fan Fair, June 1986 – Nashville, TN. Courtesy Marlon Hargis.

Farm Aid II press conference, July 4, 1986. Courtesy Marlon Hargis.

Farm Aid II. Courtesy Marlon Hargis.

Exile dressed as women on Hee Haw *circa 1986. Courtesy Steve Goetzman.*

Sonny on Hee Haw *with a flower in his hair.* Courtesy Lee Carroll.

Lee on Hee Haw. *Courtesy Lee Carroll.*

J.P. sporting a wig and a beard. Courtesy Lee Carroll.

Steve in the Hee Haw *dressing room. Courtesy Steve Goetzman.*

Exile with Kenny Rogers in 1986. Courtesy Steve Goetzman.

Exile performing with friends on Nashville Now in 1986: (left to right) Steve Sanders of The Oak Ridge Boys, Michael Martin Murphy, Les, John McKuen, Steve, Juice Newton, J.P., TNN's Terry Mead on trumpet, recent addition Lee Carroll, Sonny Lemaire.

Steve and Lee with Johnny Cash. Courtesy Lee Carroll.

Lee at a festival in his early years with the band. Courtesy Lee Carroll.

Paul soloing intensely. Courtesy Lee Carroll.

Lee on keytar. Courtesy Lee Carroll.

156

Sonny on 4-string bass. Courtesy Lee Carroll.

Les and J.P. jamming on electrics. Courtesy Lee Carroll.

Paul and Lee. Courtesy Lee Carroll.

Steve with a snare. Courtesy Lee Carroll.

Exile backstage at The Late Show Starring Joan Rivers *with Los Angeles disc jockey, Gerry House: (left to right): Sonny, J.P., Les, Gerry House, Lee Carroll, Steve. Courtesy Steve Goetzman.*

Exile in Los Angeles with Kentucky disc jockey, Coyote Calhoun: (left to right) Sonny, Coyote Calhoun, Les, Lee Carroll, J.P., Steve. Courtesy Steve Goetzman.

Exile in 1987 with Kentucky governor Martha Layne Collins. Courtesy Steve Goetzman.

Rickman was replaced by two musicians, one of which was singer/keyboardist Mark Gray. Gray had an impressive, powerful voice, and he was also an aspiring songwriter. Chapman arranged for the band to meet Gray while they were in Los Angeles. Gray was hired soon after, leaving Exile with three keyboard players. "I remember at the time Jim Morey saying, 'Buzz, that's going to be yet another keyboard player,'" remembers Buzz.

Buzz didn't initially worry about the three keyboard situation, but the move was a nail in the coffin for his involvement with the band. Gray wrote on the keyboard, and he preferred to play while he was singing. "It did start to grate after a while," admits Buzz. "Then I got to the point where, 'Ya know, I really don't care.'" That this personnel move affected Buzz is unfortunate, because Gray's keyboard skills had little to nothing to do with why he was hired. "It was mainly, I wouldn't say a prop because he was a good keyboard player, but he was more integral as a singer rather than a player, really," explains Marlon.

Gray is remembered as an easy person to get along with, but his dedication to Exile was shaky at best. "He had quite a few other things going on musically besides us, and I think that at times it took away from his total dedication to the band," said J.P. Nevertheless, his personality allowed him to work effectively with Exile. They felt as though he might be able to bring them back to the top of the pop chart with his songwriting and vocals. "We felt like we'd really found a superstar, and I believe he really was a superstar," said Steve. "He was a little torn, I think, between wanting to be a star and wanting to be a band member."

Gray was given the nickname "pink baby" by the other band members due to his hairless appearance. "We'd go into his hotel room to check on him," said J.P. "He'd be sitting up in the bed with his little pink, hairless body drinking coffee, smoking a cigarette, or whatever." Unlike most of the members of Exile, Mark was not a native Kentuckian. He was born in Vicksburg, Mississippi.

Introducing Les Taylor

Mark was Chapman's choice as a replacement vocalist for Stokley, but J.P. was also looking for possible replacements in Central Kentucky. One of the more impressive vocalists from the area was Les Taylor. J.P. knew Les from their days playing at The Youth Center in Martin during the 1960s. The Exiles used to trade sets at the center with Les' group, The Ovations. They first discussed playing in a band together during an Ovations show at Speck's. "They were playing at Speck's and I was talking to him on the break, and I said, 'Hey, one of these days we oughta join up and play together,'" recalls J.P.

Les had a voice to be reckoned with, and he was equally capable of singing soaring lead parts or providing high vocal harmonies. He was also a gifted guitarist, but he largely abandoned lead playing after he joined Exile. J.P. began attending Les' solo shows on Thursday nights at a Lexington bar called The Camelot around the same time that the group was in the process of releasing Rickman. "I would go back to the guys and say, 'Hey, you know, you need to hear him sing if you haven't,'" said J.P.

Les' show included a variety of popular music styles, and he also played lead guitar. "He was doing a lot of that Bob Seger stuff and really good Santana songs, and I just felt like he would be an awesome fit for us," continues J.P. Les was asked to join the group, joining Mark Gray to form a seven-piece Exile with two guitarists, a bass player, three keyboardists, and one drummer. Les and Mark were excellent vocalists, and the talent level of the band peaked during this brief period.

Les Taylor was born in Oneida, Kentucky, an unincorporated community in Clay County. His family moved to London, Kentucky following his birth. "I have a lot of aunts and uncles and cousins, and so on and so forth down there," said Les. He and his cousin started learning to play the guitar on the same day when they were about 12-years-old. They spent time at Les' uncle's tire shop learning how to play, sometimes asking customers questions about the guitar. "We would find out that they played guitar or something like that, and we would nab them and have them show us a few chords or something," remembers Les.

They eventually formed a band playing the same instrumental guitar-based tunes that J.P. grew up with such as "Red River Rock" and "Walk Don't Run." Les and his cousin were trading lead guitar parts at the time. "He was playing more of the lead stuff than I was at that point," explains Les. Their set was completely instrumental until one of their friends, their "manager," suggested that someone needed to sing. Les was elected to be the vocalist. The first song that he learned was "California Sun," a song popularized by The Rivieras. The manager named the band Little Caesar & the Romans, with Les acting as "Little Caesar." Les isn't sure when he realized the full potential of his distinctive high-tenor voice. "I still don't think I know it," says Les. He was always shy, but he was especially shy about singing. This is surprising, as his voice has been and still is his claim to fame. While he's certainly no slouch as a rhythm guitarist, Les' soaring lead vocals and harmonies were major factors in Exile's success as a country band. In some instances, he needed added courage in order to perform. Les:

I was real shy. I had to have a little taste before I went onstage. I was just kind of embarrassed or something. It took me a long time to get out of that, but the music was definitely a world that I felt better in when I was onstage.

At some point in the mid-1960s Les left Little Caesar to join The Ovations, a group based in Corbin, Kentucky. They played a mixture of rock and soul, but they tried to stick to Top 40 covers from the Billboard chart. "Back then it was singles—45s that you bought more so than you did albums," explains Les. Radio was less of a niche market in the 1960s, and audiences expected diverse entertainment. "We'd do a Stones tune and then turn around and do an Otis Redding song," said Les.

Les developed a love for soul music during his time with The Ovations, and he cites Otis Redding and Wilson Pickett as influences. "From the minute that I heard my first R&B record, I just really liked that kind of music," said Les. The Ovations had a five-piece lineup consisting of two guitarists, a keyboard player, a bassist, and a drummer. There were three vocalists in the band, and Les developed an ear for singing harmonies while he was with The Ovations. Cecil Jones became the booking agent for the band, and they were soon playing gigs throughout Eastern Kentucky and East Tennessee. Performance venues included a roller skating rink in London, The Youth Centers in Corbin and Martin, fraternity parties at The University of Kentucky, various events at The University of Tennessee and Centre College, and two clubs in Hazard, The Colonial and the VSW. "The fraternity gigs were absolutely crazy," remembers Les. "People gettin' drunk and throwin' up everywhere."

That the Martin Youth Center, a venue located in a town with less than seven hundred people, would play a crucial role in the Kentucky music scene is somewhat surprising. "There would be four hundred of them in The Youth Center," jokes Les. In the late 1960s, The Ovations split gigs at the Martin Youth Center with The Exiles, and Les met several members of the band including Stokley, whom he remembers as "laid back" and "a great guy." "We would set up on one end of the building, and they would set up on the other end of the building, and we'd sort of switch off sets and stuff," said Les. There seems to have been no animosity or spiteful competition between the groups. The Exiles were a few steps ahead of The Ovations at the time with their intricate vocal harmonies (four or five vocalists), horn arrangements, and occasional light show. "I remember back then I always wanted to be a part of that band, even back in those days," remembers Les. Les traveled to Richmond in order to attend several of The Exiles' shows at Speck's during the mid-1960s, and got to know J.P. in the process.

Les would have to wait several years and play with several bands before he would get to play with Exile. His success with Exile in the 1980s may lead some to believe that he was raised singing in the honky-tonks of Kentucky, but he had to move to Indianapolis to play with his first country band. Les played guitar in this four-piece group, which also included a vocalist, bassist, and drummer. He soon discovered that his soulful-southern voice fit the genre, and after about nine months, he moved from a sideman role to fronting the band after the vocalist departed. After fifteen months in Indianapolis, Les returned to Kentucky. "Had to do a lot of country music stuff up there, which I didn't mind, but after a while I just kind of got the longing to be in a bigger band and stuff and do some different kind of music," said Les. This experience with a country band would pay off for Les down the road. He cites George Jones and Merle Haggard as influences.

Les started playing in the house band at a club called Marty's in Lexington soon after he returned to Kentucky in 1970. It was located just off of Richmond Road, near where The Burlington Coat Factory currently resides. "It held about 550 people, something like that," remembers Les. The house band was called upon to provide accompaniment when artists were not self-contained. They had the opportunity to play behind a number of national acts while Les worked there, including Freddy Cannon, Ronnie Dove, and Rufus Thomas. "Basically they would just send us a song list, and we had to fend for ourselves as far as getting the record," explains Les. Bob Seger, Mitch Ryder and the Detroit Wheels, Jerry Lee Lewis, The Box Tops, and Strawberry Alarm Clock are among the acts that played at Marty's during Les' tenure at the club. Seger was at a particularly low point in his career at the time, and was trying to keep his band together after he failed to follow up on the success of "Ramblin' Gamblin' Man." "I think they only paid him, like, $850 dollars," says Les. Local acts played at Marty's as well, including The Exiles.

Les played in a number of bands after his three-year stint at Marty's. In 1973 he left Lexington to go on the road with a show band out of Louisville. The Johnny Greene Show featured two vocalists, Greene and a female singer, and a band. There wasn't much choreography, but there were occasional skits. "Basically where you just have…he and the girl come out and use the dance floor and stand out there and sing songs," explains Les. "There wasn't a whole lot of production to it, but they were called a show band." The band included musicians who would later go on to play with Charlie Daniels, including keyboardist "Taz" Digregorio. Les played with The Johnny Green Show for four months before joining another show band called Gary Edwards and Sage. Edwards did impersonations of famous singers such as Elvis Presley, Gene Pitney, Tom Jones, and Engelbert Humperdinck.

After leaving Gary Edwards and Sage, Les joined a ten-piece jazz-rock group called Cyclone. Cyclone was committed to musical diversity. Their show included arrangements of the music from *Star Wars* and the theme from Stravinsky's *Firebird Suite*. "There was a guy out of Vegas…his name was Joe Zito, and this guy had like, I don't know, three degrees in music," says Les. Zito was skilled in the art of writing charts, and he arranged the band's music. "They said if he did sleep, he would sleep, like, thirty minutes, and then he would be up rarin' to go again," continues Les. The hard work paid off, as Cyclone became a tight unit including guitar, bass, keyboards, drums, a five-piece horn section, and a vocalist. They were based out of Elkhart, Indiana, but the group spent a lot of time on the road. Les eventually left Cyclone, choosing to, once again, return to Kentucky. He joined a Lexington-based rock and roll cover band called Sunburst in September of 1978. They played a few original songs, but their show was primarily built on hit songs by popular rock bands such as Foreigner and Styx. Les left Sunburst in August of 1979 when J.P. invited him to join Exile. "There had been some changes made in Sunburst from the time that I started playing with them up until that point, and it was changes that I didn't really like," said Les. "It was kind of starting to get to me, so when J.P. asked me about coming to work with Exile, I just literally jumped at the chance."

Les and Mark Gray started rehearsing with Exile on the same day. They joined Exile at a difficult time in the band's history, but Les remembers it as an exciting time. "It was just a whole lot of fun, and it was just great to be in an organization like that that was really professional," remembers Les. Exile was struggling, but they had topped the charts and they had a record deal. Les was thrilled with his new situation. "From that standpoint it was great to come into a band that already had a record deal, and things were really looking good for the band," continues Les. By this point Exile had three talented lead vocalists, three keyboard players, two first rate songwriters in J.P. and Mark, and two guitarists. This resulted in a thick sound, and a soundman's nightmare. "It was just blowing me away because there was just so much talent there," said Les. He didn't have any difficulty fitting in with the band, musically or personally. "Les is an absolute joy, one of the funniest guys," remembers Buzz. "He can come out with a line, and deliver it with such a straight face—have you on the floor laughing. Anything that happened to him was always so much bigger than if it happened to somebody else." Buzz remembers one particularly humorous Les adventure involving a cherry to-mato and a rather posh restaurant. Buzz:

> He picked up this very small tomato, this little cherry-like tomato like an hors d'oeuvre. He put it in his mouth—the thing exploded! He sat there just dumbfounded. He said, 'It exploded!' You wouldn't have thought anything that small could have made that big of a mess. He was full of stuff like that. And he could tell stories....

The seven-piece lineup worked for a little while, and the unit toured South Africa. The musicians worked well together, but it soon became clear that something was going to have to give.

As optimistic as the times were for Les, they were equally disheartening for Buzz. While J.P., Steve, Sonny, and Marlon remember the making of the third Exile album on Warner-Curb as a positive experience, Buzz was not enjoying the process. "It just seemed like the deck was starting to be stacked against us," remembers Buzz. "We'd all run out and bought houses. I started really worrying about whether or not we were going to be able to generate enough income to keep what we had bought, because it didn't look like the hits were poppin'."

The addition of a third keyboard player was an irritation, and Buzz's talents as an arranger were being pushed to the background as Mark assumed more of the songwriting duties. "That's when Mike (Chapman) started going, 'hmmm,'" said Buzz. For some time, Buzz had been somewhat out of the loop, working at his parent's shop in Bybee, while J.P., Marlon, and Steve, played on sessions at Lemco. He never took to the more country-oriented direction that the group seemed to be moving in at times.

Another problem surrounding the recording of the album, which would ironically be titled *Don't Leave Me This Way*, was the absence of Mike Chapman. "I remember seeing him two or three times when we were cutting," said Buzz. *Don't Leave Me This Way* was produced by Chapman's engineer, Peter Coleman. Chapman's marriage was continuing to fall apart, and it was affecting his work. This led to a lack of record company interest, and it didn't seem to the group that the album was promoted as aggressively as previous efforts. "Chapman was becoming more and more distracted with the success of Blondie and Nick Gilder, and Pat Benatar now coming up, and then he started working on The Knack, which means his focus at the record company was not entirely about us either," said Sonny.

Chapman had a lot of pull at the record company, but he was spreading himself too thin. Exile reached the big time through their connection with

Chapman, but they were sinking with him as well. "I don't think he was fit to be in the studio with anybody," remembers J.P. "He was going through divorce, and I don't think he was in top mental condition at the time." The record company was probably aware of Chapman's condition, a situation that did not bode well for Exile.

Exile would eventually turn themselves into a self-contained songwriting group during the country years, but they were largely viewed as a vehicle for Chapman's talents during their pop era. The record company was interested in Exile solely because they were produced by Mike Chapman, and the fact that they recorded songs written by the "Chinnichap" songwriting team. There were no Chinn-Chapman compositions on the *Don't Leave Me This Way* album. It was beginning to look as though the group might get dropped at the end of their four-album deal.

The circumstances surrounding the recording of *Don't Leave Me This Way* didn't keep the band from recording arguably their best album from the Warner-Curb years. J.P., Steve, Marlon, and Sonny remember the album fondly. "For me, the *Don't Leave Me This Way* album just song for song, pound for pound, is my favorite album out of the pop stuff," said Sonny.

Peter Coleman was a less demanding producer than Chapman, and he gave the group some freedom to run their own sessions and to pursue their creative ideas. Coleman was a drummer, and Steve enjoyed working with him. "Sometimes he would kind of build on what I was doing, and that was the first time that had occurred," remembers Steve. "And I was given a lot of freedom. He didn't dictate so much to me the parts he wanted as Mike Chapman had done."

Coleman had strong musical instincts, even if he didn't have the greatest feel for what would work well in the pop music market. "We knew that certainly as an engineer he was capable, and we also knew that he was musically capable, too, because you just get that sense when you're in the studio with somebody a lot," said J.P. Unlike *Mixed Emotions* and *All There Is*, the album was recorded entirely in Glendale, California. *Don't Leave Me This Way* didn't produce any hits for Exile, but it contained songs that worked to catapult Alabama to the top of the country charts. Alabama's versions of "Take Me Down" and "The Closer You Get" topped the country chart in 1982 and 1983, respectively, a phenomenon that would eventually encourage Exile to shift genres.

Don't Leave Me This Way opens with a Mark Gray/Greg Guidry composition entitled "You're Good for Me." Guidry was an established songwriter at the time. The newly layered sound of the band is evident from the start as multiple guitar tracks interweave with the sounds of acoustic piano, electric piano, and synthesizers. The synthesizers, viewed as a crucial, innovative part of the musical landscape in 1980, date the album. Mark's voice sounds nothing like Stokley's, and it is immediately clear that the band had a strong, assured lead vocalist in tow. "You're Good for Me" was released as a single, and it reached No. 105 on the pop chart.

The second song on the album was a Pennington/Lawley composition entitled "Nobody's Hero." "I don't even know what that song's about," said J.P. The lyrics concern the plight of an egotistical man who breaks hearts unflinchingly. ("You know he's going to spend his life being nobody's hero," etc.) J.P. wrote the music, and provided lead vocals. Lawley wrote the lyrics. "When she would write she would think pretty abstractly, and that wasn't something that we were too used to as writers," explains J.P.

"Don't Leave Me This Way" is a "power-ballad" composed by J.P., featuring a lead vocal from Mark. J.P. was writing on the piano more and more by this time, and "Don't Leave Me This Way" shows his growing maturity as a pop craftsman. The song ends climatically, with multi-tracked vocals, swirling synthesizer lines, and a powerful guitar riff. J.P. and Mark composed "Take Me Down." It's easy to see why the song appealed to Alabama. The laid-back, soulful groove and J.P.'s pleading lead vocal showed that Exile still had a way with romantic love songs. The otherworldly sounds of the synthesizers work well in the song, and the layered background vocals add to the urgency of the lyrics. It's unlikely that the band had any indication that the song could be a country hit. It peaked at No. 102 on the pop chart for Exile. Songs such as "Take Me Down" and "The Closer You Get" indicate that, for a brief moment in the band's history, Mark was developing the songwriting partnership with J.P. that Stokley could never establish.

Side one closes with "Smooth Sailin' (Rock in the Road)," a song that Mark would revisit on his second solo album, *This Ol' Piano*. Mark wrote this ballad with Johnny Slate and Steve Pippen, two diverse songwriters associated with the Nashville music scene. This ballad falls a bit flat, and it wasn't very successful when Mark later released it as a solo artist. His solo version peaked at No. 43 on the country chart. This would break Mark's string of three top ten country hits, and signal the decline of his career.

Side two opens with "Jailbait," a song that shows Mark's penchant for writing songs with unorthodox lyrical themes. It was co-written with songwriter Ed Setser. The hard rock vibe of the song sits somewhat uncomfortably on an album full of love songs, but it also provides a bit of variety. The lyrics, concerning a rock and roll musician's encounter with an underage fan, present the frustrating side of stardom in less than glamorous terms.

The J.P. penned "There's a Love" features Les on lead vocals. Les proves himself to be a capable vocalist even if the full potential of his voice would not be demonstrated until the next album. "The Closer You Get" features another soulful vocal from J.P. The country-esque influence is a bit more pronounced on this track than on the more pop-oriented "Take Me Down." The closing overlapping vocal arrangement shows how powerful the band was vocally by this point. "It Takes Love to Make Love" was composed by Mark, Sonny, Jeff Silbar, and Sam Lorber. Silbar is perhaps best known for co-writing "Wind Beneath My Wings," a song that was recorded by multiple artists including Bette Midler who took it to the top of the pop chart in 1989. Lorber would go on to write songs for several well-known artists including The Pointer Sisters and Wynonna Judd. "It Takes Love to Make Love" is a soft-rock, Doobie Brothers-style song driven by the group's three keyboard attack.

"Let's Do It Again," another J.P. composed song with a lead vocal provided by Les, closes the album. The feel-good vibe of the music masks the fact that the lyrics dwell on a lost love. Nevertheless, the optimistic outlook of the song works to close the album on a positive note. The band did indeed want to "do it all over again," but *Don't Leave Me This Way* would not save the band's career in the pop music industry.

Don't Leave Me This Way was Buzz's last album with Exile. "I became more and more estranged from the group," remembers Buzz. "It just seemed that things were coming to a bad end." Buzz could sense that the group was moving into a country music direction, and he had absolutely no interest in playing in that style. Mark, J.P., Marlon, and Steve had significant country music experience, and the various staff songwriters strewn across the *Don't Leave Me This Way* album seemed to point the group away from the pop/rock sounds they developed in the 1970s. The group owed Warner-Curb another album, but Buzz would not participate in the recording. Buzz:

> I got a call from Jim Morey one day, and I was in the shop. And he said, 'Buzz, how's the routining on the album going?' And I said 'Well, I've been in the studio several times, and I've yet to play a note on it.' He said, 'That's what I want to talk to you about. You all need to talk.' I knew they were in the studio that day. I was at the shop. I just drove to Lexington. Marlon did the engineering for us, for our demos and things. He said, 'Okay, let's talk.' Everybody else left. I said, 'Things are getting really bad.' And he said, 'Yeah, I know. Who knows where the group is going? You're not happy, Buzz.' I said, 'No I'm not. I don't know that I want to give up my gig, but at the same time, I'm scared.' He said, 'I look for us to have to start

all over again, Buzz.' I said, 'What do you mean?' He said, 'Well, we're getting ready to go in and do this album.' I said, 'Yes, and nobody's heart seems to be in this album.' He said, 'Well, this is probably the last rock album.' I said, 'We're going to go in and record this album with no faith?' He said, 'We owe another album, and we're going to do the album.'

Buzz left the group in January of 1981. He listened to the group's fourth Warner-Curb album, *Heart and Soul*, and wasn't impressed with the results. "When I listened to it I thought, 'That's not good,'" said Buzz. "I thought, 'They're gonna get dropped.'"

Leaving the band was a difficult experience for Buzz. He lost touch with Chapman, Chinn, Peter Coleman, and his former band mates, and continued to work at his parent's shop in Bybee. "I didn't miss a day of work," said Buzz. "I got some calls from people wanting me to do this, and wanting me to do that." After years of pursuing the Exile dream, Buzz found himself struggling with various social and financial pressures. Buzz:

> I was so caught up in being able to maintain my lifestyle in my home and everything else, that that was all that started mattering to me. I didn't want to leave Kentucky. I didn't want to leave the job that I had. I didn't want to leave the security. I was determined that, No. 1, I wasn't going to lose my house, nor was I going to miss a beat with all this. I should have sold the house immediately, and moved back either to California or over here to Richmond. I continued with that house until 1989. I left in 1981, January of 1981. It was stupid. It was crazy of me. I had my value system all twisted around. Somehow I thought there would be some kind of a judgment on me if people saw that I'd lost the house. I really cared more about what everybody else would think than I did about even me. That was just really stupid. It took me a few years to realize that.

Buzz's post-Exile career can hardly be considered a failure. After his departure from Exile he went back to EKU and completed his theater degree. After some reluctance, he returned to EKU and earned a Master's degree in English in 1994. His family business continued to thrive especially during the time John Y. Brown was governor of Kentucky. Brown's wife, Phyllis George Brown, was deeply interested in crafts. She founded the Kentucky Museum of Art and Craft in Louisville. "She did this big push of Kentucky Crafts, and I was able to help with that and push the shop," said Buzz.

At the time of this writing Buzz is living in Bybee. He is active in local theater, and has recently worked with students at Madison Central High School. In the summer of 2011, he was hired as an office manager for Eastern Kentucky University's Upward Bound department.

Buzz was just over thirty years old when he left the group. He had spent almost half of his life chasing a dream that few others aspire to. "I'd really gotten into the group much too early, much too soon," confirms Buzz. "I had never, ever developed as a human being really to know my own worth." Buzz also believes that the other members of the band were a bit more stable at the time. "They all seemed to all have their feet on the ground a lot more than I did," remembers Buzz. He found it easier to communicate with group members individually than he did at group meetings. "When I would talk to them as a group, it always seemed there was the group and me," explains Buzz. "When I would talk to them individually, it was always like 'we're in total agreement with this and that.'"

Buzz has an intense personality, and he is capable of telling a person exactly how he feels about something. He takes music very seriously, and he expects a level of professionalism that isn't always present in the pop music world. "At that period of time I was capable of being slightly holier than thou, and I realize that now," admits Buzz. Steve:

> Buzz is great, too. I didn't like him when I joined the band. I was a lot more sensitive then as an individual, and he was always hurting my feelings. He was always saying just snide, sarcastic remarks. In life, I hadn't learned how to deal with that very well at that point in time. I didn't like him much. But after a year or two, I started liking him very much. Now of all the guys from the old days that I rarely see anymore, he's by far my favorite.

Buzz has since reconciled with his old band mates. He attended the benefit for Jimmy Stokley in 1984 and the band's thirty-year reunion at the The Kentucky Horse Park. "I love 'em to death," says Buzz. "There hasn't been a time that I haven't gotten with them and just had a wonderful time." It's interesting to note that Buzz was the last remaining member from the Exile lineup that was first discovered by Peggy Rogers in 1966. None of the Exile members from the *Heart and Soul* sessions were playing on that fateful night at Speck's in Richmond.

Mike Chapman returned to the producer's chair for Exile's fourth and final pop album, *Heart and Soul* (1981). The six-piece lineup of J.P., Mark, Sonny, Les, Marlon, and Steve was still loaded with talent, and Les had high hopes for the album and the Chapman/Chinn penned title-track. He was still relatively new to the band, and he looked forward to working with Chapman for the first time.

Les remembers the *Don't Leave Me This Way* sessions as a positive experience and he believes that it was a good album, but he felt that working with Chapman would increase the group's chances of success. "After working with Peter Coleman…I mean he's a great guy and stuff like that and he's a great engineer, but he's really not a producer and there's a difference," said Les. "He's not a real strong song guy for one thing."

Les' sentiments seem to contradict Buzz's reservations about working on the album, and it's clear that the latest additions to the group were important in the push to continue. Les believed that the entire group was excited. "When we went in to do the *Heart and Soul* album everybody was excited because the guys that had been there, with the exception of Mark Gray and myself, the guys that had been there were obviously excited to work with Mike again," explains Les. "Mark and I were excited to work with Mike for the first time, so it was definitely a good time at that point."

J.P., on the other hand, admits that there was some trepidation. "We were a little bit worried about our standing with Warner-Curb by the time we made that album," admits J.P. The *All There Is* and *Don't Leave Me This Way* albums failed to chart, and no single had cracked the top forty since "You Thrill Me" reached the bottom rung of the Top 40. J.P. knew that a lot was riding on the *Heart and Soul* album.

The title track was the only Chapman/Chinn composition on the record, but the group hoped that it would be another "Kiss You All Over."

"We knew it was a hit song," said Marlon. "And course it was, just not for us."

The song would eventually reach the No. 8 position on the Billboard Hot 100 chart when Huey Lewis and the News released it in 1983, but it peaked at No. 102 for Exile, perhaps due to lack of record company support.

"We were getting airplay, but for some reason, I don't know, I don't think the label promoted that record good," said Les.

Chapman was known for recycling material. For instance, he wrote "Kitty" for Racey in 1979, but Tony Basil changed the name to "Mickey" before taking the song to the top of the charts in 1982. Exile's arrangement of "Heart and Soul" is similar to Huey Lewis' version.

"It sounds so much like our version it's pretty uncanny, really," said Les.

Les and Huey Lewis had voices with a somewhat similar timbre, and the heavy guitar riff and driving beat are evident in both versions. The Exile version is longer (6:11) than the 1983 version (4:13), with longer instrumental interludes. Exile just missed the advent of MTV in late 1981, and Huey Lewis and the News had the benefit of a stylish video to promote the song.

Marlon discussed the song with Lewis at an awards show. "Actually, he came up to us and he said, 'Frankly,' he says, 'Hell, we just copied the demo,'" said Marlon. "He'd be the first to admit it. Actually they're one of my favorite bands."

Exile continues to play "Heart and Soul" in their show, relaying the history of the song to those more familiar with their country period. "We tell that story now in our show, and it's one of the highlights of our live show now," says Marlon.

Heart and Soul opens with the title track. By this point Exile was deeply associated with the soft-rock movement, but "Heart and Soul" presents them as a slightly harder-rocking outfit. Les' somewhat detached vocals fit the robotic-rock sound of the music. The alternating mellow-ethereal verses and hard-rock, riff-based chorus make the song memorable. It is followed by "Take This Heart," a mellow R&B tune written by J.P. and sung by Les. Les sounds more like Michael McDonald here than usual, sometimes reaching into his falsetto. Les' lack of vibrato as an R&B vocalist is notable, and it helps to make his voice distinct.

"The bluegrass in me, I guess, or something," explains Les.

"Take This Heart" was covered by Kenny Rogers in 1982 on his *Love Will Turn You Around* album. "Till the Very End," a ballad composed by Mark and Sonny, was the second single released from the album. It failed to chart. After "Heart and Soul" tanked, the record company seems to have lost a good deal of optimism. "Till the Very End" was released as an afterthought, and probably suffered from a lack of attention from the record company.

Musically, "Till the Very End" is a well-crafted ballad. Lyrically, it's a fitting swan song for this era of the band. "Can't Love You Anymore" is another mid-tempo R&B/soft-rock tune. J.P. provides the lead vocal. "One More Night for Love" is another foray into country music. This time it's a ballad, and a vocal showcase for Les. Les' high notes near the end of the song provide an effective climax for the end of side one.

"You ought to hear the demo, though," exclaims Sonny.

Sonny composed the song with Mark and Dobie Gray, a singer-songwriter living in Nashville and known for writing hits such as "The 'In' Crowd" and "Drift Away." "One More Night for Love" is a precursor to the ballads that Sonny and J.P. would write during the band's country years in the same way that "Stay with Me" predicted the more up-tempo numbers from the mid-1980s. Country music was beginning to change in the early 1980s, and Exile would soon be at the center of that development.

"It didn't have to be so traditional sounding," said Les. "Alabama and The Oak Ridge Boys certainly opened those doors up, I think."

"One More Night for Love" is swarmed with country inflections, but it also wallows in a sea of reverb. "When the album was mixed, Chapman at that time…there were these reverb machines that he used on that project," explains Sonny. "The whole album is swimming in reverb, and from a technical point of view, I mean, I hated it."

Chapman was always looking for gimmicks, and they often came in the form of new sounds in the pre-MTV era. While the effect works better on songs such as "Till the Very End," it keeps "One More Night for Love" from sounding like the great country song that it is. "The demos we used to do in Lexington of all our stuff is much dryer and in your face, which is kind of what music is today," said Sonny.

Side two of *Heart and Soul* is more eclectic, making it the band's most diverse album. This was due in part to the increased number of writers and songwriting partnerships.

"At that point in time with the writing, I was writing with Mark, Mark was writing with J.P., J.P. writing with other people—the writing was a bit scattered," said Sonny.

Mark's "Baby It's Me" is as close as Exile ever came to arena/progressive rock territory with its heavy guitar line, pulsing synthesizers, modulations, powerful vocals, and sing along chorus. Sonny and Mark were among the co-writers on "Werewolf of Love," which is one of the oddest songs in the band's discography.

"I remember we played the song live some, and it always kind of got a good reaction, but it was just something totally different," said Marlon.

Mark provides the lead vocal. The song includes lyrics that represent an unusual take on sexual prowess, werewolf howls, and an unorthodox guitar solo from J.P. Musicians will note that he makes use of the whole-tone scale in the solo, a series of musical pitches associated with classical composers such as Claude Debussy. J.P. came up with the whole-tone guitar line, but he soon tired of having to play it live.

"Because of the speed of it, it was really hard," explains J.P.

Despite the fact that Exile always had their eye on the commercial market place, they weren't afraid of musical boundaries.

"We'd always try something," said Marlon. "It may not have worked, but we'd try it."

J.P. sang on the next two cuts. Sonny was a co-writer on "Dixie Girl," a funky tune that wouldn't sound out of place on an album by The Doobie

Brothers or Little Feat. The song has an earthy feel that helps to balance the band's lush, romantic sentiments. "Someone Like You" is a shuffling soft-rock composition composed by J.P. and Mark. It doesn't stand up to their collaborations on *Don't Leave Me This Way*, but it's a pleasant enough slice of optimistic pop-rock. "What Kind of Love Is This" benefits from Mark's powerful vocals, and a hard rocking musical arrangement. J.P.'s "Still So in Love with You" closes the album. The 12/8 doo-wop feel of the song works to enhance the uplifting lyrics.

Heart and Soul would prove to be Exile's last album with Mike Chapman. Chapman's reputation had taken a hit by this point due to his controversial interview and a feud with The Knack. Chapman experienced the height of his success in the late 1970s when he was producing hit albums for Blondie and The Knack. At that time he started referring to himself as "The Commander." He included the following on the back of the *Don't Leave Me This Way* album:

> Exile-
>> There is so much, yet so little to say. My friends, my brothers. This is the group that made me what I am today. Deep in my heart there is a very special place for Exile. You could say they promoted me from private to commander.
>> From my friends and from me,
>> we love you,
>>> The Commander

Ironically, this message from The Commander appeared on an album that he did not produce. J.P. recalls that the group used to "call him that as a term of endearment, and then he started taking it all pretty seriously." Chapman's liner notes on *Don't Leave Me This Way* are humble compared to his writings on The Knack's . . . *But the Little Girls Understand*, released the same year. Chapman:

> Making a Knack album is like dying and going to heaven. It's like making a cake. It's like making a mistake. It's like making out. We spent just a few days doing it and we **really** did it this time.
>
> We had one disaster though—Houston kicked Pittsburgh's ass and Prescott stole my money—Doug laughed—Bruce collapsed and Berton went home. But I was in total command the whole time.
>
> As you listen to this album you will discover the many different sides of The Knack. Side 1 and Side 2. The songs are an assortment of feelings

and emotions expressed redundantly as only The Knack can. From the basic street language of '**Baby Talks Dirty**' to the intellectual mystery of '**Rave Up**,' we find ourselves wandering through a wilderness of pleasure, pain, passion and lust.

This record is very dear to me and my bank manager. Please buy another copy for a friend...it's a bargain at half the price.

The Knack has become a way of life to me. They are special people and, I believe, the future of rock 'n' roll.

The Commander

The liner notes were probably meant as good natured ramblings, but they came across as conceited at the time. The Knack fell out with Chapman soon after, and their third album, *Round Trip* (1981), was produced by Jack Douglas. When the album peaked at the No. 93 position on The Billboard 200, the band was dropped from their label. Chapman's career began to take a major downturn soon after.

"He was a big part of rock music in those days, and he came off not looking too good—came off looking pretty arrogant," said J.P. "To me he never was."

Reports on Chapman differ, and it's clear that he had an explosive personality. "We all loved him, and still do, but he was just...boy...he was a pill," said Steve.

Chapman wanted to produce hit records, and as a result, he was constantly concerned about trends and the marketplace. "I mean, we were under pressure to deliver to the label something that fit the market, so on every album there had to be something that was disco-ey," continues Steve. "Most musicians really hated disco."

Despite his burning desire to succeed in the pop marketplace, Chapman also seems to have a patient, understanding side. "I always found Mike to be just a very warm, caring person, real level-headed," said J.P. Still, J.P. hasn't stayed in touch with the demanding producer. J.P.:

I haven't talked to him in years. It's just one of those things. He eventually moved out to Connecticut from L.A. He's been in Connecticut now for a lot of years. After he moved out there, he married and had some children. And so did I, and it's just one of those things where you just sort of...Outta sight, outta mind. I miss Mike.

Chapter Six

GIVE ME ONE MORE CHANCE

E XILE WAS DROPPED FROM the label after *Heart and Soul* failed to reach the charts, marking the end of their soft-rock, pop-disco phase. While there are several underrated gems among the Warner-Curb albums, the 1977-1981 era is the period in which the members of Exile were most inclined to compromise their artistic integrity. It had happened before on their singles for Date Records in the 1960s, but this time it was done on a much larger scale.

They achieved mainstream pop success with "Kiss You All Over," but it was fleeting and not particularly satisfying from an artistic viewpoint.

"When we went out and they started marketing us, it was almost like we had to become what the marketing was," said Steve. "Being naïve we did that, or we tried to, and I found that to be exceedingly uncomfortable."

The label tried marketing the band as a group in a number of ways including a semi-homoerotic album cover for the *Heart and Soul* album featuring the band hunched together, an image that the guys in Exile could never pull off. Their Chapman-produced albums were also heavily produced affairs, often featuring large doses of overdubs and studio effects.

"He'd put eight tracks of background vocals," said Steve.

Exile never gained much respect from rock critics, and they were largely viewed as a one-hit wonder pop band. For instance, they didn't place on VH1's 100 Greatest Artists of All Time, and they weren't included in the third edition of *The All Music Guide to Rock*. Exile was a legendary band in the Central Kentucky area, but to the world at large they were a soft-rock band known for "Kiss You All Over."

"I remember a review we got in *The L.A. Times*," said J.P. "We opened a show for Seals and Crofts at The Greek Theater. He went on and on and on about how great Seals and Crofts was, and the last paragraph of the review said, 'I only wish that I hadn't rushed through traffic to see Exile.'"

The band was aware that they were being used in a trendy, overtly commercial fashion, but there were always attempts to salvage their artistic integrity. And unlike many of the pop acts, the members of Exile were always first rate musicians. In the age of Auto-Tune and overly produced product, some of the music from the Mike Chapman period holds up better today than might be expected.

"I never expected people to think we were great, but I thought we were better than that," said J.P. in regards to the negative review.

Exile, a small town band, was always somewhat at the mercy of the record companies, even more so than the average act. The Knack was able to draw a good deal of record label attention before they were signed; Exile was lucky to get on a label. It looked as though Exile was coming to an end when they were dropped in 1981, but it turned out to be the best thing that could happen to the band from an artistic standpoint. It would also pay off commercially.

Exile would soon move into an era of complete artistic control, but they would have to change genres, lose another member, and go through a brief period of inactivity in the meantime.

"I joined a band playing in a bar in Winchester for about eight or nine weeks, something like that, playing four nights a week just to have something to do," said J.P.

Larry Cordle, a future co-writer for Exile and others, was among the members in the band. Cordle has also recorded with the band Lonesome Standard Time.

Jim Morey was still acting as the band's manager, and it was he who suggested that Exile move into the field of country music. Morey had a strong working relationship with Buddy Killen, the owner of a large publishing company in Nashville called Tree International. Killen worked with pop and country artists throughout his career, and Morey felt that he would be an effective producer for Exile. Alabama and Kenny Rogers were recording Exile songs, Dave & Sugar reached No. 6 on the country charts with "Stay with Me," and Janie Fricke scored a No. 1 country hit in 1982 with "It Ain't Easy Bein' Easy," a song composed by Les, Mark, and Shawna Harrington-Burkhart. Morey believed that Exile should go ahead and market their songs toward country radio.

Morey called a band meeting in 1982 in order to explain his reasons for moving the group in a new direction. "I literally looked at him with disbelief, and I thought he had lost his mind," said Sonny.

With the exception of J.P., the members of Exile were not deeply interested in country music. They were influenced by R&B and rock, and that didn't change when they became a country band.

"I was not a huge country fan," remembers Marlon.

Country music was changing by this time, but it was still much more traditional than it would become in the 1990s. In addition, Marlon was not a fan of the urban cowboy movement that was popular in the early 1980s.

"I just thought it was kind of crap," says Marlon.

The other members of Exile also had reservations about moving in a country music direction. "Motown, Stax, that kind of stuff is really where my heart was," said Steve.

Even J.P., the member most responsible for the band's stylistic shift, was more inclined to play pop, rock, and rhythm and blues.

"The Beatles and The Young Rascals and a lot of the R&B singers of the day seemed to suit my palette," explained J.P.

There are several reasons why Exile was able to make a smooth transition to country. Members of the group had experience playing behind country artists at Lemco, J.P.'s country roots ran fairly deep, country music was changing, rock bands in Kentucky were often required to play country music, and Les and J.P. had voices that *sounded* southern. Songs such as "Stay with Me," "One More Night for Love," "Take Me Down," and "The Closer You Get" suggested that the group could easily make a transition to country.

Country music was incorporating sounds from pop music during the early 1980s, and it turned out that Exile's soft-rock approach had crossover appeal. Exile would switch genres, but they would do so on their own terms as they became pioneers in the modernization of country music. They also played the instruments on their records, an uncommon liberty in Nashville at the time.

"At that point in Nashville that wasn't happening," said Sonny.

Exile was a tight unit by this time. Their background as a pop-rock band and as session musicians prepared them to play on hit songs. "We were a very organic, self-contained band," said Sonny. "We wrote them, we recorded them ourselves, we sang them, played them."

The first step in Exile's move toward country was to rehearse new material including covers. The group moved into the basement of a house owned by Steve, and they rehearsed for six weeks. They worked on material from their pop-rock albums and various medleys. They worked up a 15-minute Beatles medley, a 15-minute Motown medley, an Everly Brothers medley, and they added country songs by artists such as George Jones and Merle Haggard. "We went from doing ninety minutes to four hours," explains Les.

The Motown medley would prove especially important in the band's quest for a record deal. "The Motown medley that we did as an encore was what really persuaded them to sign us to Epic," said Steve.

The medley included five songs: "I Can't Help Myself (Sugar Pie Honey Bunch)," "Ain't Too Proud to Beg," "My Girl," "Signed, Sealed, Delivered I'm Yours," and "Stop! In the Name of Love." Lexington crowds enjoyed the medley, and the group continued to perform it after they were signed. Opinions differ on whether or not the band was playing music from their first country album by this point.

"I don't think we ever did play any of those songs out before they were recorded," said Les. "Not that I can remember, anyway."

J.P. remembers playing the material. Whatever the case, the band was playing country music in addition to rock and soul.

After six weeks of intense rehearsals, Exile secured a weekly gig at a club called The Rebel Room located in Southland Bowling Lanes on Southland Drive in Lexington, just down the street from where Lemco was located on Longview Drive.

"Our reason for going into The Rebel Room was to hone our country thing," said J.P.

They were also getting tighter, with J.P. and Marlon providing solos while Les played rock solid rhythm guitar parts. J.P., Sonny, and Les developed a three-part harmony sound that would be a signature of the group. "It was just an osmosis there with our blend," said J.P.

The band played five nights a week at first, but eventually it was dropped to four. Exile played to enthusiastic audiences at first.

"As far as Lexington was concerned, we were still a really big band, pop band, and artistically it was really good," said Steve. "It was really cool playing to a small audience again like that, and people that we knew."

During that period Exile played exclusively at The Rebel Room. They didn't look to play elsewhere. Exile was compensated like a club band, a far cry from the money they made while they were on a major label. "We played three sets a night, and I think we were maybe paid a couple hundred bucks a week," said Marlon.

Exile was invited to play a brief tour of South Africa soon after they started playing in Lexington. "Kiss You All Over" had been successful in South Africa, and songs such as "You Thrill Me," and "How Could This Go Wrong" fared much better there than in the United States. Exile had played a two-week run at a theater in downtown Johannesburg while they were a pop band, often to enthusiastic crowds. Exile's return visit to South Africa in 1982 was even more successful, as thousands of fans gathered to meet them at the airport. The band was exhausted and a bit worn out after consuming all of the wine on the plane when they noticed the crowd.

"And our eyes were almost virtually hangin' out of our heads," remembers J.P. "That just hit us like a ton of bricks."

At first the group didn't realize that the crowd was for them. "It was something like you'd see in a movie," remembers Marlon. "We really didn't know what was going on, and of course we're all coming off all hung over and dirty."

Mark Gray traveled with Exile to South Africa in 1982, but he left when they returned. "When we got back, he quit," said Steve. "We figured out that he had planned to quit, but he hung in long enough to get that tour."

Another factor in Mark's departure was his decision to live in Nashville. Exile was committed to playing in Lexington, and they didn't feel the need to move.

"When we started making the transition from pop to country we were doing that in Lexington, and he was living in Nashville and he felt excluded," said Steve.

Mark was also interested in a solo career. The success of "Take Me Down," "The Closer You Get," and "It Ain't Easy Bein' Easy" demonstrated that he was becoming a first rate songwriter in country music circles. The connections made during the recording of "It Ain't Easy Bein' Easy" proved especially important in Mark's quest for a solo deal. Mark signed to Columbia records after he left Exile, where he began working with Bob Montgomery, Janie Fricke's producer. His solo career as a solo country artist/balladeer was short lived, sizzling out by 1988. He recorded three full-length albums for Columbia. His highest charting country single (No. 6) was a duet version of Dan Hill's "Sometimes When We Touch" with Tammy Wynette. Mark also reached the country music top ten with "If All the Magic Is Gone," "Diamond in the Dust," and "Please Be Love." New versions of "Smooth Sailing (Rock in the Road)" and "Dixie Girl" were included on his 1984 album, *This Ol' Piano*.

With Mark's departure, Exile settled into its most stable lineup. The five-piece group consisting of J.P., Marlon, Steve, Sonny, and Les was the smallest lineup in Exile's history up to that point. Exile was now down to a single keyboard player, and the leader of the band was clearly J.P. Pennington. He was the only original member of the band and, with Mark's departure, was the most established songwriter. Marlon and Steve lacked the desire or the ability to write songs, and Sonny had not yet fully blossomed into a first-rate composer of hit songs.

"I really wasn't that good a songwriter," said Marlon.

Les experienced success as a co-writer on "It Ain't Easy Bein' Easy," but he had difficulty getting his songs on Exile albums in the 1980s. J.P. was the primary writer, lead guitarist, and one of two lead vocalists for the group. He would be a major force in Exile's successful country run from 1983–88.

The fan reaction in South Africa differed greatly from what Exile experienced when they returned to The Rebel Room. It was an interesting study in how popular culture can differ geographically. The experience in South Africa had been good for morale, and much needed. "Then it's funny cause you'd come back to The Rebel Room, and you're playing for fifty people," said Marlon.

181

The crowds were enthusiastic at the band's early gigs at The Rebel Room, but attendance eventually dropped off. It's hard for any band to draw consistent crowds three or four nights a week, and Exile was becoming just another local band.

"What we thought would be about a six week process turned into two years, so it became a grind," said Steve. Exile began to tire of the Rebel Room. They eventually moved to Breeding's, another Lexington club.

It was during this period that Jim Morey introduced Exile to Buddy Killen. "Buddy was like 'Mr. Nashville' as far as the music business went," said J.P.

In addition to owning a large publishing company, Killen was producing acts and he owned a club in Nashville called The Stockyard. Jim Morey and Ray Katz, another well-known manager, approached Killen concerning Exile.[2] "I told them that the Exile record 'Kiss You All Over' was one of my all-time favorites," said Killen.[3]

The Stockyard was divided into a restaurant and bar. The bar was called The Bullpen. It was in the lower level of the building. Through Killen and Morey, Exile was invited to play a series of showcases at The Bullpen.

"They invited all the right people to see us, and we were passed on by virtually all of them," said J.P. Only Rick Blackburn, from Columbia and Epic, saw something in the band. Exile was signed to Epic, and they began work on their first country album.

Exile's first album on Epic was another self-titled effort. The decision to call the album *Exile* may have been to mark a new era in the band's history, far removed from the group's 1973 album of the same name. J.P. is listed as a co-writer on nine of the album's ten songs, but Sonny was also becoming an important songwriting contributor by this point. Sonny co-wrote half of the songs on the album, including one of the singles, "I Don't Want to Be a Memory." Mark Gray's influence as a writer was still felt as he contributed to "Red Dancing Shoes" and "High Cost of Leaving." "I Just Came Back to Break My Heart Again" was written by J.P. with Larry Cordle. Les and J.P. handled the lead vocals on the album. Les sang lead on six of the songs, but J.P. provided lead vocals on two of the three tunes released as singles.

There was an effort to make *Exile* appealing to country music audiences, but the band continued to function as a tight R&B unit. "We were concerned that our lyrics would be concise and understandable, and just what country music lyrics were," said J.P. "And we put an acoustic guitar on everything."

They didn't add a pedal steel guitar, and with the exception of a solo from well-known country/bluegrass artist Ricky Skaggs on "Take Me to the River," Exile records didn't utilize the fiddle. Almost all of the instruments on Exile records were played by members of the band. "As far as I know, we were the first country band of any consequence that played all of their own records," said J.P.

Exile also underwent an image makeover during this period in order to become more acceptable to country music audiences. The makeover was welcomed by the band, as they had suffered through some awkward promotional ideas during their pop years.

"As I recall, the best part of it was the way that we were marketed," said Steve. The record company realized that the members of Exile were down to earth guys from Kentucky, and there were no efforts to promote them as eclectic free spirits. "So when we went country what they did was they got very close to us, and they figured out what we were and what we were made of and then they designed the marketing around that," said Steve. "So that was very comfortable."

Buddy Killen's approach to producing Exile was different from Mike Chapman's. "He would just kind of sit back and listen," said Marlon. Exile was an experienced studio band by this point, and they didn't need a lot of guidance. Marlon was a skilled engineer, and the musicians knew what to play.

"A lot of times we might work on some tracks for maybe most of the day, and Buddy would come in at the end of the day…and they were always good suggestions," said Marlon. Steve remembers Killen as more of a referee than a producer. "He would just kind of sit there and listen, or take care of business on the phone," said Steve. "But when we would want to re-record something, because one of us hadn't done the best job we thought we could do he would say, 'Wait a minute guys. Listen to the feel. Just listen to the FEEL of what you've recorded.'"

The production methods in Nashville were earthier than in the pop world, and the sound of the albums reflected how the band sounded on stage. Killen wasn't interested in layering vocals or finding new synthesized sounds. He understood that the power of the group's playing and the strength of their three-part harmony singing would drive the music. Killen understood the radio, and he knew a hit song when he heard it.

Exile's first country album opens with "Take Me to the River," a high energy tune that the group uses to open shows. J.P. composed the music and the lyrics. It was never released as a single. The driving arrangement and J.P.'s strong vocals and guitar solo work to erase any doubt about the band's ability to play country flavored music.

"It's natural for me to go back and play country music," said J.P. "I just kind of understand it."

Ricky Skaggs' fiddle solo helps to add a country vibe to the tune, and J.P.'s fishing lyrics fit the music well. J.P. was aware of the Al Green-composed "Take Me to the River" that was popularized by Syl Johnson and The Talking Heads. "I was smart enough to know that I needed to stay away from anything that sounded like that song, and I also knew that you can't copyright a title," said J.P.

"Woke Up in Love" is one of Exile's best known tunes. A strong southern gospel/black gospel influence is evident despite the fact that J.P., the lone writer of the song, did not grow up playing in church. He developed an affinity for the style by listening to the records that his mother used to play around the house. "She liked black gospel music," said J.P. "She liked Mahalia Jackson a lot."

J.P. had tried to write the song on several occasions. He had the title in mind before he wrote the words. "I just remember one day being down in my basement, and this sort of gospel groove just came to me," said J.P.

The chord progression is a common one in gospel music, but Exile was able to take the energy of the church setting and place it in an infectious secular context. It's hard to listen to "Woke Up in Love" without singing along, and the group played the tune with more energy in live settings, sometimes closing with a sped-up chorus. J.P. and Marlon, the primary instrumental soloists in the band, trade tasteful leads in the middle of the song, both demonstrating their country-esque chops.

"Red Dancing Shoes" was composed by Sonny in collaboration with the departed Mark Gray. It wasn't released as a single, perhaps because its strong R&B feel was more in line with the group's previous albums. Les provided the lead vocals on "Red Dancing Shoes," and the five songs that follow it.

"'Red Dancing Shoes,' we get a lot of requests for that song, and so hopefully we're going to put that back in the show at some point," said Les.

"We've Still Got Love" is a ballad composed by J.P. and Sonny. All of Exile's country albums include slow ballads with strings, but the group didn't have a hit in this style until they released "She's Too Good to be True" a few years later. "I Just Came Back to Break My Heart Again" opens with a tejano music inspired guitar line before settling into a mellow country groove. The addition of strings and electric piano give the song a pleasant, breezy quality.

The second half of *Exile* maintains the high standard of the first five songs. "This Could Be the Start of Something Good," another Pennington/Lemaire tune, continues the mellow vibe established on "I Just Came Back to Break My Heart Again," but with less of an overt country influence. The influence of Chet Atkins' finger picking is readily apparent during the introduction of J.P.'s "After All These Years (I'm Still Chasing You)." "High Cost of Leaving," a Pennington/Lemaire/Gray composition, was this version of the group's most determined stab at traditional country music. The music is in ¾, a common time signature in country music, and the influence of George Jones is apparent. A lush string arrangement accompanies the rhythm section driven by Les' acoustic guitar. Sonny, Mark, and J.P. wrote the song, possibly with the intent of giving it to another artist.

"They actually, I think, wrote that song for George Jones, and then after we got this country deal, then we decided to do it ourselves," said Les.

The last two songs feature J.P. on lead vocals. "I Don't Want to Be a Memory" was a successful country single. It marked the beginning of the Pennington/Lemaire songwriting dominance within the band. Despite the commercial success of the song, Exile doesn't always play it at their live shows. "It's just one of those that doesn't compute over to live very well," said J.P.

Musically, "I Don't Want to Be a Memory" has a doo-wop, 1950s rock and roll feel. J.P.'s "Here I Go Again," a mysterious, galloping minor-key tune, closes the album.

"High Cost of Leaving" was the first single released from the album, and it stalled at No. 27 on the country chart. J.P. was proud of the song, but he didn't feel like it was representative of the band. "The label, I guess their thinking was, and maybe our thinking, too, was our first release needs to let radio know that we can play country music," said J.P.

Les retains a positive view of the song. "If it would have been a second or third single it would have probably been a No. 1 record, really," said Les.

The second single, "Woke Up in Love," was Exile's breakthrough country single. It reached the No. 1 spot on Billboard's country chart early in 1984. Like the rest of the band's No. 1 country hits, it would hold the top spot for a single week. "We were all just thrilled to death," said J.P. "We had quite a few years there of doubt about whether or not the band could survive. It was nice to be back with a record company that believed in us, too."

Having missed out on the "Kiss You All Over" experience, Les was particularly excited to be playing on No. 1 records. "It's kind of hard to describe – the ultimate feeling of finally, and all the hard work has paid off, and the dues paying and all that stuff, and the believing that we could make this happen again," remembers Les.

"I Don't Want to Be a Memory," the third and last single pulled from the album, also reached the No. 1 spot on Billboard's country chart. "As I recall, I was more excited about "I Don't Want to Be a Memory" than I was "Woke Up in Love," because I felt like it really validated us," said J.P. "We weren't a one hit thing."

By this point the members of Exile were more experienced and were better able to enjoy their success. They also had a more advanced understanding of the business. "For my money, anyway, it was a much more pleasant run of success than the pop had been," said Steve. *Exile* peaked at No. 10 on Billboard's country album chart, signifying a trend in their career. Their country singles sold better than their albums.

J.P. and Sonny began to develop a strong songwriting partnership while the band was working on *Exile*. With the exception of "Comin' Apart At the Seams," a song composed by Les with Jerry Paul Marcum, the next two Exile albums would consist entirely of Pennington/Lemaire collaborations.

"I think we just really jelled as friends, and we found that we really had a lot of the same sensibilities music-wise, too," said J.P.

They wrote on guitar and keyboards, and they worked hard and often. Ballads such as "She's Too Good to Be True," were composed on the piano. "Usually one of the two of us would have a title," said J.P. "If not, a title encompassed in the chorus or part of a chorus, and we'd just take it from there."

Due to a busy touring schedule and the success of their first album, the band was more pressed for time when trying to write for subsequent albums. J.P. and Sonny took on the songwriting responsibilities, and it was constant. "He and I would both catalogue song titles, ideas, and we'd schedule time off the road," remembers Sonny. "So we were touring, and we'd come off the road, we'd write, we'd go back on the road, tour, come off it, tour." Despite the pressure, the grueling schedule was worth the effort during these exciting times for the band. Still, the pressure would eventually take a toll. They had two years to put their first country album together, but subsequent albums would have to be completed at a much faster pace. "It was a little harder to cobble the second one together with only, like, nine months time," remembers J.P.

Exile's second album, *Kentucky Hearts*, was released in 1984. It was the only Exile album to top Billboard's country album chart. J.P. provides lead vocals on the first three songs. The album opens with "She's a Miracle," a song that J.P. has cited as one of his favorite Exile tunes. "She's a Miracle" comes across as a male-female relationship song on the surface, but J.P. and Sonny wrote the song about their daughters.

"When we wrote it, Sonny's daughter was just a little girl, and Suzie and I were expecting," remembers J.P.

The group's trademark three-part vocal harmonies are on display during the sing-along chorus. Marlon provides boogie-woogie piano lines throughout this R&B inflected country song. The second song, "I've Never Seen Anything," retains some of the southern gospel feel from the previous album, but with somewhat more advanced piano and guitar solos and western swing/boogie-woogie sensibilities.

"You Make It Easy" is another song concerning a low stress relationship. Musically, the song is an R&B tune with country touches courtesy of J.P.'s guitar licks and the group's southern-sounding vocal harmonies.

"Comin' Apart At the Seams," a ballad that Les composed with his high school friend Jerry Marcum, almost didn't make the album. "I took that song in to the guys and to our producer Buddy Killen, and it almost didn't get recorded because the guys kept saying—Sonny and J.P. mostly—were saying that it really doesn't sound like an Exile song," said Les. "And I thought 'Well, you know, probably "Minute by Minute" didn't sound like a Doobie Brothers song either, but Michael McDonald made it one.'"

Buddy Killen convinced the band to include the song on the album, but it was never released as a single. Les knew Marcum from his days playing in the London/Corbin area. "When we were all growing up down there, he had a group, too, called Jerry and the Decades," said Les.

Members of Exile have always been good about remembering where they came from, as the involvement of songwriters such as Jerry Marcum and Larry Cordle suggests. Marcum's contributions were primarily lyrical. He came up with the main idea of the song. Les provided the musical arrangement, helped out with the lyrics, and was the lead vocalist. Les always had a desire to write songs, but "Comin' Apart At the Seams" marks a turning point in his desire to push for his material to be included. This would remain a frustration for Les throughout the rest of his career with Exile. "He was never really proactive about the writing until he wrote 'Comin' Apart At the Seams'" said J.P.

"Just In Case" is another southern gospel flavored tune that emphasizes Les' abilities as a vocalist. The Forester Sisters recorded a version of the song in 1985, and it became a No. 1 country hit. "They were looking for songs when that album was out, and I think maybe my publisher must have pitched it to them," said J.P.

"Give Me One More Chance" jump starts the second half of the album by blending the southern gospel feel of "Woke Up in Love" with the group's harder rocking tendencies. It features one of the band's catchiest chorus sections, and the verses are just as infectious, if not more. It features one of J.P.'s most enthusiastic lead vocal performances.

"That was fun to play—always get a positive reaction outta that song," said J.P.

As in "Woke Up in Love," the instrumental section near the middle of "Give Me One More Chance" includes solos from J.P. and Marlon. Marlon's boogie-woogie, country style of playing is perhaps best represented on the *Kentucky Hearts* album. It seems as though he had embraced the style.

"Somethin' You Got" showcases Les' abilities as an R&B vocalist. The chorus is particularly memorable, and the song could have possibly been a hit despite the absence of a country music influence. Les provides the lead vocal on "If I Didn't Love You," a slow ballad similar in style to "Comin' Apart At the Seams" and "We've Still Got Love." "Ain't That a Pity" is a boogie-woogie style tune, clearly inspired by Fats Domino's similarly titled "Ain't That a Shame." Marlon provides an inspired 1950s style piano solo, and Les sings the lead vocal. It's not one of their more memorable songs. "Crazy for Your Love," one of the band's better known mid-tempo ballads, closes the album. The influence of The Eagles' "Best of My Love" is evident.

"When Sonny and I wrote it I don't recall if we ever actually talked about or said 'Hey, let's write an Eagles sounding song,'" said J.P. "It just sort of came out that way." J.P. provides the lead vocal track, and Sonny and Les add subtle harmonies.

In addition to reaching the top of Billboard's country album chart, *Kentucky Hearts* produced three No. 1 country singles. "Give Me One More Chance," "Crazy for Your Love," and "She's a Miracle" topped the charts, and the band was riding high in the midst of their most successful period. A video was produced for "She's a Miracle," and it was part of CMT's early rotation. The video shows footage of the band dancing around a horse park and trying to woo beautiful women.

This was also a time of stability for the band. Exile released four pop albums with essentially four different lineups, but their first two country albums and the subsequent *Hang on to Your Heart* featured the same five-piece lineup and producer. Exile was finally beginning to stabilize into a successful country hit making machine. But as with many situations that seem too good to be true, Exile would only be able to ride this wave of success for a short time before internal and external forces began to gnaw away at the band.

News of Jimmy Stokley's failing health began to spread in 1984, and it became apparent that the singer was deathly ill from problems with hepatitis. He was admitted to Pattie A. Clay Hospital in Richmond, and several of his old band mates showed up to visit.

"I went to see him the first time he was in the hospital there," said Mike Howard. "He didn't want anybody to know."

Mack Davenport also recalls dropping in to visit Stokley. Billy Luxon, by this point a successful businessman in Richmond, helped to arrange a benefit to help Stokley pay medical bills. Exile was invited to play the benefit.

"We had a committee that actually had planned that for about three months I guess, and Ralph Hacker was probably the chairman if we had a chairman," said Billy. "But we did it through WVLK, and several of us tried to work on all the angles so that we could ensure that everything went the way we planned it."

The involvement of Hacker, one of the radio announcers for University of Kentucky basketball at the time, and the attendance of Governor Martha Layne Collins worked to show the high level of respect for Stokley in the Central Kentucky area. "It was a pretty full house," remembers Billy.

The benefit was held on October 29, 1984. Former Exile members such as Mike Howard, Mack Davenport, and Buzz Cornelison were in attendance. They were invited on stage. The intention was for Stokley to sit in with the band, but he was much too ill.

"The original plan was he was going to sing, but that really wasn't in the mix at the time we finally got it going," said Billy. Stokley insisted on walking across the stage by himself. "We kind of had to push him on stage—wheelchair deal," said Billy.

The benefit was a success, and Stokley was able to pay off his debt. "He had $18,000 worth of medical bills piled up, I think, that he couldn't pay," said Steve. The band raised just enough to cover the bills. "We came out of there with $18,000, almost to the penny what he needed to pay off his debt," said Steve.

Stokley continued to suffer from hepatitis, and passed away on August 13, 1985 at the age of 41. The tragic news had to have an impact on the members of Exile. The hard reality is that Exile never would have hit the big time without Stokley, but they wouldn't have been able to continue with him. One could easily argue that Mike Chapman could have found a better way to handle the situation during the band's pop years, but Stokley, a rocker at heart, didn't have the voice or the songwriting skills needed to move the band into country music. It's hard to argue with the success that J.P. and Sonny had as songwriters in the 1980s, and they never would have been able to assume those responsibilities as freely if Stokley were still a member of the band.

Nevertheless, Stokley's situation was tragic, and some who remember Exile as a rock and roll band from Richmond will never accept the country years. For some, Jimmy Stokley was Exile. He WAS the driving force of the band for many years. By continuing on, the band was following Stokley's example. He didn't believe in giving up, and he always put the band first.

Ronnie Hall, Paul Smith Jr., Mike Howard, Mack Davenport, Bill Kennon, Kenny Weir, Bernie Faulkner, Billy Luxon, Bobby Johns, and Danny Williams never got to experience the success of "Kiss You All Over," and Stokley, the clear leader of the band before the Mike Chapman years, was willing to make the personnel changes when he needed to. The music business is fierce and often ugly, and always about survival. Musicians often live in poverty while they try to get a record deal, but Stokley was willing to do whatever it took within the realms of sanity to make it. Exile was his life.

The one thing that could slow him down, his health, eventually affected his voice and his ability to perform. In order for the band to survive and keep their gig with Mike Chapman, they had to let him go. It was a decision that still haunts the band to this day, but in retrospect it was probably the best decision they could have made in terms of survival despite the harsh realities of the situation.

Exile was at the absolute zenith of their country success when Stokley passed away. *Hang On to Your Heart* (1985) was another hit album for the band. "*Hang On to Your Heart*, I guess, is my favorite of the country albums," said Steve.

The first two singles released from the album, "Hang on to Your Heart" and "I Could Get Used to You," gave the band their sixth and seventh consecutive No. 1 hits on the country chart, and rank among their best and most recognizable songs. "Super Love," the third single released from the album, would break the streak peaking at No. 14, but it has become one of their most popular songs. The album also included the first two No. 1 hits featuring Les on lead vocals, "It'll Be Me" and "She's Too Good to be True." "We wrote those songs specifically for him," said J.P.

Nevertheless, J.P., the singer most associated with Exile by this point, sang lead on all of the other songs on the album. There wasn't a need for the band to make many changes by this point. It seemed as though they could do no wrong in the country music world. "We were rolling pretty hot by that time," remembers J.P. *Hang On to Your Heart* was the most diverse album from the band's country years, showcasing the influence of several styles including R&B, funk, rock, and, somewhat surprisingly, rap. It's an uneven album, but the highlights, which are many, represent some of the best music of the band's career. All of the songs were composed by the Pennington/Lemaire songwriting team.

Hang On to Your Heart opens with "Promises, Promises," a less memorable version of the gospel inflected music that the band developed with "Woke Up in Love" and "Give Me One More Chance." The tight arrangement and the solos, once again provided by Marlon and J.P., demonstrate that Exile was continuing to grow as a country ensemble.

"I Could Get Used to You," essentially an R&B tune with an almost Caribbean feel, is one of Exile's best and most popular songs. The chorus is highly memorable, and audiences enjoy the feel-good vibe of the tune. The rhythmic nature makes it ideal for dancing. Les' high harmonies work to enhance the passionate chorus sections, encouraging listeners to sing along.

Exile was rapidly becoming known for country-style love songs such as "I Could Get Used to You." This can be seen as a continuation of the themes they developed in their pop career with "Kiss You All Over" and other tracks. The instrumental hook at the beginning of "I Could Get Used to You" is as catchy as the chorus. "I think if you'll analyze most of our songs there's usually an intro hook of some sort, and then that hook usually reoccurs at some point," said Marlon.

The title track is more in a pop-rock vein, and it also includes a memorable opening riff, one of the band's most instantly recognizable instrumental sections. The lyrics describe the beginnings of a love affair, and J.P.'s vocals are enthusiastic and triumphant. It's one of his best vocal performances. The band's sense of song craft seems to have peaked by this point, as the infectious verse and chorus sections seem to flow into one another in a seamless fashion. It's hard not to feel good after listening to "I Could Get Used to You" and "Hang On to Your Heart" back to back.

These highly effective tracks are followed by two less distinguished songs. "She Likes Her Lovin'" is a moderate rocker that fails to distinguish itself as more than pleasant filler, although it does continue the band's move toward sexually suggestive country songs. J.P.'s bluesy solo is rooted in his rock and roll background. Listeners were probably not prepared for "Music," a funky track that includes a rap courtesy of J.P. "We think it was the first country rap song," said J.P. "At least that's what we were thinking when we wrote it."

J.P.'s rap doesn't hold up well today, but it should be noted that mainstream rap was much less developed in 1985. J.P.'s foray into rap sounds better compared to 1985 standards. The most important thing about "Music" was that it showed the band's willingness to experiment with new sounds. "I'm not sure how they let us get away with putting it on an album," said Marlon. The lyrics are a celebration of diversity in music, and the joy that a song can bring. It is an extension of the lyrical concerns that started to develop on "Don't Do It" from *Mixed Emotions*, a song concerning the joys of music and being a musician.

The second half of *Hang On to Your Heart* includes some the group's most popular songs. "Super Love" is a funk-inspired track, and it received some resistance from country radio. "We were so high on that song that we begged our record label to release it as a single, and they were resistant because they felt like it was a little too far left of center," remembers J.P.

The funkiness of the track translates well to the clubs, and it's not uncommon to hear bands in the Central Kentucky area play it on any given weekend. In 2010, Exile was using it for their encore. Unfortunately, it broke their string of seven consecutive No. 1 hits.

"It'll Be Me" is a mid-tempo R&B tune with country touches. Les demonstrates his vocal range, especially during the bridge section. J.P.'s guitar solo helps to give the song a country edge. After the disappointing chart performance of "Super Love," the group rebounded by releasing "It'll Be Me," their eighth No.1 country hit, and their first featuring Les on lead vocals.

"Practice Makes Perfect," another driving rocker showcasing the group's three-part harmony, is one of the more forgettable songs on the album. "She's Too Good to Be True" is Exile's most popular slow ballad, and the peak of the style that J.P. and Sonny had been developing on "We've Still Got Love" and "If I Didn't Love You." Les felt as though the song should be released as the third single instead of "Super Love." "Because when that song came out, we hadn't had a ballad out in over four years," said Les. "If for no other reason I thought that song should have been the single instead of 'Super Love.' That was the song I was lobbying for."

The internal controversy surrounding whether to release "Super Love" or "She's Too Good to Be True" showed a few cracks in the band's chemistry. J.P. was the lead vocalist on Exile's first seven No. 1 country songs, and Les, a gifted vocalist in his own right, wasn't getting as much mainstream attention as a lead vocalist. His background vocals were always an essential element of the group's sound, but the ballads showcasing his voice were often passed over as singles for up-tempo love songs. This stirred emotions within the band as they tried to keep their streak of No. 1 songs intact.

"The majority of the band and the majority of the people at the label… 'cause I remember we had lots of meetings about it and all that stuff…they wanted to try to keep that rolling, and I said 'Well, the way to keep it rolling in my opinion, guys, is to release 'She's Too Good to Be True,'" said Les. His opinion turned out to be the right one in terms of chart success. When it was released in 1987 it became the fourth No.1 hit from the album.

The album closes with "Proud to Be Her Man," an up-tempo Western swing influenced tune that blends elements of country, jazz, and boogie-woogie.

Photo session circa 1987 after Lee joined the group: (left to right) Les, Steve, Lee, J.P., Sonny. Courtesy Lee Carroll. Below are other shots from the photo session.

With Dolly Parton, circa 1987. Courtesy Lee Carroll.

Exile in full Roman garb, 1987. Courtesy Lee Carroll.

Les as a Roman warrior. Courtesy Lee Carroll.

Sonny with a spear. Courtesy Lee Carroll.

J.P. circa 1987. Courtesy Lee Carroll.

Lee wielding a sword. Courtesy Lee Carroll.

Exile with Dennis Hopper circa 1987: (left to right) Lee, J.P., Les, Dennis Hopper, Sonny, Steve.

Lee with Dennis Hopper, 1987. Courtesy Lee Carroll.

Somebody spelled the name wrong. Courtesy Lee Carroll.

Above: Les in a wild pose, 1987.
Courtesy Lee Carroll.

Left: Sonny and J.P. in front of
the tour bus. J.P. left the band
shortly after this photo was taken.
Courtesy Lee Carroll.

Exile with CBS staffers in Nashville celebrating the success of "Just One Kiss," a No. 9 country hit.
Courtesy Lee Carroll.

J.P. on the set for the "I Can't Get Close Enough" video. Courtesy Lee Carroll.

Sonny, Les, and J.P. on the set for the "I Can't Get Close Enough" video. Courtesy Lee Carroll.

Last photo shoot with Les and J.P. in 1987. Courtesy Steve Goetzman.

One of the last shows with J.P. and Les in 1987. Courtesy Lee Carroll.

199

A rare photo from the period in which J.P. and Paul were both in the band, 1988. Courtesy Lee Carroll.

Another photo from the J.P./Paul period. Courtesy Lee Carroll.

Les would leave the band soon after this photo was taken. Courtesy Lee Carroll.

An autographed photo of the new lineup for 1988: (left to right) J.P., Lee, Paul Martin, Sonny, Steve. Courtesy Lee Carroll.

J.P. in 1988 near the end of his 21 year run with Exile. Courtesy Lee Carroll.

Steve Goetzman

Managment

GALLIN · MOREY · ASSOCIATES

8730 Sunset Blvd. Penthouse West
Los Angeles, CA 90069
(213)659-5593

XXXX

WILLIAM MORRIS AGENCY
(615)385-0310

Lee Carroll

Paul Martin

exile

Sonny LeMaire

ARISTA
MUSIC CIRCLE NORTH
NASHVILLE, TN 37203
615/780-9100

(615)329-0022

Exile after J.P. left the band. Courtesy Lee Carroll.

Steve, Paul, Sonny, and Lee on the set for the "Nobody's Talking" video. Courtesy Lee Carroll.

Another shot from the filming of the "Nobody's Talking" video.

Sonny, Steve, Paul and Mark with Dolly Parton. Courtesy Paul Martin.

Mark, Paul and Sonny in the early 1990s. Courtesy Paul Martin.

204

Promo shot of the band as a four-piece circa 1990. Courtesy Lee Carroll.

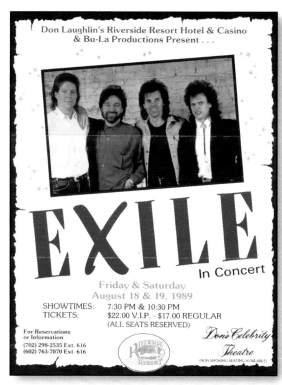

Poster for a show at Don Laughlin's Riverside Resort Hotel and Casino in Laughlin, Nevada. Courtesy Lee Carroll.

The four-piece Exile lineup circa 1990. Courtesy Lee Carroll.

Clockwise from left: Sonny LeMaire   Mark Jones   Steve Goetzman   Lee Carroll   Paul Martin

MANAGEMENT:
GALLIN, MOREY
8730 Sunset Blvd.
Penthouse West
Los Angeles, CA 90069
(213) 659-5593

Evelyn Shriver Public Relations
1313 16th Avenue South
Nashville, TN 37212
(615)383-1000
fax (615)383-1966

exile

The
Bobby Roberts
Company, Inc.
POST OFFICE BOX 3007
HENDERSONVILLE, TN 37077-3007
(615)859-8899

Promotional poster after Mark Jones became a full-time member of the band. Courtesy Paul Martin.

*Exile performing as five-piece with Mark Jones: (left to right) Mark Jones, Paul, Sonny, Steve, Lee.
Courtesy Lee Carroll.*

Promotional photo for Justice *circa 1991: (left to right) Sonny, Mark Jones, Lee, Paul, Steve.
Courtesy Lee Carroll.*

*Paul providing vocals.
Courtesy Paul Martin.*

*In the spotlight – 1990s. (Left to right) Mark Jones, Lee Carroll, Paul Martin, Sonny Lemaire.
Courtesy Paul Martin.*

Album cover for Exile's self-titled debut album: (left to right) Buzz Cornelison, J.P. Pennington, Kenny Weir, Bernie Faulkner, Bobby Johns, Billy Luxon, Jimmy Stokley.

SIDE A
SING A SONG (ASCAP 4:30)
WHATEVER MOOD YOU'RE IN (BMI 2:32)
ROCK N' ROLL WOMAN (ASCAP 3:47)
LEAVE ME STANDING (ASCAP 4:55)
WE CAN WORK IT OUT (BMI 5:09)

SIDE B
GOIN' DOWN (BMI 3:25)
THE BOBBER (ASCAP 2:55)
NEW WAYS—TRAIN, TRAIN (ASCAP 11:02)
DON'T IT FEEL GOOD (BMI 3:55)

RECORDS ARE YOUR
BEST ENTERTAINMENT

Produced by **Bill Traut**
Arranged by **Exile**
Recorded and remixed by **Barry Mraz**
Manufactured from masters owned by Wooden Nickel Records, Inc.

Jimmy Stokley *lead vocals and percussion*
Billy Luxon *vocals and percussion*
Buzz Cornelison *RMI, piano and vocals*
Jimmy Pennington *lead guitar, rhythm guitar and vocals*
Bernie Faulkner *organ, acoustic guitar and vocals*
Kenny Weir *bass and vocals*
Bobby Johns *drums*
Ted "Curly" Whitaker *Road Manager*
Doug Shelton *Lights*
Danny Poe *Stage*

Recorded June 1973 at Paragon Recording Studios, Chicago, Illinois,
and LIVE at Reflections, Cincinnati, Ohio, using the remote
recording facilities of Metro Audio, Detroit, Michigan.
Mastered at The Mastering Lab, Hollywood,
California.

Special thanks for the recording help of Marty Feldman, Steve
Kusiciel and Jim Atlas of Paragon, Chuck Buchanan of Metro, and
Ken Kornell of Reflections. Thanks also to Tom Thacker, Charlie
Tompsley, Marti Grota, and Traynor Amps.

Art Director — **Acy Lehman**
Photographer — **Nick Sangiamo**

RCA
AFL1-3087—STEREO
This album is also available on 8-track — AFS1-3087 and Cassette — AFK1-3087

Stage Pass *album
cover.*

211

Album cover for Mixed Emotions.

All There Is *album cover.*

Don't Leave Me
This Way *album
cover.*

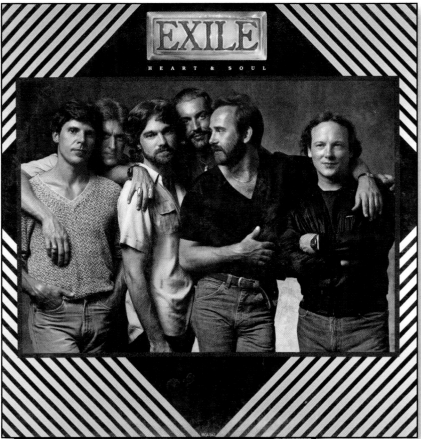

Album cover for
Heart and Soul.

Album cover,
Exile *(first country album).*

Album cover of
Kentucky Hearts.

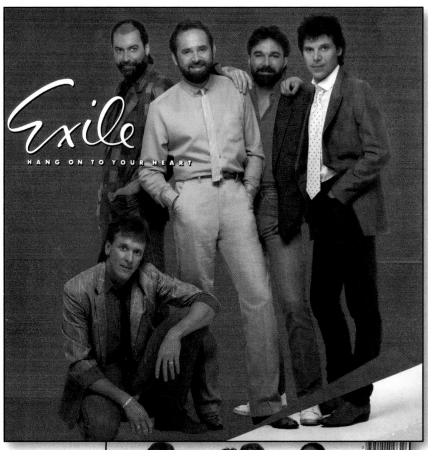

Hang On To Your
Heart *album cover.*

Greatest Hits,
album cover.
Courtesy M. Frene
Melton.

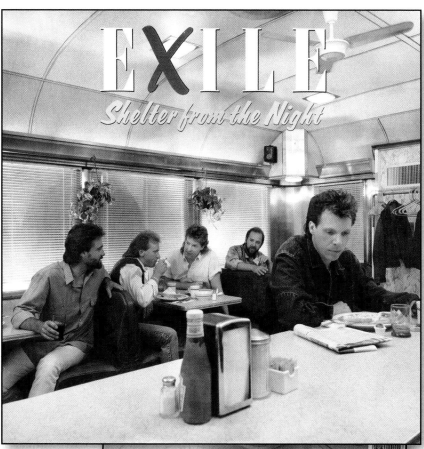

Shelter from the Night, *album cover.*

Album cover for Still Standing. *Courtesy Lee Carroll.*

Album cover for Justice.

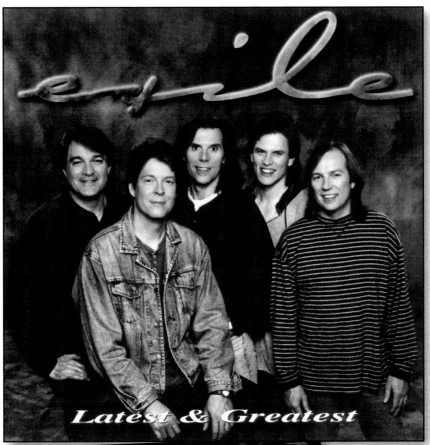

Latest & Greatest,
album cover.

For Bookings:
artist events, inc.
Gary Kirves
Office: 615.309.0458

Website address:
www.exile.biz

Reunion photo circa 2010. Courtesy Marlon Hargis.

Chapter Seven

SHOWDOWN

B Y LATE 1986 *HANG ON TO YOUR HEART* had produced three No. 1 country hits, and it seemed as though Exile was still on a role despite the fact that their streak at the top of the charts was no longer intact. "It'll Be Me" and "She's Too Good to be True" started a new streak, and proved that Les' voice could prove as popular on country radio as J.P.'s. The band looked stronger than ever, and they seemed poised to continue on as one of the most popular bands in country music.

Marlon remembers meeting one of his heroes in Nashville at a late night bar around this time. "I was sitting there with Pam Tillis and some other people, just basically drinking and partying," recounts Marlon. "Someone taps me on the shoulder and says, 'Hey man, I just wanted to come over and tell you I really like what y'all do.' As I turned around he said, 'I'm Steve Cropper.'"

Cropper, a member of Booker T. & the MGs and a major player in the history of Stax Records, recognized the synthesis of country music and soul in Exile's music. Stax artists such as William Bell and Booker T. Jones experimented with country sounds, and other performers from the world of soul/ blues not associated with Stax such as Ray Charles, Al Green, and Bobby "Blue" Bland had successfully experimented with country-soul hybrids. It's not surprising that Cropper was a fan of Exile, as the Stax sound was virtually absent in R&B at the time. The soulful sounds of Otis Redding and Rufus Thomas were more likely to be heard among blues artists by this point, and Exile was continuing the country-soul hybrid that began to develop over twenty years earlier at Stax and elsewhere.

Exile received recognition throughout the music industry. They performed multiple times at The County Music Association Awards (CMAs) and The Academy of Country Music Awards (ACMs). They were nominated six times at the CMAs, but they never won. Les remembers that the group was also nominated for awards on multiple occasions by the Academy of Country Music, but, once again, they didn't win the prize. It appears that, despite their success, Exile may never have been truly embraced by a majority of the country music industry as a "pure" country band. That recognition was saved for

Alabama, a group as intent on doing what it took to make it big in the music industry as Exile ever imagined.

By this point there was internal friction within Exile, and the record label drove the band to make some bad decisions. Some of the internal friction was influenced by band members' tendency to indulge in partying and the nightlife. Buddy Killen:

> The strongest song material that we recorded came in the first couple of albums. But, with any artists who become hot and start touring day and night, there are many distractions. If they're not careful, their songwriting can take a back seat to everything else. This happened with Exile. It is also easy for musicians to start depending on stimulants to sustain energy levels that are necessary if they are to travel and perform day and night. When this happens, it can severely affect a group's recording qualities; their focus becomes blurred and it is much more difficult to achieve a good performance. This also happened with Exile. Some of the members became restless, and it was hard to keep them in the studio physically while we were trying to record.[4]

The members of Exile don't deny that there was significant partying going on at the time. J.P. remembers it as distraction, but emphasizes that it wasn't out of the ordinary. "That's not something that was unusual, and it's really not something that I like to talk a whole lot about, to be honest with you," said J.P. "It was so counter-productive. That's the word that comes to mind."

Steve remembers the party atmosphere as something that all of the members indulged in. Everyone was affected by it, but Marlon was the first member to reach the breaking point. In a way it's not surprising, as he had more free time than some of the other members of the group. Marlon wasn't writing songs, and he wasn't a primary vocalist for the group. His role as engineer would soon be erased, as the label looked to pair the group with better known studio veterans. Marlon:

> I think a combination of too much partying—everybody got burnt out. Egos. The same old B.S. that every other band goes through. I can't think of any particular occasion—'I think I'll quit.' No one tried to talk me out of it. Thinking back, it was probably stupid. On the other hand, I got to do some other interesting things after that, so I can't say there's any regrets.

It's clear that the internal issues went beyond substance abuse. Twelve years of striving for mainstream success had taken its toll on the keyboardist/engineer. "Of course, none of the rest of us were doing any partying whatsoever, ever," said Steve sarcastically. When I asked Steve if there were any members of the band who went home every night, he responded with the following: "Not that I can remember." Les talked about Exile in the mid-1980s:

I don't know. Maybe we partied a little bit too much. You know, of course, success changes people whether you want to admit it or not. It seems like we handled it all pretty good. I thought we did. We never took our shows for granted. We never took our audiences for granted and our fans. We did the most that we could do, I think. There's probably some things that maybe that we would have done differently if we had it to do over again. It felt like to me that we were handling it pretty good. Even though, the band had had success before, it was the fact that...not of this magnitude. We didn't go to many European countries and play country music like they did with 'Kiss You All Over,' but still the success here in the States was pretty strong. I thought we handled it pretty well.

Performance footage from the era shows the band as an energetic, tight ensemble capable of holding their own in any performance setting, both as vocalists and instrumentalists. The musicianship was at a peak even if the chemistry was not. J.P. and Les were more than capable as lead vocalists, and Exile's three-part vocal harmony was among the best in country music. They would sometimes tag the end of "Woke Up in Love," playing the chorus section in a fast gospel style. If substance abuse was playing a debilitating role, it wasn't always evident by the video-taped performances.

Marlon left Exile in early 1987 before they started to work on the *Shelter from the Night* album. He continued to live in Nashville. "I worked with Jerry Reed for a couple of years; I had a club band in town for 5-6 years; worked with Steve Goetzman for about a year at a management company; ran a music store for a few years—while playing and producing sessions all along," said Marlon.[5]

While running the music store he met Felix Cavaliere, one of his early influences. Cavaliere was looking for a keyboard, and Marlon decided to talk to him about the keyboard solo in "Good Lovin.'" "So I play him the solo and he's going, 'Well, you got it just real close, and here's one little trill you're doing different,'" said Marlon. Marlon remembers that he liked the *Shelter from the Night* album, especially "I Can't Get Close Enough," but he lost interest in Exile after J.P. and Les left a few years later. "It was a good band, but it was just a different band," remembers Marlon.

Introducing Lee Carroll

Marlon's replacement was Lee Carroll, a talented young keyboardist from Cave City, Kentucky. Cave City is located between Louisville and Nashville off I-65 and is best known for Mammoth Cave. Lee didn't study jazz or classical music when he was in high school, but he found musical motivation from a fellow student named Max Williams. Williams played guitar, piano, and trumpet. He was also interested in Led Zeppelin and Jimi Hendrix. He showed Lee how to play various musical ideas on the piano. "The very first song he showed me was Vanilla Fudge's version of 'You Keep Me Hangin' On,'" remembers Lee.

Lee proceeded to buy records and play along with them. Music became his escape, and helped him to cope with the loss of his father. "So I look at music for me as a gift, because I was at a point in my life where I could've gone crazy," said Lee. Instead of developing some of the bad habits that plague many young men, he immersed himself in music and spent hours in his room practicing. Lee enjoyed improvising on the piano, but also taught himself how to read music.

Lee chose to attend The University of Kentucky when he graduated from high school, majoring in pre-med. He soon realized that he wanted to be a musician, not a doctor. Instead of attending class he would stay up late at night playing the upright piano in Haggin Hall. "I had no role model of any kind growing up as to how you could actually make a living as a musician, so you just don't consider it," said Lee.

In 1972 he met bass player Chip Graham, and they rented a house together during Lee's sophomore year of college. Guitarist/vocalist Mark Jones, Graham's friend from Hopkinsville, Kentucky, was among those who dropped by the house on occasion. It wasn't until Lee met harmonica player/vocalist Rodney Hatfield and drummer David White that he began playing professionally. Hatfield and White invited Lee to join their band, The Hatfield Clan, which he did. They played gigs in the Lexington area.

Lee continued to work on his keyboard skills playing in bands, and he was eventually accepted to Berklee College of Music in the mid-1970s. His acceptance was partially due to a recommendation letter written by Vince DiMartino, a well-known trumpeter/educator in the Central Kentucky area. Mark Jones, another future member of Exile, was aware of Lee's decision to go to Berklee, so he decided to apply as well. The two musicians and another keyboard player named Keith Hubbard traveled from Lexington to Boston in Mark's deceased grandfather's Oldsmobile during the middle of winter.

"It was so damn cold," said Lee. "It was just bleak and dismal and we were out walking around there—and the wind whipping through those buildings...Man!"

Mark was able to earn a degree from Berklee in 1980, but Lee never stayed long enough to finish. After four semesters in Boston, Lee returned to Lexington and played in small jazz bands. He then returned to Berklee for two more semesters. During this time he formed an eight-piece jazz-fusion group with Mark called Fly by Night. The band consisted of four horn players and a four-piece rock rhythm section featuring Mark on guitar and Lee on Fender Rhodes electric piano. Lee spent time composing a high percentage of Fly by Night's material, and he dropped out of school once more.

Fly by Night hit the road in the early 1980s, often suffering through meager circumstances. They reached a breaking point in January of 1983. Lee:

> Mark and I are out on the road with our jazz/fusion band, and we're playing Baker's Keyboard Lounge, which is a renowned jazz club in Detroit. Nobody shows up to see us. Guy gives us five bucks a day to eat. This was after a long string of...you know, jazz/fusion music was basically going nowhere. So we get in the car and head to the next gig, which is in Florida. We get about halfway there and pull over in the middle of the night, and basically there was a rebellion in the band. And the guys said, 'We're going back to Boston. It's not worth it. We don't want to do this anymore.'

Mark and Lee realized that they would have to explore other styles of music in order to stay active as a band. They didn't have a vocalist that could effectively pull off R&B material, so they realized that the change would be rather drastic. They turned to music videos for inspiration. MTV began broadcasting in 1981, heavily influencing the music industry in the process.

"And the guys...regrettably...the guys had been watching MTV when it was really beginning, and so they were all into this 80s...so all the music was da-da-da-da-da-da-da-da-da," said Lee. "We cut the sleeves off our t-shirts and got funny haircuts, and we started trying to book into the rock clubs."

Lee's involvement with this project lasted about six months, and he eventually tired of the Boston music scene. Some of the reasons included the fact that he had to get a job parking cars at a hotel in order to make ends meet, and the new band was not playing his original compositions.

"I had written some of the dance stuff, but my heart wasn't in it anymore," said Lee. "I was starving to death, and we'd been starving for years. But to starve doing something you don't like is different, and I just said, 'I'm getting the hell out of here.'"

The music scene in Boston was competitive despite the fact that the city is not considered one of the major centers of the music industry. The fierce competition didn't seem worth it. Lee decided to go to a music industry town. This narrowed his choices to New York, Los Angeles, or Nashville. He chose Nashville, a city known for country music. "I don't even like country music," admits Lee.

Lee knew three people in Nashville when he arrived. One friend from outside of the music business became his roommate. He also knew Joe Turley, a pianist/songwriter, and Dave Innis, the keyboard player for the country band Restless Heart. Lee met Turley in Lexington during the 1970s while playing with The Hatfield Clan. Innis had heard Fly by Night play in Nashville. For nine months Lee played any gig that he was offered.

"Now, when you first move to Nashville you do two things: you play showcases and don't get paid for them, you know, singer-songwriter showcases, or you do what's called a spec session, which is to go in the studio and records people's demos and not get paid for it," said Lee. He had to get a job waiting tables while he was playing music for free in order to meet people. "Well, the good news is that I played piano, not guitar," said Lee. "There are no piano players in Nashville." Innis was busy at the time, and he began throwing spec sessions Lee's way. Some of the gigs were for pay.

A job supporting Christian rock artist David Meece proved to be especially important. Lee was thrilled to be offered $700 for two rehearsals and two gigs. Unfortunately, he had to decide between playing the gig or attending Joe Turley's wedding. After receiving Turley's blessing, Lee decided to play the gig with Meece. Several Nashville musicians played on the gig including guitarist Don Potter. Shortly after the gig with Meece, Potter was asked to put a band together for The Judds, an up-and-coming musical force in Nashville. The Judds had fired their band and were looking for new musicians. Potter was impressed with the rhythm section from the David Meece gig, and he invited them to audition. The musicians learned the first Judds album in its entirety, but the audition was rough. "And we came real close to not being hired," said Lee. "Don said 'Listen, these guys can play. Just give them some time. I'll work with them.'" Lee admits that the music was challenging.

"People think country music's simple and that it's easy to play, but that's not the case at all," said Lee. "There's definitely a pocket you gotta put things in, and a touch to it."

Lee started playing with The Judds shortly after they signed to RCA. The Judds were becoming highly successful by this time, and they were pleased with their new backing band. It was an opportune situation for Lee. RCA decided to make The Judds the next big act on their label, a situation that made the backing band nervous. They feared that the backing band would be fired in favor of Nashville studio players. "And Don Potter said something I'll never forget…to this day it's part of my way of dealing with life is…He said, 'Guys, if you want to keep your jobs, make yourself invaluable,'" said Lee.

Lee recognized the importance of the job, and he worked hard to keep it. He understood that The Judds had tremendous upside. They had a compelling story, and were making an impression throughout Nashville. "I tried out for Crystal Gayle the week before I took that gig with them," said Lee. "I'm glad that I went the way that I did, because The Judd's career exploded." Lee remembers opening for artists such as Reba McEntire, Kenny Rogers, and Conway Twitty. Next, The Judds started playing small theaters as headliners. Eventually, they acquired their own bus, and their stage shows began incorporating elaborate choreography. "Then we were doing choreographed shows where they brought guys in from New York, and staged our shows and told us where to stand," remembers Lee.

The country music circuit was small in the mid-1980s, and Lee remembers running into the members of Exile on several occasions while he was with The Judds. Lee had been aware of Exile since 1968. "In fact, the first concert I ever went to was a Dick Clark Caravan of Stars at the E.A. Diddle Arena in Bowling Green, Kentucky, and the opening act was Exile," said Lee. He was only 15-years-old at the time. Lee later heard about Exile when he was playing clubs in Lexington during the 1970s. "They were just the hottest regional act in Kentucky, so I knew who they were," said Lee. Fly by Night played in Lexington in the early 1980s while Exile was playing at Southland Bowling Lanes. Lee:

So I'm touring with Fly by Night, and these guys, for young guys, these guys were just fabulous musicians. We had some of the best young musicians out of Berklee playing in our band. Not a lot of self-control, but tremendous chops and tremendous energy. So we had this jazz-fusion band that only musicians came to see. I mean we could blow out the back wall with this horn section and with the rhythm section that we had.

> But the music was so obtuse, nobody except a musician liked it. We just never really got that part of it. But we were playing in Lexington, and I heard that Exile was playing at a bowling alley lounge. The Rebel Room, or whatever the hell they called it. And so we went by to see them. And it was one of the saddest things I've ever seen. 'Kiss You All Over' had gone through the roof, and then that was it. Their career just skid to a halt, and all of a sudden they were bottomed out. We just walked into that bowling alley lounge right when they bottomed out. Life was over as they knew it, and here we were young and full of piss and vinegar.

Things had turned around for Exile the next time Lee ran into them in 1985. They had reached the top of the country charts several times and were one of the most successful bands in country music. "So now they're back on their game again," remembers Lee.

Lee had been playing with The Judds for two and a half years when J.P. approached him about joining Exile. Lee was serving as the band leader for Naomi and Wynonna's backing band by this point, but he still wasn't playing on their records. "And basically all we were going to do is they were going to hand us a record every year and say 'Learn these songs,' and we'd go on tour with them," said Lee.

He was earning a middle class salary with The Judds, but he wasn't earning retirement money. The Judds were a bigger draw than Exile at the time, but Lee saw the advantages of accepting J.P.'s invitation. He thought he saw an opportunity to get involved in the creative process with Exile, and he knew that he would be able to play on the records. It was still a difficult decision, because Lee saw The Judds as approaching "major league" status in the music world. "Exile was definitely firmly entrenched in the minor leagues where they were doing what they loved to do, but they were making a middle class living," said Lee. After consulting with his wife, Lee decided to join Exile. The departure from The Judds was emotional. "I was the guy who basically was liaison between the girls and the band," said Lee. "They gave me their blessing, but it was very emotional." Lee joined Exile in 1986.

Lee didn't know that he was joining Exile at what would prove to be one of their most difficult periods. They were at the peak of their success commercially, but there were several problems brewing underneath the surface. Some of the major problems were instigated by Epic, their record label. There was a feeling on the part of the label that Exile songs were beginning to sound alike, and that they were adhering to formulas mainly in the form of up-tempo love songs. This seems especially odd due to the fact that *Hang On to Your*

Heart was the band's most diverse album from their country era. It's also difficult to understand why the label would meddle in the affairs of a band that had reached the top of the country charts with nine of their last ten country singles. (This discounts re-releases of "Stay with Me" and "Dixie Girl," neither of which had much success.)

J.P. had a bad feeling when Rick Blackburn left Epic. Blackburn had been criticized for firing Johnny Cash from the label among other things.[6] He was replaced by Roy Wunsch. "And one of the first things I remember hearing out of Roy's mouth was, 'We feel like there's a sameness in your music, and we would like for you to entertain two things, another producer than Buddy, and outside songs,'" said J.P. "I don't know about the rest of the guys, but it really set off an alarm in my head."

This came at a time when Les and Lee were looking to provide creative input, and it was clear that they weren't going to get many songwriting opportunities. "The implication was that if you're in the band you get to pitch your songs like everybody else," said Lee. "One of the difficulties in a band is that once somebody is in creative control, once their writing has been what has propelled the band to that point, it's not all that easy," said Lee. "And truth of the matter is, and I'll be perfectly honest here, I don't really like country."

Firing Buddy Killen was not a good move for Exile, but it appears they had little choice in the matter due to pressure from the label. "And then finally our manager (Morey) came on board with the label, and then that was it for us," said Steve. "We had nowhere else to run, so we fired him."

Killen, a very successful figure in the music scene over the years, didn't take the situation well. "He goes, 'Well, why would you change producers? We're having all these hits and success. Why would you change horses in the middle of the stream?'" said Sonny. "Which was a very logical question to ask, but we were following the directions of the record company at the time."

Despite Exile's success, there was a feeling that their records were getting more resistance from radio programmers. "The complaint from radio was that every Exile record sounded like the last," said Steve. "That was what they were up against, so that pointed to the producer." After an enormously successful career in the music business, Killen was beginning to get a reputation as an old-school producer oblivious to current production methods. In retrospect, he was the perfect producer for Exile in the country music field. Steve:

Firing Buddy was a big mistake, and it happened at a very bad time in his career. People around Nashville knew that he wasn't a great producer...an ear for songs and he had great instinct, but in terms of what a producer normally does, Buddy wasn't good at that. That perception of him had cycled back, and he was getting wind of it. It was really hurting him, and then in the midst of it all we fired him. That was like putting up a billboard on music row: 'Buddy Killen doesn't know how to produce.' It bruised him badly, so when he wrote his book he spent a couple of pages talking about the drugs and alcohol in the band, and how much trouble he had trying to keep us in the studio. And I'd have to say it was all probably accurate. I don't think that he stepped out of bounds. I think what he said was probably true.

It was probably the worst period in the band's history in terms of substance abuse, as music industry pressures and life on the road began to take a toll. "Once I got into the bus, you know, and we're pulling out on the road and I'm watching what's going on around me and I…not that I'm a saint… but I was not in the league these guys were in," said Lee.

Exile replaced Killen with Elliot Scheiner, a producer/engineer who had worked on many albums in the pop music field including Steely Dan's *Aja* (as engineer) and Bruce Hornsby and the Range's *The Way It Is* (as co-producer). The record company intended to gradually move Exile back over to the pop music market in order to sell more albums. "I do recall at the time that one of our competitors, Restless Heart, had had a song that had crossed over way up into the pop charts, and I think that had an effect on us, too," said J.P. "And, of course, we wanted to do it, too."

Restless Heart's "I'll Still Be Loving You" had indeed crossed over into Billboard's pop chart, peaking at No. 33 in 1987. Country music was beginning to move in a more commercial direction, a trend that would come to full fruition with the success of Garth Brooks in the early 1990s. Exile got caught in the middle of these changes, and it didn't work to the band's benefit. On paper, they seemed a natural fit for the changing musical landscape. After all, they had already been a pop band. They were a self-contained band capable of writing and performing their own material in the studio, and they would have little trouble adjusting to the arena rock world. Pairing the group with Scheiner, an in-demand pop producer at the time, seemed like a sure bet. But it wasn't.

J.P. and Sonny were used to penning Exile's material, and they were not excited about recording songs by outside writers. "I don't think it concerned fellas in the band who didn't write as much as it did Sonny and I," remembers J.P. "That may sound selfish on my part, but Sonny and I were in a really good place." They knew that they could write songs and get them recorded on a major label, a privilege that a small percentage of musicians have ever enjoyed. They had it made as writers.

In addition, the band members seemed to be having a good time on stage, and the material was fun to play. "So that set off an alarm, and not only because of the writing aspect, I think more so in that we felt like a change in the regime may have not been to our benefit," said J.P.

Scheiner brought in three outside songs for the *Shelter from the Night* album, "Shelter from the Night," "Fly on the Wall," and "She's Already Gone." Despite his background as an accomplished engineer and producer in the pop music world, Scheiner was not a great "song guy" in terms of knowing country music radio. "We felt like our producer, Elliot, was a little bit out of his element as far as knowing what really worked for us in respect to country music," said J.P. "It turned out to be not the greatest experience in the world for us."

Les was the vocalist on all of the outside songs, and it's probable that they were chosen with him in mind. "I really don't think the majority of the guys wanted to do those songs," said Les. In retrospect, Les described "Fly on the Wall" as a good song: "I think it's a good song, but still not in keeping with the type of music that Exile was doing or people were used to hearing from us."

Les also provided lead vocals on "My Heart's in Good Hands," a Pennington/Lemaire composition, and a song that he co-wrote with J.P. and Sonny entitled "Feel Like Foolin' Around." The remaining five tracks were composed by the Pennington/Lemaire songwriting team, all featuring J.P. on lead vocals. None of Lee's compositions were included on the album. "J.P. and Sonny had a stranglehold on the creative side, and even though it was stated that everybody had the same shot, the truth of the matter was that was not the case," said Lee. "But I was handicapped by the fact that I was not a country songsmith."

Shelter from the Night was not recorded under ideal circumstances. Scheiner agreed to produce/engineer the album under the condition that Exile would record the album at his studio in Stamford, Connecticut. Not anticipating the physical realities of the situation, the group agreed to his conditions. After writing the songs and doing some pre-production recording, the band started making trips to Connecticut. Sonny:

> We would fly up to New York, La Guardia, or into Newark...either one, depending on where we were coming from. We would drive up, get vans. Put our equipment in, drive up to Stamford. Set up in the studio, and

record Tuesday through Thursday or Friday. Pack it all up. Drive back to La Guardia. Fly out to places we play on Saturday and Sunday. And this was for a month—well over a month. I think it was all of June of '87. So the schedule was pretty grueling itself, just doing this physically.

The recording of the album was followed by more touring, and by the end of July band members were traveling to Los Angeles to finish parts of the record and mix. J.P. and Sonny would spend time working with Scheiner in Los Angeles before flying out to meet the other members of the band for gigs. The schedule was taxing. "And honest to God, by the time we were finished with that record, I was physically...I was fried," said Sonny. "I admit it. I was absolutely exhausted just from the logistics of doing it all over the place."

Given the circumstances in which it was recorded, it's not surprising that *Shelter from the Night* is the most uneven country album that Exile released while J.P. and Les were in the band. The album opens with "Just One Kiss," A Pennington/Lemaire composition with a strong pop influence. It demonstrates that the in-house songwriting team was still able to effectively step outside of the country field, and craft catchy pop music. "Just One Kiss" would have fit comfortably on *Heart and Soul*. It seems as though J.P. and Sonny set out to prove that they didn't need the outside songwriters in order to produce quality pop music. J.P. provides the lead vocal. It's one of the more memorable songs on the album, and a somewhat underrated track in the band's discography.

The title track, composed by outside songwriters Michael Foster and David Michael Thompson, is a fairly ineffective slice of '80s pop-rock. Les provides the lead vocal, but his respectable performance can't save the song from sounding like stock material. If the volume were cranked up several notches, the song could work on a Judas Priest album with its minor key chord changes and twin guitar lines.

"My Heart's in Good Hands," also sung by Les, is a synth-heavy, moderate R&B ballad composed by J.P. and Sonny. It has brief country inflections, and is not unlike some of the material on the band's first country album. The production is a bit more polished and less organic than their earlier ballads, but the song works.

"Showdown" is another underrated Pennington/Lemaire tune, with a soulful vocal from J.P. and memorable chorus sections. The synthesizers date "Showdown" a bit, and songs such as this may have led Lee to abandon digital instruments in favor of vintage instruments later in his career. "Fly on the

Wall," composed by Bernie Taupin and Bruce Hornsby, is the most effective outside song on the album. Lee's piano drives the music, and Les is given an opportunity to demonstrate his subtle vocal abilities on this rock-influenced ballad.

The rock influenced "Feel Like Foolin' Around" was the only song that J.P., Sonny, and Les wrote together. "It had nothing to do with country," said Lee. "Feel Like Foolin' Around" isn't a bad song. It allowed J.P. to rock out in fine style, and it's a sultry, well-crafted tune that could have been a hit on country radio in the 1990s. Les' lead vocal is perfectly in line with the song's lustful sentiment.

"I Can't Get Close Enough" was the hit from the album, and it's easy to see why. It's an up-tempo love song composed by J.P. and Sonny, and it manages to milk the Exile formula while changing the music just enough (i.e. the mysterious intro) to allow the song to stand out from the group's former hits. J.P. provided the lead vocal on the studio version, but Les has been singing it recently at the band's reunion performances.

"I Can't Get Close Enough" is followed by two of the weakest cuts on the album, and it's easy to see why they were tucked away near the end of side two. John Clifford Farrar's synth-heavy "She's Already Gone" sounds like a much less effective version of the music that Don Henley was creating in the 1980s. Lee's synthesizers sound dated, and Les sounds out of place on this pop-dance track. J.P. added twangy guitar sounds to "It's You Again," but the pop-rock influence is still prevalent. The results are less memorable than much of their pop-rock material, and the fake electric piano sounds don't help. The Exile formula wears thin on this track, despite some creative guitar lines from J.P.

"As Long as I Have Your Memory" is one of Exile's most memorable ballads, and it closes the album beautifully. I asked J.P. if the lyrics were about anyone in particular. "There may have been something, subconscious there about Jimmy, I don't know," said J.P. "I don't think we were talking about anyone specifically on that song." J.P.'s mother also passed away in 1985, but he didn't mention her in relation to the song. "As Long As I Have Your Memory" is one of the great *lost* Exile songs, and I suggested that they add it to their current set-list. "I think we've entertained the thought before," said J.P. "Sometimes it's hard to work new stuff into the show, because we've been fortunate in that we've had so many hits."

Hopes were high for the *Shelter from the Night* album. The band believed they had a hit record on their hands after they listened to the playback. "It was a big ass party," remembers Lee. "People thought that it was a home run."

The prediction seemed accurate when "I Can't Get Close Enough" soared to the top of the country chart in the latter part of 1987.

A promotional video was filmed, showcasing the group performing "I Can't Get Close Enough" in a smoky room with a large painting in the background. It showed that J.P. and Sonny still had the ability to pen successful mid-tempo love songs that appealed to country music audiences. Unfortunately, this would be the group's last No. 1 country single.

Chapter Eight

LET'S DO IT AGAIN

L ES TAYLOR DECIDED TO leave Exile soon after "I Can't Get Close Enough" was released in August of 1987. "I just felt as a singer that I had pretty much done everything I could do in the organization, and I was getting kind of frustrated with the label, too, the way they were handling things a little bit," said Les. He was frustrated by his lack of songwriting input, but he was especially irritated by the fact that a high percentage of the singles featured J.P. on lead vocals.

"I felt like I could contribute to the band more than I was—had I been able to sing more, and I felt like that there was some songs on there that I did sing on the albums previously that should have been released," remembers Les. He remembers voicing his concerns to Rick Blackburn. "I remember him telling me once when we were having dinner…'Just trust me Les, we're going to put some more songs out with your voice on them and stuff,'" continues Les.

It should also be pointed out that the songwriters in the band earned considerably more money than the other members of the group, and Les was not receiving a good deal of songwriting credit. Les only received songwriting credit for two songs on the band's first four country albums: "Comin' Apart At the Seams" and "Feel Like Foolin' Around." He was making a living with the band, but the two guys he was singing with on a consistent basis were making considerably more money. "If you're in a band on the level Exile was in, the only people really making beyond a middle class living are the guys who are writing the songs, especially if they hit the radio," explains Lee, another group member who was growing frustrated by his lack of creative input.

Les knew that he had a distinctive voice, and he wanted to see if he could make it on his own as a solo artist. He certainly had the talent, and some encouraged him to step out on his own. Nevertheless, it would not prove to be a good move. "And everybody knew Les would have some challenges, because…Les is a very gifted singer, but nobody was making bets on Les as a business man, managing his own career," said Lee.

Les' decision to leave the group occurred after the success of "I Can't Get Close Enough." Subsequent singles were much less successful. "Feel Like

Foolin' Around" was the follow-up single. Its rock based approach found resistance from country radio peaking at No. 60 on the country music charts. "So what happens is you got The Judds and Randy Travis over here, sort of the traditional backlash—Exile fell through the cracks," remembers Lee. One can only speculate the reasons for Exile's fall from grace among radio programmers, but it's likely that Les' departure, Buddy Killen's influence, and the group's new rock based style all played a role. Exile clearly lost favor among some influential figures in the country music business. Lee:

> If there's, I don't know, a hundred radio stations they use to determine where the record is, and if there's three guys who control the programming at a third of those radio stations or a fourth of them...if you don't have the blessing of those three guys you don't make it to the top.

"Just One Kiss" showed some renewed promise by reaching No. 9 on the country chart in early 1988. The lackluster fourth single from the album, "It's You Again," fizzled out quickly, peaking at No. 21. The streak was over for Exile, and it looked like their hit making days might be coming to a close.

Introducing Paul Martin

Les Taylor's replacement was Paul Martin, a young multi-instrumentalist from Winchester, Kentucky. Paul was an extraordinarily gifted musician capable of playing a wide array of string instruments, keyboards, and drums. Paul's parents had a studio, and music was engrained in his consciousness from an early age. "Dad had a little country band when he was in high school," remembers Paul. "My mom, her and her brothers had a gospel trio."

His parents met at a radio station in the mid-1950s. Music would continue to be an important part of their lives as they settled into a traditional family setting. Paul's father worked jobs unrelated to music during the day, but he continued to stay in the field by recording musicians in the family living room. By the time Paul reached the age of six, the basement of the house became a studio. Paul became fascinated by music around this time, and he committed himself to learning various instruments including guitar, keyboards, drums, and electric bass. He played double bass in the middle school orchestra, and became active in choir during his high school years. His time was also spent playing on sessions at his father's studio. He formed his first rock and roll band during his freshman year of high school.

Paul also developed an interest in country music, bluegrass, and gospel. Unlike the other members of Exile, Paul was raised on a steady diet of country music. "Anything that was popular in the '50s and '60s that country was from Merle Haggard, Buck Owens, or anything of that nature," remembers Paul. "Any of the old Ray Price, things like that. That's the stuff that I cut my teeth on." Other influences included The Chuck Wagon Gang, The Louvin Brothers, Don Reno and Red Smiley, The Oak Ridge Boys, The Imperials, and The Statesmen Quartet.

In addition to this background in country, gospel, and bluegrass, Paul was also influenced by soul music. He remembers watching African-Americans record at his father's studio, and listening to the music coming out of Motown and Stax. He was on his way to becoming a first rate, diverse musician. "Most of the musicians that I've gotten to know here in Nashville over the years, they laugh because they've come to my studio and they'll go 'Paul you're the only guy I know that I could look at your CD collection and see the Osborne Brothers and Judas Priest right next to them,'" said Paul.

Paul was not a highly motivated student. His father encouraged him to go to college after high school, but Paul's stay at Eastern Kentucky University ended without a degree. He entered EKU as a music major, but changed to industrial technology after his first year. He eventually dropped out of school, insisting that he wanted to dedicate his time to playing music. He assured his parents that he would return to school if things didn't work out. It didn't take him long to land a high profile gig playing keyboards with Billy Joe Royal. He joined Exile a year later.

Paul became aware of Exile as a young boy in the early 1970s, before the success of "Kiss You All Over." "At that time they were still playing around the hometown area, playing proms and dances and things, trying to get something going," said Paul. Paul still has a copy of "Mary on the Beach" hanging in his studio. He is representative of the young musicians from Kentucky who grew up hearing about Exile.

Paul remembers playing drums behind J.P. Pennington at the Martin family studio at some point during the early 1980s. It would not be the last time that they would cross paths. Paul got a gig playing with Doug Breeding, Sonny's former band mate, in the early 1980s. The members of Exile and their tour manager, Clarence Spalding, occasionally attended the performances. After Les' departure, Paul was considered as a possible replacement. Spalding invited Paul to visit the band's office above Doug Breeding's club (Breeding's), and the young multi-instrumentalist accepted. "I went in there and met with them, and I took some stuff I'd done at my dad's studio," said Paul.

They knew a lot of the same people, and it was a relatively comfortable experience. Doug Breeding was one of Paul's supporters, and likely had something to do with the band's decision to hire him. Paul:

In all due respects, Doug Breeding's probably the key figure for me getting that job anyway, because when I walked out that day...It was very humbling, because when I walked out of the meeting that day I saw Doug," said Paul. "He walked up to me. He said 'Paul there's a lot of guys... I'd go to the wall with them. But I gotta be honest with you...I would crawl to the wall for you.'

In late 1988 Martin replaced Les Taylor in Exile. Exile now consisted of Paul, J.P., Sonny, Lee, and Steve. The new line-up would be short lived. Paul and J.P. represented two ends of the music business spectrum. Paul was the up and coming star, a multi-instrumentalist capable of inspiring awe in fellow musicians and audience members. J.P. had been a professional musician for over 25 years, played on a No. 1 pop hit, composed or co-composed ten No. 1 country hits, and toured extensively.

Despite the obvious respect that both men feel for one another, it was not a good situation in 1988. "It really affected me when Les left in a very negative way," remembers J.P. Paul was a skilled vocalist, but he was better known for his instrumental skills. Les had a voice that was difficult to duplicate. Further evidence of this can be found on J.P.'s subsequent solo album, where songs have the instrumental drive of Exile without the same distinctive vocal harmonies.

"The magic harmony that the three of us had...it went away," said J.P. J.P., Les, and Sonny had developed a sound that was hard to duplicate. Paul was thrust into a difficult situation. "Paul is a massively talented person, and I like Paul fine," said J.P. "Just something about it that was never the same." It's clear that J.P. was also dealing with burnout and some personal problems. He left the group at the end of the year. "I was just burnt out–'petual bad mood," said J.P. "I didn't handle my exit very well at all." J.P. wasn't the only one in the band having difficulties at the time, far from it. But he was the only member left from the 1960s incarnation of the group, and he had spent a lot of time on the road.

Things certainly weren't turning out the way the Lee envisioned them when he left The Judds. He had not been allowed to contribute songwriting on the *Shelter from the Night* album, and it looked as though the band was falling apart entirely. This led to tension between him and J.P. Lee:

It was J.P.'s band, for better or worse. He was the creative heart of the group. He was the only founding member. He was the person that people identified with. He was the band leader. He was also very controlling and protected his personal interest. The money is in the songwriting, and he was protective of that. Eventually, it reached a point where J.P. had to get off the road. They were partying pretty hard when I got in the band. The truth of the matter is, without being specific about anybody in the band... this is a general statement...If you have a weakness...if you have anything about you that is an addictive personality trait whether it's drugs, or alcohol, or sex, or whatever.... When you reach a level of celebrity where people actually know who you are, people give you whatever you want. If you don't have self-control, celebrity will eat you alive. That's why so very few people last. There are a lot of pressures to do the wrong thing. J.P. ended up getting off the road and going home and being with his family, and that was his choice. His own heart has to determine whether or not he did the right or wrong thing. I'm sure he probably feels he did, from a personal perspective, did the right thing, and I applaud that.

J.P. and Paul played a few gigs together in the closing months of 1988, but it was a difficult period as the group appeared to be losing the support of their record label. This didn't work to lessen Paul's excitement or dedication to the band. He was young, talented, and excited to be on stage. "I guess it gave J.P. a good kick in the rear to play because you can get real stagnant," said Paul.

For a short while it seemed as though his youthful enthusiasm might brush off on J.P. "We were together on stage one night and he came over to me in the middle of a show...because we were playing something together, some guitar thing...and he just said 'Man, you make me want to play guitar again,'" remembers Paul. This renewed enthusiasm would prove to be short lived.

Paul got married in late 1988, and things were looking up when he went on his honeymoon in November. Still, he began to worry when he was invited to a band meeting as soon as he returned. Paul feared that the other guys had decided to fire him. When he arrived at breakfast the next morning he spotted Lee, Sonny, Steve, and Jim Morey, but there was no sign of J.P. "They said, 'Sit down, Paul, J.P. has left the band,'" remembers Paul.

The other members informed Paul that they intended to continue, but that he would be required to take on an important role in the band as a lead vocalist and lead guitarist. Paul was up for the challenge. Soon after, J.P.'s last gig with Exile took place on New Year's Eve, 1988. The show was full of tension. Paul still has the board tape from the evening. "During the solo of 'Give Me One More Chance' on piano, Lee, out of his frustration…It's like he starts playing the solo and then about halfway through it sounds like he just takes his fist and starts going bam, bam, bam, bam across the keyboard," said Paul. "And it's funny, but it ain't, I guess you'd say."

J.P. and Lee were at completely different points in their careers, and the frustration reached a boiling point. After almost thirty years in the business, J.P. needed a break. "They weren't too happy with me, though, and I don't blame them—not very diplomatic," said J.P.

After leaving Exile, J.P. and Les moved on to brief solo careers. J.P. was signed to MCA Records as a solo artist resulting in one album, *Whatever It Takes* (1991). The album was produced by well-known producer/keyboardist Barry Beckett. J.P. enjoyed working with the talented producer, but he didn't enjoy working as a solo artist. "I enjoyed making the album," said J.P. I just didn't like everything else that went along with it."

The album performed poorly on the country music charts, as both singles from the album failed to crack the country music top 40. The title track peaked at No. 45, while "You Gotta Get Serious" ran out of steam at No. 72. This was unfortunate, because the album has some good tracks. It contains fewer highlights than the Exile albums, but songs such as "Whatever It Takes" and "What I Wouldn't Give" prove that J.P. could still deliver tightly crafted country ballads while "Whatcha Tryin' To Do" is an underrated country-groove tune.

The album also lacks some of the serious production mistakes (overuse of digital synthesizers, lack of soulful instrumental interplay) that work to date Les Taylor's two solo albums. This would prove to be J.P.'s only solo record. "I was just a band guy," said J.P. "I wasn't used to having everything depend on my sole decision."

Les' reputation in the country music industry in the early 1990s rested on his abilities as a vocalist, not as a writer or guitarist. This gave him substantially less control over his solo career than J.P. Les co-wrote four of the ten songs on his first solo album *That Old Desire* (1990), but he didn't play guitar on any of the tracks. There seems to have been an attempt by producer Pat McMakin to showcase Les' vocal talents while continuing to move him in a more pop inspired direction. These attempts are occasionally successful.

Songs such as "Every Time I Think It's Over" and "That Old Desire" demonstrate his impressive vocal range, and "Ole Tin Roof" (co-written by Les) is a somewhat memorable fusion of rock and country. Still, much of the album falls flat, and Les wasn't able to develop much of an identity as a solo artist.

The singles released from the album failed to move Les to the upper echelons of the country music chart. "Shoulda, Coulda, Woulda Loved You" reached No. 46 while "Knowin' You Were Leavin'" petered out at No. 58. Les was signed to a seven record deal, but he would record only one more solo album, *Blue Kentucky Wind* (1991). The highlights of the album include the haunting title track and "The Porchlight," a song with writing contributions by Bernie Faulkner. "He's an excitable guy," said Les referring to the former Exile keyboardist/saxophonist/guitarist. "You'd be having a conversation with him, and he'd say, 'Oh man, that's a hook.'"

One can only imagine what a conversation between Les and Bernie would sound like, but "The Porchlight" resulted in the most passionate, heartfelt performance of Les' solo career. Les didn't write the song, but it accurately portrays his experience growing up in Kentucky. "That song was real close to the type of life that I grew up, wading in the creek and all this kind of stuff," remembers Les. A country-rock tune entitled "I Gotta Mind to Go Crazy" was the single from the album. At first it looked as though the single would be a success, but it rapidly sunk and peaked at No. 44 on the country chart.

It seems as though country radio may have developed a vendetta against Exile and former members of the band. "That song started off gangbusters and went straight downhill," said Les. There seemed to be an attempt to transform Les into country music's Michael Bolton on tracks such as "Welcome to the Real World of Love," and "The Very First Lasting Love," a duet with Shelby Lynne. "There were some things that I would do differently," said Les. He was dropped from the label after the album failed to produce a hit.

Somewhat surprisingly, Exile was able to pull together despite the loss of their well-known lead vocalists/guitarists. Sonny Lemaire, Steve Goetzman, Lee Carroll, and Paul Martin owned the name, and they were anxious and a bit nervous about the future of the band. "But all of a sudden the four of us grew really close, real fast," remembers Paul. They ventured to Paul's father's studio in order to regroup and pick songs for a new album. Unfortunately, the group's record label at the time, CBS, dropped the band shortly after J.P.'s departure. "We were really out in the cold, and we had to make a decision to carry on or just let it drop," said Steve. Ultimately, they decided to carry on. They continued to use the name "Exile," and they proceeded to play small venues.

Introducing Mark Jones

Many of Exile's songs featured three-part harmonies, so the band needed to hire another vocalist. Lee and Steve were skilled musicians, but not vocalists. Lee decided to invite his old friend Mark Jones to join the band. Mark, now a graduate from The Berklee School of music, was still in Boston at the time. New Man, the '80s style pop band that he and Lee had founded, had broken up after recording one album and losing their record deal. Lee knew that Mark was a talented guitar player and that he could also cover the high vocal parts for Exile. Mark accepted the offer, and the last Exile line-up was in place.

Mark Jones grew up in Hopkinsville, Kentucky listening to rock groups such as Led Zeppelin, The Allman Brothers, and The Beatles. He remembers hearing about Exile in 1970 when he was sixteen years old. "The Exile story for me starts when I was a junior in high school, and I was charged with hiring the band for my senior prom in Hopkinsville," said Mark. "In going through all of that and trying to find a band, I had contact with agents all over the southeast and received materials on the group Exile from a number of them." He tried to book Exile, but they weren't able to play due a scheduling conflict.

Two years later he heard them play at The Nashville Pop Festival, and was impressed by the band's performance. "They played adjacent to Big Brother and the Holding Company, I do believe, who really were terrible," remembers Mark. "Just by contrast that was a good band for them to play next to. Here's a bunch of guys who can barely stand up and play, they're so screwed up, and then here's Exile really on top of their game sounding great, playing great, looking great." He next heard about the group while he was attending the Berklee School of Music in 1978. Mark preferred jazz by this point, but he appreciated the fact that a group from Kentucky was performing on *The Midnight Special*. Mark completed his degree, released an album on Epic with New Man, and toured with INXS, Bryan Adams, and Culture Club before he joined Exile. New Man was plunging into oblivion, and Mark decided to check out his new option.

"I love the vocal side of it, because that wasn't so much what the band I was in Boston was doing," remembers Mark. "And I wasn't the lead vocalist up there, so I wasn't getting a chance to sing as much as I wanted."

Mark's high tenor allowed him to sing many of the parts that had been assigned to Les Taylor. He proved to be the missing link for the 1990s version of Exile. At first, Mark was brought in as a sideman. It was a role that he would continue to assume throughout the recording of Exile's next album,

Still Standing. "I didn't expect to land in the camp and be automatically a member of the band instantly and an owner in the trademark instantly," said Mark.

Paul remained Exile's lead guitarist. "That was Paul's function, and I never really intended to try to challenge the status quo in that regard," continues Mark. "I'm a big fan of Paul Martin's playing—in that genre really he was better equipped than I was." Mark could easily have played solos with Exile. "I always encouraged him…'Man you want to take a solo, go ahead,'" said Paul. "It wasn't like, 'I gotta have the solos,' but he just never seemed to want to do it."

Despite his status as a sideman, Mark was major contributor to the group's first album on Arista Records, performing on every cut. "I felt like a member of the band creatively at that point," said Mark. The group auditioned for Arista as soon as he arrived in Nashville from Boston. It must have felt like a whirlwind situation for the singer/guitarist. The first recording sessions for the record took place over the course of a weekend, and Mark's vocal parts proved an important factor in the band's sound. "Because I had been involved in making those demos and they had turned out so well, I just hung in there and was a part of the whole record," said Mark.

His high pitched vocals became a critical element of the Exile sound during this period. "Sonny sometimes would sing the falsetto high part, but for the most part during my time with the band Sonny stayed out of that area and I sang the high parts," said Mark.

The first order of business for the new group was to get another recording contract. "We were playing around, and it wasn't very pretty," said Lee. "We were going in these honky-tonks and county fairs, and every now and then opening for somebody trying to convince people we were still Exile." Thankfully, this version of the band was loaded with talent, and they could always deliver an impressive live show.

Country music radio personality Ron Helton heard them perform at a show in Hot Springs, Arkansas, and was duly impressed. He brought news of a revamped, exciting Exile line-up when he returned to Nashville. Tim Dubois, the president of Arista's new subsidiary in Nashville, decided to attend one of the group's Lexington performances in the spring of 1989. Dubois was looking to establish the record company, and he felt that Exile could help. He offered them a record deal on the condition that they retain their name. Sonny didn't want to use the name, but eventually relented. "When Tim Dubois signed us to be on that label…I mean we begged him…I begged him to let us…because I said 'you know, we're not the same band anymore,'" said Sonny.

Dubois understood the marketing power of the Exile brand name by this point, and he insisted that they keep it. "He had to have somebody on this brand new Arista Records launch the label, and he wanted an act with a name," continues Sonny. The group was signed to Arista, and they had another opportunity to scale the country music charts. "It was kind of like everybody had written us off, but we didn't believe everybody," said Lee. Lee remembers this as his most exciting time with the band. They were certainly beating the odds.

Still Standing was the first album that Exile released on Arista. It is the stronger of the two efforts that they recorded for the label. The musicians seem revitalized, and Lee and Paul seem particularly ready to take on the world. Lead vocals were split between Sonny and Paul. This was the first time that Sonny had provided lead vocals on an Exile record since *All There Is*. Sonny handled much of the songwriting on the album in collaboration with Randy Sharp. Sharp, a successful songwriter for Restless Heart ("Why Does It Have to Be Wrong or Right," "A Tender Lie"), co-produced the album with Tim Dubois. Although he is listed as co-producer, Dubois clearly had the last say in major decisions. A former certified public accountant, Dubois composed hit country songs for various artists in the early 1980s including "She Got the Goldmine (I Got the Shaft)" for Jerry Reed, Restless Heart's "The Bluest Eyes in Texas," and "Love in the First Degree" for Alabama. He had a good deal of self-confidence, and the members of Exile liked him. "Anytime Tim Dubois is involved with anything it sets such a tone that it's just going to be a pleasant experience," said Steve.

Ironically, the opening cut and first single released from this new version of the group was a Pennington/Lemaire composition entitled "Keep It in the Middle of the Road." Paul, an uncertain singer in his own mind, provided the lead vocal. He was not used to being the lead singer in a band. "The first time I'm getting to sing lead it's on a major label," said Paul.

His vocals sound confident, as though he had been singing for years. He also provided the guitar intro and solos. Paul's talents as a guitarist are immediately apparent in the acoustic introduction. Paul:

> You've gotta give J.P. credit for that guitar intro. He wrote it. I just copied it and played it as written when we recorded the album. The dobro and acoustic guitar in the solo section of the song were my contributions. It was exhilarating for me to be encouraged by all the band members and producer to "stretch out" and create things that had not been part of Exile's sound previously.

Lee's piano solo is another highlight, demonstrating his talent as an instrumentalist much better than the synth-driven parts on *Shelter from the Night*. A dedicated music fan, Lee demonstrates an understanding of blues, boogie-woogie, country, ragtime, and western swing in his solo. "Keep It in the Middle of the Road" served notice that this new, young version of the band could be a force to be reckoned with. Unfortunately, this instrumental prowess failed to return Exile to the top of the country chart, and the song peaked at No. 17. It did, however, perform much better than anything that J.P. and Les were releasing as solo artists at the time, and it set the stage for the commercial success that the band would achieve with their next two singles.

Sonny was always overshadowed as a vocalist during the 1980s, but he shared lead vocal duties with Paul in the 1990s. His vocals proved especially effective on ballads such as "Nobody's Talking" and "Yet." "Nobody's Talking," an expertly crafted slice of pop-country composed by the Lemaire/Sharp songwriting team, almost took the band back to the top of the charts. Released as the second single from *Still Standing*, "Nobody's Talking" reached the No. 2 spot on the country chart. The lyrics concerning a man's inability to get to the truth mesh perfectly with the ascending chord progression at the end of the verses, creating drama. It's one of the stronger ballads in the Exile catalog.

"Yet" is another moving ballad, driven by a dual acoustic guitar progression played by Paul and Mark. "That's actually two guitars," said Mark. "Paul's playing one, I'm playing the other. I'm basically playing sort of the main part and Paul's playing a high strung guitar part on that." Lee's tasteful piano and organ playing and Sonny's passionate delivery are also notable. "Yet" was Exile's last top ten country hit, peaking at No.7. The fourth single from the album was "There You Go," a much less memorable ballad sung by Paul. It reached No. 32 on the country chart.

Videos were important for country music artists in the late 1980s and early 1990s. Exile recorded videos for "Keep It in the Middle of the Road" and "Nobody's Talking." Not surprisingly, the video for "Keep It in the Middle of the Road" showed the band playing in the middle of a road and on the back of a large truck. Paul is shown throughout, and Lee's piano playing is emphasized as well. "Nobody's Talking" shifts the focus to Sonny as he tries in vain to find his beloved. Other members of the band make various cameos as detectives (Lee and Steve), a bellboy (Paul), a cab driver (Steve), a restaurant worker (Paul) and a lonesome accordion player (Lee). The band's sense of humor is evident in both of the videos.

The strongest songs on *Still Standing* were the first three singles, but the album includes some quality album cuts. Paul provided vocals on "Bad Blood," "I'm Still Standing," "Don't Hang Up," and "Show Me."

"Bad Blood" is a galloping country-rock tune including some bluesy playing from Lee and Paul. The up-tempo title track is one of the weaker cuts on the album, as it repeats the sentiment expressed by Elton John in 1983. "Don't Hang Up" showcases Paul as an R&B/country-soul vocalist, not his strong suit. Nevertheless, his guitar playing is as tasteful as ever. "My guitar solo on that song is a one take thing," said Paul. "They wouldn't let me do it again." "Show Me" is another country rocker that fails to leave much of an impression.

Sonny provided the lead vocals on "For You" and "Only a Woman," the last two songs on the album. "For You" features some interesting piano/organ/guitar interplay, but it doesn't sound as though it was tailored toward the country music market. "Only a Woman" is a strong album cut. Never before had Exile borrowed as obviously from bluegrass music. "When Sonny came in and played that song for the first time I said 'Man, I gotta get a mandolin on that,'" said Paul. "I dabble with mandolin."

Still Standing was a successful comeback album for Exile, but hopes were high that the next album would do better. Two top ten country hits would be considered an achievement for most bands, but Exile was used to greater success. "After doing the first record, things went okay," said Lee. "We didn't knock anything out of the park, but we had a record deal." For a brief moment it looked as though the group still had a good deal of life left in it.

Sonny was the only group member to contribute songwriting to *Still Standing*. Other band members hoped to contribute creatively to the next album. In retrospect this is understandable, as he was half of the songwriting team that produced a series of No. 1 hits in the 1980s. It's doubtful that Exile would have been signed to Arista without Sonny as a member of the band. Nevertheless, this lack of input from the rest of the band created tension.

For the most part, members of the band other than Sonny were not permitted to contribute songs to *Justice*, the group's second album on Arista. Lee explains:

They started hooking us up. Everybody in the band was writing. I mean, feverishly writing. It's like finally the doors had opened and they're saying 'We're going to listen to everybody's songs.' That's how we felt, though. They were actually hooking us up with really good songwriters. We were all writing with Randy Sharp and all these different Nashville guys. We came in with about fifty songs between us. And, of course, we were listening to songs. Little did we know...Tim Dubois was in the process of going through a divorce. So here's the co-producer on our record who's the president of the label and we are all so, in retrospect...We're basically shooting ourselves in the foot because we're all so excited and so much want to...finally in our lives we have this chance to actually have creative input into what we're doing, and we started bickering. There was a lot of tension over whose songs were going to get on the record. It became a big issue. Agitated state, turmoil. Tim, I think...I think he just got tired of it, didn't want to deal with it. This is my perspective, so I don't know if anybody sees it this way or not. So he just comes in one day and he says, 'Okay, here's the songs we're going to do.' And he picks a bunch of Sonny Lemaire/Randy Sharp songs. And end of story. At that point, once again from my perspective, he just let the air out of the whole deal. That was right at the highpoint when everybody thought, 'Finally, we're going to get to make a record that's not full of a bunch'cha sappy country love songs.' And you're not going to hear that from anybody but me. From Mark you would hear something like that, or Paul maybe.

Lee's frustration is understandable. He could have easily remained a side-man with The Judds, but he joined Exile with the hope that he would be able to contribute creatively to one of the most successful bands in country music. Shortly after he arrived, the band lost two lead vocalists and its record contract. *Still Standing* was a comeback record of sorts highlighting Lee's instrumental skills, but he was not allowed to contribute to the songwriting process. By the time the group got around to recording its second album for Arista, *Justice*, it seemed as though the disappointment would continue. Lee:

> We really thought we were going to be able to make a record that meant something. That doesn't mean we wouldn't have radio appropriate songs on it, but we thought we could actually have songs on there.... Now perhaps we were fooling ourselves thinking we could actually write songs that were worthy of that, but we felt like we at least could attempt it. Because it was the same song. It was the same song Sonny had been writing for years.

Mark became a full-time member of the group prior to the recording of *Justice*. "In the last half of the time I was with the band, Lee and I became sort of the administrative partners from the band's perspective," said Mark.

"So we did a lot of the grunge work in terms of just the business administration of the group." Mark enjoyed the sessions, but acknowledges that there were some difficulties. "I think Tim Dubois, who was the co-producer of the record again at that time, had some significant personal things going on in his world that were a little bit of a distraction," remembers Mark.

The first single and the opening track on *Justice* was "Even Now," a moderate ballad composed by Randy Sharp and Marc Beeson featuring a heartfelt vocal performance courtesy of Paul. It was the last Exile single to chart, reaching the No. 16 spot. It's an underrated song in the Exile catalog. It showed that Paul's vocals could effectively carry a well written ballad. As of late he has continued to perform the song at his shows with The Martin Family Circus. A high percentage of the promotional video was shot in black and white. The band is seen performing in a warehouse environment, and Mark Jones makes his first video appearance as a member of the band.

The moderate success of "Even Now" couldn't have possibly prepared the group for the problems that would follow. The follow up single was another ballad featuring lead vocals from Paul entitled "Nothing At All." It was composed by songwriters from outside of the band, Susan Longacre and Johnny Pierce.

Exile had success with ballads on *Still Standing*, and there was no reason to believe that the pattern would change. "Nothing At All" could have been a hit, but timing was not on Exile's side. "The week that we put that single out at Arista, it was the same week that Reba (McEntire) put her first single out called 'For My Broken Heart,'" remembers Paul. Arista had a difficult time getting any activity on the single, and it was quickly pulled.

Dubois' response was to push for the release of "Somebody's Telling Her Lies," a Randy Sharp composition. It would have been the third release from the album with no songwriting contribution from a member of the band. "I think some of the band members didn't really like that song, for whatever reason," said Paul. Dubois felt as though the song was a hit, and insisted they release it. It was certainly in the up-tempo style of their hits from the 1980s, but it lacks a memorable hook on the level of their No. 1 songs. Paul, the vocalist on the track, liked the song, but was outvoted.

Likewise, Mark, the newest member of the band, was less irritated by the song than others. "I think there were some disagreements on what songs should have been released as singles, which is not uncommon between a band and a label, but I think that was more frustrating perhaps for some of the other members of the band than it was to me," said Mark. The band convinced Jim Morey, still their manager, to contact Dubois in regards to the upcoming single. "He said 'Tim, if we put that single out, how certain are you that it'll be successful enough to make a difference,'" remembers Paul. Dubois couldn't guarantee success, and the single was never released. The band asked to be released from the label, and Dubois agreed.

Justice has its moments, but it's not as strong as *Still Standing*. This time out, the lead vocals were split evenly between Paul and Sonny. The group interplay that was so evident on songs such as "Keep It in the Middle of the Road" and "Yet" seemed to get lost in the shuffle as Exile looked to spin out professional versions of songs composed by outside songwriters. The boogie/country-rock flavored "The Invisible Man," a song concerning the plight of the working man, sounds like the work of a different band. "Somebody's Telling Her Lies" and "Nothing At All" sound like less impressive attempts to revisit past glories. "One Too Many Times" includes some interesting musical ideas including an inventive bass line from Sonny and an offbeat rhythm uncommon in country music, but these musical ambitions fit somewhat uncomfortably amidst the rest of the album.

"One More Reason" was composed by Lee and Randy Sharp, but it works as a vocal showcase for Paul. Paul grew as a vocalist between the *Still Standing* and *Justice* albums. His passionate performance on "One More Reason" is effective. He also provides the harmonica solo. "Dreams Die Hard" is a fairly effective mid-tempo ballad with a title that may have seemed appropriate for Exile at this point in their career. "What You See" has a boogie/western swing feel, and it features some tasteful soloing from Lee and Paul accompanied by Sonny's walking bass lines.

"(For You, For Me) Forever" isn't one of the group's more memorable ballads, but it does include some interesting vocal harmonies. "Shot in the Dark" is a driving country rock tune that fails to leave much of an impression apart from Paul's agile fretwork. "All In Good Time" is a more effective country-rock/blues-inflected tune that manages to capture some of the band interplay that was so evident on *Still Standing*. Paul and Lee trade solos in the middle of the song, and the use of a Hammond organ helps to provide a soulful background.

The most underrated song on the album is the title track, a haunting closer that was atypical of the Exile sound. It features one of Sonny's most impassioned vocal performances and a rocking musical arrangement that accurately captures the mood of the vindictive lyrics. Mark's high pitched background vocals help to carry the emotional chorus sections.

The Arista version of the group is sometimes referred to as Sonny's version of Exile. With the exception of one song on *Justice* credited to Randy Sharp and Lee Carroll ("One More Reason"), Sonny was the lone songwriting contributor from within the group. He was in a position to see changes in the music industry and how they were affecting Exile. Dubois had signed Diamond Rio, and after a series of personal setbacks, they released their first album on Arista in 1991. "The focus shifted from the old act to the brand new act," said Sonny. "That's just the way the politics works in record labels."

Sonny eventually became friends with the members of Diamond Rio, even co-writing the No. 1 country hit "Beautiful Mess" for them in 2002, but the situation was more complicated in 1991. Diamond Rio's success coincided with a host of personal problems for Dubois, and *Justice* was destined to become an overlooked album. "Tim was distracted, but it was a pleasure to make that project—a lot of fun," said Sonny. "It's interesting, because I've listened to it recently, and I'm very proud of that record." Sonny and Dubois are friends now, but there was tension brewing in 1991. Sonny was feeling disillusioned with his career, and he was growing tired of the turmoil. They had to part ways. Sonny regrets the decision. "You talk about decisions that if I could take back, I would…" said Sonny. Sonny continues to admire Dubois and describes him as "a true gentleman" for whom he has the greatest respect.

Exile's future was further complicated by some personal issues. Just as the group was looking to get away from Arista, Lee's first son was born in need of a liver transplant. For the first time in his career, he had to miss some shows. "In my whole career…twenty-five years up till then, I had never missed a gig for any reason," said Lee. "That year I missed twenty-five shows, and they did them without me." It was during this time that Paul's instrumental skills proved invaluable. They continued to play the gigs as a four piece with Paul switching between guitar and piano. "He can play anything you put in his hands well enough to do sessions," said Steve. Lee was paid as a full-time member during this period, a gesture for which he is still grateful. Lee:

> They paid me as if I was there, and they never made me feel uncomfortable about going home and taking care of my family. That was Paul, Mark, Steve, and Sonny. We will always be like brothers. It was all heart. We took care of each other, and we got through some tough times together. J.P. and Les…I enjoyed that period of time, too. But when those guys left the rest of us that were left…that challenge that we faced, and we went through together and then this deal where I almost lost my son, and those guys came through for me…. It's created a bond amongst the guys. Now we're the guys who still own the name. So we own the name, because the last surviving guys own the name. And those guys will always be like brothers to me.

Exile continued to tour into 1993, but they weren't able to find a record label after they left Arista. The band began to run out of steam. New pop-country artists such as Garth Brooks were dominating the country music landscape by this point, and Exile got lost in the shuffle. Brooks was selling albums at an alarming rate, and Exile, a group much better known for their singles than their albums, couldn't effectively compete.

Sonny recalls that Exile was being viewed as "the old guard of country music." The band was forced into a rigorous touring schedule.

"The downside of Exile for me was, for a while there, you start playing the same songs 150 nights a year, 150 shows a year, and you don't get a chance to really stretch out and grow," said Paul.

Paul was always looking to improve as a musician, and would often resort to recording music on the road. "Everybody said on the bus 'Aw man, don't do that,'" said Paul.

He and other members of the band started to regret their decision to leave Arista. "If we had been more mature, more professional about how we dealt with business, and the whole thing about song selection, all that stuff, if we'd basically let Tim Dubois mold us into something that he thought he could sell, and not resist it, we might have had a hit on that record," said Lee. "Because I don't know what a damn country hit is." His push for creative freedom was at odds with the mainstream music industry.

One of the more uplifting moments for Exile in 1993 was the group's thirty-year reunion at The Kentucky Horse Park in Lexington. All of the former members were invited to participate. J.P., Buzz, Mike, Mack, and others attended the event. "It was really pretty cool," said Lee. Those who attended seemed to enjoy the concert. Buzz:

> We had a really good time at the 30th anniversary that was at the horse park. That's when they called me onto the bus and said 'we have something we need to tell you.' They said 'New Year's Eve will be our last performance as Exile. Your name is still on so much stuff, Buzz. We're going to have to stay in touch.'

Buzz agreed, and he heard from some of his old band mates shortly afterward. J.P. and Les decided to regroup with new musicians in 1995, and they wanted to use the name "Exile." Buzz didn't stand in their way. "We've got product out there that can still sell," said Buzz.

Former members of Exile were invited onstage during the reunion show. "When we go up we just clown around and get on the microphone and sing background with them or something, shake a tambourine or whatever," said Mike. "It was fun."

The event gave J.P. an opportunity to make up with his band mates from the late 1980s. "We finally made up," said J.P. "It took me being a man about it, and apologizing to them."

He had continued to monitor the progress of his old group after departing, and was a fan of their Arista albums. "Yeah, I liked them," said J.P. "Yeah, I thought they were good—to hear Sonny doing some lead vocals. Yeah, I was glad about that."

Exile held out hope for a record deal until the fall of 1993. Morey continued to promote the band, but he wasn't having any luck. The band was robbed near the end of 1993, and things seemed to be spiraling downhill. Paul:

> Right as Exile was getting ready to quit touring in '93, somebody broke into our bus and stole all of my guitars, and they stole Sonny's bass. They stole all our stage clothes, our stereo equipment...the band decided to call it quits in a meeting held in a hotel room on the road. It was up to Sonny to end the band. He just kind of said, 'Well guys, I think that, you know, I want to give my notice.'

It was the right move to make at the time. The band couldn't realistically continue without Sonny, and no one tried to keep it going after he announced his decision. Paul, Mark, and Sonny performed at Dollywood as a trio in the summer of 1994, but the band was officially defunct.

Chapter Nine

AFTER ALL THESE YEARS

E XILE WAS OFFERED ONE more chance to record in late 1994. Sonny, Steve, Lee, Paul, and Mark accepted an offer to re-record some of their biggest hits and a few new songs for Intersound Records. "Intersound is a label for washed up country acts," said Lee.

The *Latest and Greatest* album was recorded in January and February of 1995. The album includes four new songs as well as re-recordings of "Yet," "Nobody's Talking," "Keep It in the Middle of the Road," "I Can't Get Close Enough," "Give Me One More Chance," "Woke Up In Love," "Kiss You All Over," and a "special dance mix" of "Super Love."

Mark was especially active during the recording of the new compositions, contributing songwriting to two songs and singing lead on one. The most memorable new track was "How Bad Can It Be," a song composed by Sonny and Mark. Sonny provides the lead vocal.

Mark composed "In the Blink of An Eye" with Larry Winslow, a friend from Boston. Randy Sharp was also involved in the project collaborating with Sonny on "L-O-V-E Spells Trouble" and "Heart of Steel." Paul was a co-writer on "L-O-V-E Spells Trouble," his only songwriting contribution to the Exile catalog. "The way I tended to write, it just didn't seem to fit what the band was about," said Paul.

He was also careful to save his best work for future solo projects. "At the time I would have pitched more stuff for that project, but I was working on a solo thing so I was kind of thinking 'Well, I don't want to throw what I feel might be my best stuff out there for this,'" admits Paul.

Lee didn't contribute any songs. "That record was not a serious attempt to make art," said Lee. "Let's make a couple of bucks doing this and get back together and enjoy each other again."

The album closed with a new dance mix of "Super Love" arranged by Paul, Mark, and assistant engineers Dave Hieronymus and Chris Milfred. Lee never heard the new version of "Super Love." Lee: "You know what? I don't want to hear it."

Paul remembered hearing songs such as "Strokin'" played at the clubs, and he felt as though "Super Love" could be used for similar electric slide situations. Paul's friend Duncan Mullins was brought in to provide drum programming, and additional sequences and samples were added. Sonny played electric bass in the verses, and Paul played synthesizer bass during the chorus. All of the additional keyboards were played by Paul. "Everybody kind of balked at it, so it never really got off the ground," remembers Paul. The group disbanded after the release of *Latest and Greatest*, and the band members went their separate ways.

Mark Jones moved into artist management after Exile broke up. Clarence Spalding had moved into artist management after leaving his job as Exile's tour manager, and he proved to be an important connection for Mark. "After I came off the road with Exile, I eventually ended up working with Clarence, and that's what I do now here in Nashville,' said Mark. He works for Spalding Entertainment managing artists such as Sarah Evans and Pat Green. He also performs with Tin Can Buddha, a musical collective formed by Lee Carroll. "I play a little music with my seventeen-year-old son and my wife and some friends, and then Tin Can Buddha here and there," said Mark.

Steve Goetzman also moved into artist management. "I wanted to get off the road," said Steve. "I had two daughters, and I wanted to be a dad." At first he had a difficult time choosing a career path. After all, he had been a professional drummer for most of his life.

Luckily, successful country star and fellow Arista label mate Steve Wariner was looking for a manager as Exile was breaking up. Wariner believed that Steve Goetzman could do the job. It was a lucrative deal for the Exile drummer, and he started the new job during his last month performing with Exile. "He paid me a lot of money," said Steve. "It was a lot less than what he was paying his former manager."

Steve managed several groups, including a country group from the Soviet Union called Bering Strait. "They were playing in a Mexican restaurant in Moscow, if you can believe that," said Steve. Steve also hosted a short lived radio program called *Country Memories*, but it never got off the ground. "We did fifteen shows and we only got two stations," said Steve. Lately he's been taking part in the Exile reunion and functioning as the group's manager. In addition, he works part-time at a drug and alcohol rehab center called Cumberland Heights.

Sonny had a successful post-Exile career in the music business. After leaving Exile, he formed a group in 1995 called The Loose Cannons with Marc Beeson (acoustic guitar, vocals) and former Southern Pacific keyboardist/vocalist Kurt Howell. They were augmented by studio musicians on their only album. They changed their name to Burnin' Daylight before recording the album on Mike Curb's label in 1996. "I'm very, very proud of that project," said Sonny.

The pop country tendencies of Exile's Arista years are evident on songs such as "Say Yes," but other tracks such as "Nice Work (If You Can Get It)" and "Cut and Run" have a strong, bluesy feel. "Love Worth Fighting For," a Beeson/Lemaire/Howell composition and the first single released from the album, shows that this group was capable of producing well-crafted pop-country and tight vocal harmonies. It peaked at No. 49 on the country chart. "Say Yes" fared slightly better, reaching No. 37 in 1997. A third single, "Live to Love Again" failed to generate much airplay, and the band disbanded shortly after.

Most of Sonny's post-Exile commercial success took place as a songwriter for other artists. He and Beeson composed the crossover hit "When She Cries" for Restless Heart in 1992, a song that enjoyed crossover success reaching No. 11 on the Billboard Hot 100. Lemaire began a songwriting partnership with Shane Minor and Clay Mills following the break-up of Burnin' Daylight. The partnership resulted in three pop-country top five hits on Billboard's Hot Country Singles and Tracks chart: "Beautiful Mess" for Diamond Rio (No. 1, 2002), "She Thinks She Needs Me' for Andy Griggs (No. 5, 2004), and "Fall" for Clay Walker (No. 5, 2007). Pop artist Kimberly Locke also released a version of "Fall." Her version reached No. 1 on the Billboard Hot Dance Club Party chart. This chart success doesn't represent Sonny's more artistic inclinations, but it did show that he knew how to write effectively and consistently for the pop-country market.

Paul looked to start a solo career after leaving Exile. Things looked up when he scored a gig playing steel guitar with Kathy Mattea while working on solo material. Nevertheless, Paul's solo career never got off the ground. His first attempt was financed by a producer who wanted to create Exile-inspired music. Tony Brown, the head of MCA Records, heard the demo and invited Paul in for a meeting. "He said, 'Tell him to come down and bring his acoustic,'" remembers Paul. Paul brought his acoustic to the meeting and proceeded to play a song that he had written. "After I got done Tony said, 'Man I like that song better than I like the stuff on your demo.'" He encouraged Paul to pursue his own path instead of Exile part two.

Paul took Brown's advice. He decided to record some of his own, eclectic material. Unfortunately labels were looking for guys with cowboy hats and Garth Brooks clones by this point, and Paul's more eclectic approach was rejected. "The label guys, like Tim Dubois and Tony Brown both, always had an open door policy for me," said Paul. "When they played it for the staff they would scratch their head going, 'How we gonna market this?'"

Paul continued to stay active in the music industry singing and playing keyboards and steel guitar with Kathy Mattea and working as a session musician. He also toured with The Oak Ridge Boys for four years before going on the road with Steve Wariner. Paul is currently a member of Marty Stuart and His Fabulous Superlatives, a four-piece band. Paul provides bass and vocals for the group in live settings, and additional instruments such as piano and vibes in the studio. All members of the band are involved in the creation and production of *The Marty Stuart Show*, a weekly television program now in its 5th season on the RFD-TV Network. Stuart is a musician known for his respect of country music as a serious art form, and the show features guest appearances by influential country musicians. Paul has been involved with the show since its inception, and is referred to as "Apostle Paul Martin." Other members of the Fabulous Superlatives include "Handsome Harry" Stinson and "Cousin Kenny" Vaughan.

In 2010 Paul played on Stuart's *Ghost Train: The Studio B Sessions*, an album recorded at the legendary RCA Studio B in Nashville. The studio had been closed since 1977. "The studio is basically only used for teaching classes and they take tours in there, so Marty wanted to go back there and capture that vibe of that room," said Paul.

The musicians quickly found that they couldn't play too loud. They had to play to the room. Paul played upright bass on most of the songs, and added piano on a few tracks. "I said, 'Man, all my life I trained in my dad's studio to play this kind of music,'" said Paul. "I really analyzed all those old country records and stuff."

Paul was familiar with the work of session musicians such as "Pig" Robbins and Bob Moore, and playing with Stuart gave him the opportunity to properly acknowledge those influences. *Ghost Train: The Studio B Sessions* also contains "Hangman" a song written by Stuart with Johnny Cash. It was finished four days before Cash's death, making it his last song. Paul also started the Martin Family Circus, a group that includes his wife, two sons, and two daughters. Their album includes covers of Toto's "Africa," The Beatles' "Nowhere Man," and the Oak Ridge Boys' "Elvira," as well as Exile songs such as "Keep It in the Middle of the Road" and "Even Now."

Unlike Paul, Mark, Sonny, and Steve, Lee decided to leave Nashville. "I turned the country music network off on my TV," remembers Lee. "I didn't touch a piano for ten years."

Lee got an offer to go into business together with his brother running a Papa John's franchise in Harrodsburg, Pennsylvania. "I went and got a book on franchising, and I knew Papa John's," said Lee. He moved his family to

Pennsylvania, and quickly immersed himself in the business. "I didn't know any musicians, so I just hunkered down and built eight pizza shops," said Lee. "Very lucky to have, you know, done well."

Lee won the 2004 franchise operator of the year for small groups in the Papa John's organization. He continued to raise his son, and music was not a priority. Lee became involved in the community, but after a while he began to meet musicians. He finally came out of his shell at a Thursday night jam session held by the Blues Society of Central Pennsylvania. "So I went up on the last song, and I walked up to the stage," remembers Lee. "Nobody was playing organ, and I said, 'Hey, can I sit in?'" The musicians agreed, and Lee fell into the groove.

"And I love playing the blues," said Lee. "That's really what I am. I'm not a country guy." He had a great time, and this led to repeat visits to the weekly jam sessions. "Within a month I had about six bands ask me if I would play with them," continues Lee. He soon realized that guitarist/vocalist/didley bow player Mitch Ivanoff was one of the best musicians in the area. Mitch invited Lee to play some gigs, and they enjoyed playing together. "Mitch turns around and says 'E' and starts playing," said Lee. "And that was it. We never rehearsed." They continue to eschew rehearsals preferring to focus on simple tunes that rely on feel and improvisation.

Lee and Mitch eventually formed Tin Can Buddha with Rodney Hatfield, the vocalist/harmonica player who had played with The Hatfield Clan during the 1970s. The band formed through a series of coincidences. Lee returned to Kentucky periodically for Papa John's related business, and has since moved back to the state. Lee and Rodney decided to put together a show at The Quilt Box in Louisville, a house with a seven foot Steinway, quilts hanging on the walls, and forty folding chairs. It had been used for piano recitals and jazz events, but Rodney convinced the owner to host a blues performance.

Mitch was playing at a festival in Clarksdale, MS that weekend, and Lee invited him to drop by the performance on the way back to Pennsylvania. "An hour before we play at The Quilt Box, Mitch pulls his truck up…he had never met Rodney," explains Lee. The performers jelled, and a good time was had by all. "It's like they'd been together for years," continues Lee.

They returned to The Quilt Box less than a year later, this time with a bass player in tow. They recorded their second show, and it was released in 2008 as *Tin Can Buddha; Live at the Quilt Box*. Once again, there was no rehearsal or practice. All of the songs were reworked versions of blues and country covers as well as public domain songs.

Blues tunes included Muddy Waters' "I Can't Be Satisfied," Willie Dixon's "Little Red Rooster" (originally popularized as "The Red Rooster" by Howlin' Wolf), and Ivory Joe Hunter's "Since I Met You Baby." They also performed versions of "The Tennessee Waltz" and Hank Williams' "I'm So Lonesome I Could Cry," reaffirming the fact that Lee just can't get away from country music. "There's a lot of great country music that's deep and soulful," admits Lee.

He seems to prefer classic country vocalists. "I like music that's honest, and if you're talking Hank Williams Sr…. Just going on back—George Jones…," continues Lee. After a few edits and overdubs, Tin Can Buddha released their first album. Rodney came up with the name Tin Can Buddha, and subsequent photos of Mitch served as the band's image. It was financed independently.

A second album was recorded in 2009 at The Quilt Box entitled *Congress of Wonders*. It also featured reworked covers songs, but the influence of free-jazz is also apparent. "The Congress of Wonders" is a free improvisation built on a short story by Ed McClanahan. McClanahan guests on the track reading his prose while the musicians create avant-garde soundscapes in the background before moving into a bluesy improvisation.

The group's third album *Wake Up* (2010) was even more adventurous. It's a double CD including a reggae version of Marvin Gaye's "Inner City Blues," contributions from eclectic female vocalist Gail Wynters, and a forty minute, Miles Davis/Fela Kuti-inspired improvisation divided into two parts entitled "Skip Zone." "The way it works is we've all played all different kinds of music, and we've played it together," said Lee. "One was the Miles Davis electric stuff, the way the music worked and the other was I've been listening to a lot of Afrobeat and African pop music." Percussionist/educator Tripp Bratton played an important role in bringing "Skip Zone" to life. "He's been to Africa to study," said Lee. "Tripp's a tremendous asset to the band."

Tin Can Buddha was invited to play at The Kentucky Center for the Arts after the director of the venue saw them perform at the Quilt Box. Their first performance in the Center took place in the lobby, an area that also housed Rodney Hatfield's art. They promoted the gig and Lee estimated that 200 people showed up.

This led to a performance in one of the auditoriums. Lee didn't think that Tin Can Buddha could fill a 650 set auditorium, so he proposed another idea. He proposed that they turn the concert into a history of blues/boogie piano entitled *88 Shades of Blue*. The show included contributions from jazz pianist Harry Pickens, and Lee's old friend, Joe Turley. The next step was to look for corporate funding. The corporate funding was rejected, and Lee is now looking to apply for non-profit status. "I don't know if we'll ever catch up, but it doesn't matter," said Lee. "We're doing this to be around creative people."

Regardless, attendance for *88 Shades of Blue* was impressive, and the show was a success. "We made money on the show the other day, and the Kentucky Center's happy," explains Lee. He's quick to point out the fact that Tin Can Buddha exists for artistic reasons, not for profit. Rodney, Mitch, and Lee have never taken money from Tin Can Buddha performances, preferring to pay the musicians they work with. "We're never going to allow ourselves to be put in a position to where we have to make decisions about what we're going to do as to what songs, style of music, anything," insists Lee. "We want total freedom. It's very liberating when you don't depend on music for the money."

After Exile broke up in 1995, J.P. quickly looked to reform the group. He and Les were performing with a new version of the band by the end of the year. This version of the band included local musicians on bass, keyboards, and drums. They had to speak with previous members in order to use the name. An Exile line-up consisting of J.P., Les, Steve Richmond (drums), Ray Salyer (bass), and Jason Witt (keyboards) recorded *Live at Billy Bob's Texas* in 2005. This live document contains performances of the group's biggest hits and a short medley of hits that J.P. and Les co-wrote for other artists. The medley on *Live at Billy Bob's Texas* included "Take Me Down," "The Closer You Get," and "It Ain't Easy Bein' Easy." It would later expand when Sonny rejoined in 2008, and the group continues to play the medley at their live shows.

J.P. also worked as a staff writer in Nashville after he left Exile, a job that he wasn't particularly fond of. He was signed to two publishers in Nashville over a ten-year span. "It all revolved around co-writing with all these people that my publisher would put me with, not only from our own staff but from other companies and around town," said J.P.

This setup didn't work well for J.P., a musician used to working in a band context. "I thought, 'Man, Look at all the success I've had as a writer, I'll go down there and I'll set the world on fire,'" said J.P. "Not!" He didn't have Exile to record his songs, and it was different functioning solely as a songwriter. "I can't say that I got a whole lot of enjoyment out of it," admits J.P.

The 1980s version of Exile reformed in 2008 after playing a benefit for a hospitalized former employee of the band. "It was just one of those things that even if you haven't talked to someone in a while that you had that common connection, and you just call them because of the seriousness of it," said J.P.

Steve, Marlon, Sonny, Les, and J.P. reformed for the benefit hosted at a club called The Blue Moon in Lexington, and the proceeds were given to their friend. The event was sold out. The group had a great time performing together, and decided to reform. "Playing the stuff now is a whole lot of fun, and I'm really, really enjoying it," said Sonny. After a few rehearsals, they were invited to play at The Kentucky Theater in downtown Lexington. "Now we're all back together and dedicated to seeing how far we can sustain it from this point on," said J.P.

The 1983-1985 version of Exile has remained active. They have been touring consistently, and they released a new EP-style compact disc in 2010. The EP contains five songs. It includes songwriting contributions from Sonny's songwriting partners, Shane Minor and Clay Mills. Minor co-wrote "Bread on the Table" with the Pennington/Lemaire songwriting team, while Mills co-wrote "There You Go Again" with them.

"Bread on the Table" is a hard rocking country tune that relates to the recession. It brings back memories of songs such as "Give Me One More Chance." "It's Gotta Be You" is a groove-based R&B tune composed by J.P. and Sonny. "There You Go Again" is a ballad that isn't far removed from the more moving ballads on J.P.'s solo album. J.P. sings lead on all of the original tunes, but Les gets a songwriting credit on "I Can't Be Your Fool." J.P. and Larry Cordle were also co-writers on the song.

The EP closes with a version of Curtis Mayfield's "People Get Ready." The song is performed a cappella by Les, J.P., and Sonny. J.P. provides instrumental interludes on guitar. It's a vocal tour de force, and it shows how talented they are as vocalists. Les steals the show on this track.

Exile re-recorded "Kiss You All Over" with Trace Adkins in 2011. The recording was part of a television show on the Great American Country (GAC) station entitled *Hit Exchange*. The show is designed to allow current stars to record the songs that inspired them to pursue a career in music. Adkins was inspired by "Kiss You All Over," and his deep bass vocal brings a new perspective to the song. J.P., Sonny, Les, Marlon, Steve, and Stokley were inducted into the Kentucky Music Hall of Fame in 2012. The exclusion of several previous members was likely controversial.

The Exile saga continues. Hardcore musicians are born with talent and a desire to express themselves. Several of these musicians passed through Exile—some for longer periods than others. Friendships were made, and feelings were hurt. Some riffs remain, some have healed. But when these artists have come together under the name "Exile," the music has created a bond. The Exiles have created an enduring legacy. They reached a level of success and professionalism that continues to resonate throughout the Central Kentucky region and beyond.

Endnotes

[1] http://archive.rollingstone.com/Desktop?s=198008079#/19800807/14

[2] Killen, Buddy and Tom Carter. *By the Seat of My Pants: My Life in Country Music*, page 249, Simon & Schuster, June 1993.

[3] Ibid.

[4] Killen, Buddy and Tom Carter. *By the Seat of My Pants: My Life in Country Music*, pages 250-251, Simon & Schuster, June 1993.

[5] http://exile.biz/

[6] http://www.cmt.com/news/country-music/1698266/retired-record-executive-rick-blackburn-deat-at-70.jhtml?rsspartner=rssDaylifeFeedFetcher

About the Author

R ANDY WESTBROOK TEACHES AT Eastern Kentucky University and Bluegrass Community and Technical College. He received a Ph.D. in Musicology from The University of Memphis.

Westbrook has been consistently active as a keyboard player over the last fifteen years performing on over 1,000 gigs in the Central Kentucky and Memphis areas.

INDEX

269

270